The Story the Soldiers
Wouldn't Tell

The Story the Soldiers Wouldn't Tell

Sex in the Civil War

Thomas P. Lowry, M.D.
with a foreword by
Robert K. Krick

STACKPOLE
BOOKS

Published by
STACKPOLE BOOKS
5067 Ritter Road
Mechanicsburg, PA 17055

Printed in the United States of America

10 9 8 7 6 5 4 3 2 1

The C. C. Jones letters are courtesy of the Charles Colcock Jones Collection, Manuscripts Department, Howard-Tilton Memorial Library, Tulane University, New Orleans, Louisiana.

The Henry Schnelling letter is courtesy of the William F. Hertzog Papers, Archives and Manuscripts, Chicago Historical Society.

The Edward Carpenter interview is courtesy of Mr. Allen Ginsberg.

"Jeff Davis' Dream" is courtesy of the Patrick Keran Papers, Ohio Historical Society, Columbus, Ohio.

William C. Chambers's report on Nashville prostitutes is courtesy of the Library of the Western Reserve Historical Society, Cleveland, Ohio.

The Vance Randolph stories, copyright 1976, are reprinted with permission from the Board of Trustees of the University of Illinois.

The Oren A. Hammer and Hugh D. Cameron Letters are reprinted with permission from the John McLean Harrington Papers, Special Collections Library, Duke University, Durham, North Carolina.

Library of Congress Cataloging-in-Publication Data

Lowry, Thomas P. (Thomas Power), 1932–
    The story the soldiers wouldn't tell : sex in the Civil War / Thomas P. Lowry : with an introduction by Robert K. Krick.
      p.   cm.
    Includes bibliographical references and index.
    ISBN 0-8117-1515-9
    1. United States—History—Civil War, 1861–1865—Social aspects. 2. Soldiers—United States—Sexual behavior—History—19th century. 3. Sex customs—United States—History—19th century. I. Title.
E468.9.L69   1994
973.7′1—dc20   94-1401
                                        CIP

To the Memory of

Private Michael Conrad Lowry
Company L, 39th Pennsylvania Volunteers

Lieutenant Samuel Lowry
Company C, 54th Pennsylvania Volunteers

Private William Henry Simms
Company L, First Michigan Engineers

Private John Suhrie
Company D, 133d Pennsylvania Volunteers

Contents

࿔

Foreword

❧

TWENTY YEARS AGO I listened with the feckless awe of a neophyte as one of the leading authorities on Civil War soldiery delivered a group portrait of the men who fought the war. In discussing the proclivities of mid-nineteenth-century America under arms, the putative expert declared unctuously, "Rape, of course, was unheard of in that era." The proclamation gladdened me, I recall, because that kind of restrained behavior reflects precisely the way things ought to be. The authoritative verdict, sad to say, was based on whimsy rather than research.

Dr. Thomas Lowry's *The Story the Soldiers Wouldn't Tell* is based on diligent investigation of primary sources rather than on ex cathedra pronouncements. As a result it sheds major new light on Americans of the Civil War era. That no one yet had produced a competent, detailed report on the subject is remarkable. The inexplicable unwillingness of many historians to use the rich lode of manuscripts in the National Archives left Dr. Lowry an open field for his endeavor. With a prominent American essayist of the last generation, I am an avid admirer of competence "in any art or craft from adultery to zoology . . . for it is very rare in this world, and especially in this great Republic." Lowry's competence stretches instead from adultery to venereal disease. Its result is new light shed on our Civil War ancestors.

Armies since the beginning of recorded history have featured an auxiliary corps of camp followers. A captured French officer remarked to the Duke of Wellington in 1810, "You, Sir, have an army—we have a travelling brothel." Napoleon's underling doubtless had been deceived by brief exposure to the British army, for a century before an Englishman had written sardonically: "'Tis hard for a poor woman to lose nine husbands in a war, and no notice taken; nay, three of 'em, alas, in the same campaign."

Recurring matter-of-fact reports in Confederate newspapers make clear the simple fact that large numbers of Southern soldiers carried on with prostitutes when they had the opportunity. The Richmond *Whig* in 1864 reported on a police raid that temporarily closed a public nuisance near the Exchange Hotel and Ballard House, upper class stopping places. Although escaping crowds "were pouring out of the [raided] building," the long arm of the law snared nineteen women and thirty men. The mayor exacted $300 to $500 from each woman in court as surety to keep the peace (apparently none had difficulty paying that amount—three *years'* pay for a private soldier). A journalist described the legal hearing in uncom-promising terms: "The court room was crowded by a throng of the admirers of the women, and a horrid looking set they were—flat-headed, big jawed, greasy and flashily dressed." The tableau does nothing to conjure up the South of *Gone with the Wind*.

The notion that earnest, stalwart Americans avoided such amorous alternatives during their great Civil War crusade cannot survive in the face of the material Dr. Lowry has marshalled. He shows us that almost a quarter of a million Yankees suffered reported cases of venereal disease (to say nothing of unreported cases), contracted of course in the immemorial fashion; that in a major Union military department, nearly one-half of the men were infected at one time during 1862; and that the United States Army organized and supervised legal prostitution in Tennessee in 1863, with good results as measured at sick call. Napoleon and the Iron Duke would have recognized the phenomenon with no difficulty, however much it might astonish American Civil War writers of the romantic genre.

Students familiar with Civil War letters recognized the prevalence of the time-honored custom of disloyalty by the women of absent soldiers—reported in what came to be known during more recent wars as "Dear John letters." As Alan Moorehead wrote of a nineteenth-century soldier home-ward bound after African campaigning, "He had discovered, like so many soldiers returning from the wars, that his girl had abandoned him for another man." Equivalent infidelity by soldiers away from home appears less boldly in Civil War correspondence because it was more random and ribald, and therefore less likely to break through the Victorian sensibilities that governed written communication.

Chapter Four of *The Story the Soldiers Wouldn't Tell* provides forty-four notes by way of documentation. All but one refer to unpublished primary sources. Chapter Twelve goes to such materials for three-quarters of its notes, and Chapter Thirteen also is based nearly entirely on manuscripts. Some of Dr. Lowry's subjects were not susceptible to that kind of docu-mentation. When the author is obliged to rely upon secondary sources and manuscripts once seen by someone else but now mysteriously missing, the strength of his material is much diminished; we can hope for further enlightenment in the future as more sources turn up.

Lowry's sedulous work in Federal court-martial records cannot be duplicated in Confederate records for the good reason that those documents burned with Richmond in April 1865. Accordingly, we can only postulate how much less Southerners came to trial for debauchery. The land in the sway of Sir Walter Scott, which never gave its soldiery over to unfettered license on private property, seems likely to have maintained considerably more decorum—but it certainly would be interesting to see the records of its military courts!

Dr. Lowry's diligent industry has uncovered a wealth of new material. The book that he crafted from that new information supplies valuable insights in Civil War America and Americans.

Robert K. Krick
Fredericksburg, Virginia

Acknowledgments

ʝ∂

ANYONE WRITING HISTORY accumulates debts. More facts, more debts. The community of Civil War historians is filled with patient and generous people, who are extraordinarily kind in sharing their treasures and in pointing down the road to where the next bonanza lies. These brief acknowledgments fall far short of expressing my obligation to many wonderful people.

It is altogether fit and proper that authors make public their debt to their wives, for evenings stolen from family life and for preoccupation with events long ago, to the detriment of domestic bliss, but this would be wholly insufficient here. Beverly Lowry not only typed the entire manuscript—twice—but spent long hours in the National Archives deciphering faded handwriting, to the betterment of this book. For her continued affection in the face of such demands I will always be warmly grateful.

I owe a special debt to William C. "Jack" Davis of Stackpole Books, who saw the potential in my awkward first draft and, with his associate, Sylvia Frank, piloted the book to its final form.

At the National Archives, Michael Musick gave us the benefit of his twenty years in that treasure house, and pointed us toward material we never would have found independently.

To Robert K. Krick, chief historian at Fredericksburg National Military Park, I give my warmest thanks for his broad knowledge and accurate coaching. His willingness to introduce me to other historians was invaluable.

Also at the National Archives, Stuart Butler aided us in the art of finding courts-martial, and Michael Meier and DeAnn Blanton were additionly helpful.

Robin Lockwood of Bookman Productions and Hal Lockwood of Penmarin Books gave us friendly encouragement and priceless technical instruction.

Over the past seven years, dozens of people helped me by answering questions or giving advice. With my apologies in advance to those whom I have neglected, a partial list includes Gary J. Arnold, Beverly D. Bishop, James H. Blakenship, Jr., Tom Broadfoot, James S. Brust, Susan Butler, Mike Cavanaugh, Gordon A. Cotton, Jennifer L. Davis, Mary Lou Davison, Henry Deeks, Linda Grant De Pauw, David Evans, James C. Frasca, Deborah C. Gaudier, Dale F. Giese, Barbara D. Hall, James O. Hall, Richard Harwell, James H. Hutson, Whitmel M. Joyner, James C. Klotter, Robert

E. L. Krick, Francis Lord, Howard Madaus, Susan Manakul, Carl Mautz, Jim and Judy McLean, Wilbur E. Meneray, Myra Morales, Russell Norton, Mike Ostrowski, Herb Peck, Russ A. Pritchard, Michael Rhode, Charlotte Rittenhouse, Carol Roark, Jerry Russell, Donna J. Seifert, Charlie Shively, John J. Slonaker, Franklin G. Smith, Richard Soloway, William F. Stapp, Buddy Thompson, Robert M. Utley, and Ross A. Webb.

Amie Freling, at the Sign of the Whale, saw to our nutrition and made evenings in Washington, D.C., more enjoyable.

Special recognition must go to the late Bell Irvin Wiley, who fifty years ago first gave prominence to the life of the common soldier, in a remarkable series of classic books, and to Robert W. Waitt, whose Civil War Roundtable talks in the 1960s drew together earthy material from the great conflict.

As always, the author bears sole responsibility for interpretations, errors, and omissions.

Introduction

๛

THERE WAS NO SEX during the Civil War. Everyone knows that. Just consider some of the leading actors in that greatest of America's dramas.

Take, for example, Abraham Lincoln. Never was a man's soul so revealed as by that new invention, the camera. Gaze at the Alexander Hesler portrait of 1857, four years before the war. We see a beardless man in the prime of middle adulthood, the facial flesh full, almost unlined, the nose prominent but not beaky. Only three years later, in June 1860, Hesler photographed Lincoln again. Now the crease between mouth and cheek has deepened, the brow has begun to furrow, and the chin is more firmly set.[1]

Mathew Brady's inaugural portrait was taken a year later. The new president has grown a full set of chin whiskers, but the mouth and eyes are not hidden; around the mouth the furrows are more indented. Already the eyes are deeper set, darker; he has seen the horror and the bloodshed ahead, the first flicker of the lightning of the terrible, swift sword.

Leap ahead three years—three long years of war—to the February 1864 portrait, again by Brady. The cheeks are beginning to sink in and the whiskers are sparser, but the eyes are fierce—the eyes of a hawk, gazing into the far, far distance, seeing the rivers of blood, the suspended liberties, freedoms forgone to save a greater freedom.

In that same month, February 1864, the famous "Five Dollar Bill" portrait was taken, the one that graces our currency today. Lincoln's eyes still have a far-off look but are directed slightly downward, creating the expression seen in Eastern art in sculptures representing the Buddha of Infinite Compassion.

A year later, in February 1865, Lincoln sat again for his portrait. The lines around the mouth are not just furrows, but deep creases, almost ravines; gray hairs pepper his short beard, and the eyes—the eyes! They see a million miles away. They are the eyes of a man of sorrows, of a heavy heart, of a weary melancholy, aching to reconcile and to heal. Beneath those pools of tired sadness are dark pouches of flesh, criss-crossed with a thousand tiny wrinkles. In two months he will be dead (as were hundreds of thousands of soldiers before him), but a portion of him seems already departed. The man behind that dolorous gaze surely was freighted with cares that would deny all lust. The indicators of physiognomy all point toward a man whose passions were at work in arenas far from the carnal.

1

And what of his famous sense of humor? The scholar P. M. Zall[2] has collected 325 authenticated Lincoln jokes, told by the "Old Railsplitter" himself. Most of these jokes deal with greed, pomp, vanity, and avarice. There are several scatological stories and only nine jokes with a sexual theme (a mere 3 percent, most of these dating to the years in Illinois, before the war). Sex as a subject in his humor seems to have evaporated as the cares of the presidency piled in upon him.

It is hard to imagine old Father Abraham in those war-weary years turning to the first lady and saying, "Mary, are you feeling loving tonight?"

And what of Mary Todd Lincoln, his partner in life? They were drawn together by their mutual passionate belief in antislavery politics. Their love was sorely tested by the tribulations of her being First Lady. Washington society was Southern, and the wife of an antislavery president (even though she was Southern-born herself) was looked upon as almost a traitor. The Southern society ladies despised her, while the upper-crust Yankee women in Washington thought she was a Dixie agent.[3]

She was advised (and very bad advice, indeed) that the road to social success would be vast expenditures on clothes and entertaining, but the result was only more criticism.

Her sensitive nature and eccentric ways compounded each other. Her fearful headaches grew worse. Her temper and suspiciousness were widely known in the Capital. The death of her two children and of her half-brother completed the wreck. She began to have hallucinations.

It is hard to imagine that the president, weighted down with the sorrows of the bloody and protracted conflict, and the first lady, overcome by grief and social spite and wracked with blinding headaches, were able to find the energy for sexual union.

And what of that greatest of Southern men, Robert E. Lee? Not only in myth is he like Bayard, le Chevalier Sans Peur et Sans Reproche, but in reality also. Bobby Lee was bred to moral uprightness and ethical behavior, for in his own family he had seen and felt the hideous fruits of lust and wantonness.[4]

His father had been that hero of the American Revolution, "Light Horse Harry," formally Lt. Col. Henry Lee, a dashing and romantic figure, future governor, and a hopeless and destructive financial failure. Light Horse Harry married first the "Divine Mathilda," sired Henry Lee, Junior, wasted Mathilda's vast inheritance, and upon her death married the heiress Ann Carter, with whom he sired Robert E. Lee and Carter Lee.

By the time Robert was of an age to understand the world, everything he saw was a disaster. His father had destroyed the fortunes of both of his wives and fled from creditors and sheriffs. His mother lived on the pity and charity of family. His half-brother, Henry, by now married to the morphine-crazed Anne McCarty, sired a child by Anne's teenage sister and embezzled the young girl's money. Driven from society, having earned the nickname "Black Horse Harry," Henry was never mentioned by his brother Robert. To compound the mischief, Carter, Robert's full brother, spent the last of the family money on high living.

No wonder Robert heeded the advice of his mother to "practice self-denial and self-control." In the decades to come, Robert was utterly faithful to his often-difficult wife, and, from the testimony of his own troops, never was known to utter an oath. Robert E. Lee, too, joins the ranks of the unstained, almost-celibate, and totally nonadulterous Civil War figures.

Now let us regard Lee's most valued lieutenant: Gen. Thomas J. "Stonewall" Jackson.[5] In our day, it may be hard to comprehend how bred-in-the-bone were the ethical and religious values of such men. After the Battle at Cedar Mountain, Jackson announced that "God has blessed our armies with another victory," and ordered a day of thanksgiving. About the battle, he wrote to his wife, "If God be for us, who can be against us? . . . whilst we attach so much importance to being free from temporal bondage, we must attach far more to being free from the bondage of sin."

While his underlings quarreled over matters of pride and discipline, Jackson hoped to illustrate the rigors of duty with his own example: Although he longed for home and family, he denied himself those pleasures and had not been under his own roof in almost two years, had not seen his beloved wife in a year, and had never seen his newborn child. All this, in spite of many of his officers getting leave to go home for romantic encounters.

Later, after Jackson's terrible wound, while death crept near, he summoned his chaplain, Tucker Lacy. Was Jackson's concern his own salvation? No. He wanted to be sure that Lacy was working among the troops to ensure observance of the Sabbath. And as Jackson sank further, he and Mrs. Jackson sang together all six verses of "Show Pity, Lord," Watt's hymn based on Psalm 51.

Just before the growing delirium carried him away from this world, his wife, at the bedside, said, "Well, before this day closes, you will be with the Blessed Savior in his glory." In a final moment of coherence, Jackson replied, "I will be an infinite gainer to be translated." Such words, such sentiments, such devotion are part of a different age, but they tell much about the man. To even attempt to imagine lechery or adultery in such a man as Jackson would be to trivialize him and his powerfully held code of ethics.

Consider next Kate Cummings, the Confederate nurse whose published journal is one of the classics of the Civil War.[6] Miss Cummings, who worked valiantly in tending the great flood of Confederate wounded, waged two additional battles: against the Southern women who would not nurse the wounded because medical work was "immodest," and against drunkenness among the hired help. She also was quite explicit that during four years of travel throughout the South, both officers and enlisted men were, without exception, perfect gentlemen. She saw no act and heard no word that would offend even the most fastidious and refined woman.

Another witness to the spotless morality of military life was Carlton McCarthy, a Confederate soldier whose observations were published in 1882 under the title of *Detailed Minutiae of Soldier Life*.[7] His general opinions were that Rebels were proud, generous, and brave, while Yankees were greedy, rich, overfed, and lazy. On the subject of morals, McCarthy describes a visit by a mother or a sister of one of the soldiers; such visitors were "treated with the greatest courtesy and kindness by the whole command. But the lady visitors! The girls! Who could describe the effect of their appearance in camp! They produced conflict in the soldier's breast. They looked so clean, they were so gentle, they were so different from all around them." He describes in infinite detail the courtesy and modesty that all soldiers displayed toward women.

McCarthy goes on to tell the amusements of a soldier on furlough: "Food, shelter and rest, the great concerns, being thus all provided for, the soldier enjoyed intensely his freedom from care . . . living as near a man may, the innocent life of a child. He plays marbles, spun his top, played at football . . . and hopscotch."

McCarthy further remarks upon the fear "that the bivouacs, the campfires and the march would accustom the ears of their bright and innocent boys to obscenity, oaths and blasphemy." Not so, he insists, indeed quite the opposite: "No parent could watch a boy as closely as his messmates . . . merciless critics who demanded more of their protege then they were willing to submit to themselves." He concludes, "The gospel took hold of the deepest and purest motives of the soldiers, won them thoroughly, and made the army as famous for its forbearance, temperance, respect for women and children, sobriety, honesty and morality as it was for endurance and invincible courage."

In McCarthy's army, all was blushes and modesty, noble brows, lofty sentiments, and high-minded good will. There were no hints of degradation, of sins of the flesh.

A faint dawn of prurience appears in the title of a collection of Col. James Garfield's wartime letters: *The Wild Life of the Army*.[8] Garfield, later president of the United States and victim of an assassin's bullet, was a voluminous correspondent. His letters were not collected and published until 1964, and the title that hints of naughty deeds was added by the editor. A careful reading of the hundreds of epistles reveals four recurrent themes: his annoyance at his military superiors; complaints about his almost-constant diarrhea; descriptions of the agonies he suffered from hemorrhoids; and professions of undying love for his wife and daughter.

If "wild life" meant having his piles tortured by hours in the freezing rain, pounding on a military saddle, then Garfield had wild life aplenty. But as for boozing, womanizing, or any hint of lecherous activity in the army, we may look in vain.

It would appear thus far that we have an event unparalleled in history: a war free of sexual activity.

And yet . . . and yet, in the decade from 1860 to 1870, the population of the United States increased by 7,111,051 persons. In spite of the millions of war casualties, in spite of most able-bodied men being away from their wives and sweethearts for four years, new citizens outstripped the ones who died by over 7 million. There is no historical record of an epidemic of immaculate conception in this era; all these new souls were conceived in the time-honored way.

Another cold statistic lights our way in this dimly lit corridor: the answer that 12,000 men gave to Alfred Kinsey in the 1940s about their private lives.[9]

Civil War scholar Everett B. Long, in his monumental *Civil War Day by Day*,[10] states that the average soldier was age twenty-six. Dr. Kinsey's informants at that age averaged 3.2 orgasms per week. Human biology did not change much in the eighty years that separated the Civil War and Dr. Kinsey. In spite of disease, privation, fatigue, and moral preaching, it is likely that the testosterone tickle, the devil on the left shoulder, the still small voice of lust, cried out as strongly to men in 1862 as in 1942.

And yet . . . and yet, there is almost no mention of the sexual side of life in the thousands of books written about our country's greatest war. Today our contemporary books and magazines seem obsessed with sex, but in 1862 such an accusation would have been difficult. It is as if a great, gray veil was drawn across an entire area of human activity.

Sex, in our society, has always occupied a peculiar place. It produced all of us; it is the thread that links every generation; it intrudes into the thoughts of most adult men (and many women); and it is at the same time denounced, hidden, mocked, and trivialized. It is at once the highest and the lowest, the brightest and the darkest. The ruler of American sex would be the Prince of Ambivalence. And, indeed, sex contains within itself both the best and the worst of human possibilities.

If you asked the author's own views of sexuality in human life, his answer would parallel that of the legendary Southern senator when asked by a constituent about his views on whiskey: "Sir, you have asked my stand on the subject of whiskey. Well, if by whiskey you mean that degradation of the noble barley, that burning fluid which sears the throats of the innocent, that vile liquid that sets men to fighting in low saloons, from whence they go forth to beat their wives and children, that liquor the Devil spawns which reddens the eye, coarsens the features and ages the body beyond its years, then I am against it with all my soul. But, sir, if by whiskey you mean that diadem of the distiller's art, that nimble golden ambrosia which loosens the tongue of the shy, gladdens the heart of the lonely, comforts the afflicted, rescues the snake-bitten, warms the frozen and brings the joys of conviviality to men during their hard-earned moments of relaxation, then I am four-square in favor of whiskey. From these opinions I shall not waver."

The author's opinions on the matters with which this book is concerned might be stated in similar fashion. "If by sex, you mean that engine that moves the terrible wheels of lust, that carnal burr under the saddle that hurls men of the Gospel down from their pulpits, that tickle that causes kings to abandon their thrones for a sniff of some sweet thing, that demon that turns the heads of captains and generals, so that they whisper breathless nonsense and military secrets into the ear of some doe-eyed double agent, that frenzy that leads men of common sense to thrust aside their loyal wives, weeping children, and vested pension funds to run off with secretaries with half their years and education, that terrible strength that enables an underweight young man to couple with twenty different partners between Friday and Monday in a poorly lit Turkish bath, that dizzying blindness that allows those who brush twice a day and floss every night to risk heartbreak, herpes, AIDS, syphilis, gonorrhea, chlamydia, and lymphogranuloma venereum for the sake of a pelvic spasm, that force that causes altar boys to flog themselves silly in a soapy bathtub, torn between guilt and excitement, if that is what you mean by sex, then I am irrevocably opposed to it.

"However, if by sex you mean that delectable gift of heaven that showers its blessings upon the committed souls so that their hearts beat as one, that force that inspires the long-married to walk holding hands in the cool of the evening, that urge to enjoy the fruit of such unions and provide the twenty-two years of endurance, orthodontia, and tuition hikes that such offspring engender, that force that quickens the pulse when the loved one's footsteps are heard on the porch, that ever-flowing font of shared memories, of binding pleasures, or that drive that causes a pair of geese to mate for life, ever-faithful to their troth, generous, companionate, and true, then I am four-square in favor of sex."

Clearly, the Prince of Ambivalence has not been dethroned. And because of the two-sided nature of the subject, even the mention of sex in the same breath with the Civil War (or War for Southern Independence, as my Dixie-born high-school history teacher called it) is enough to excite scorn and denunciation. Why? Quite simple. The Civil War was our Holy War, our jihad.

In the collective unconscious of America, where our national archetypes dwell, no other war was a Holy War. The Revolution was too long ago, a vague patchwork of Valley Forge and Paul Revere; the War of 1812 has been forgotten by all but candidates for television quiz shows; the Spanish-American War was a Hearst creation that has left us tangled in the Philippines still; the First World War was a bloody affair that we somehow entered to save the French; the Good War, as Studs Terkel has titled it, was good, but not holy; Korea and Vietnam were both painful lapses that Americans try to forget; and finally, the Gulf War was a victorious battle without a victory. All these wars, no matter what their real significance, have failed to capture the American imagination as has the Civil War.

Somehow, the camp followers of the American Revolution, the girls of Paris greeting the doughboys, the sailors' farewells in San Diego, and the whores of Pusan and Saigon are all plausible, all acceptable.

But sex in the Civil War? Never. It is indeed a sacred war. I have even been advised by colleagues not to write this book. Why would that be? Let us go back to Robert E. Lee for our answer.

Just as Charlemagne was the matter, the central motif of France and King Arthur the matter of Britain, so, too, is Robert E. Lee the matter of Dixie (and to a lesser extent the North, as well). He contains in the fullest measure all the glories, the contradictions, and the heartbreak of the South. He is the cavalier, the patrician and feudal gentleman who embodied the ennobling virtues of the past, in a war made unwinnable by the weak industrial base of the South, a lack that could have been cured only by destruction of the very same feudal system of plantations and small farms that were and are the fabric of the Southern legend.

Not the least of the origins of this Southern miasma of self-delusion were the works of Sir Walter Scott. His themes of twilight-of-a-nobility and exiled aristocrats struck such a resonant chord that the soul of Dixie swelled to a tsunami of antebellum nostalgia, even before there was a "bellum" to be "ante." Sentimental feudalism of the most saccharine type was the soil in which fictitious colonels came to believe in the reality of their ranks, and it also nurtured the rampant contempt for Yankees, who failed to appear sufficiently noble. Scott helped the South to gaze at its hopelessly obsolete system of feudal land-holding and brutal hand labor and see itself as a nobility.

Mark Twain, with penetrating insight, noted that Scott set "the world in love with dreams and phantoms . . . with the silliness and emptinesses, sham grandeurs, sham gauds and sham chivalries, of a brainless and worthless long-vanished society. . . . Sir Walter . . . is in great measure responsible for the war."[11] (Such insights, however, were scarce on either side of the Mason-Dixon line in 1861.)

Part of this interlocked system of legend and morality is the theme of Honor, especially the honor of white Southern womanhood, a distillation of the most rarefied Scottian courtly love, Anglican Victorianism, and bedrock American puritanism: Separate men from women; separate race from race; separate body from spirit; separate angels from devils; separate the forces of light from those of the Prince of Darkness. And in operant terms, no sex.

If the collective will of the South had created the perfect man to lead the Confederacy, he would have resembled Lee in every detail. But since Lee actually existed, since he actually embodied every virtue wanted of him, he did not need to be invented. Once found, he needed only to be cherished, honored, and obeyed. For a Southerner to doubt Lee, he had to doubt himself. In peace, such self-doubt is rare; in war, impossible.

To raise the specter of a sexual side of the Civil War is to question the very symbol of that age. But just as in Red China, where nothing is to be believed until it has been officially denied, in the record of the Civil War the almost total absence of sexual mention tells us that something is there. In that classic cliché of old adventure films, "It's quiet out there tonight—too quiet."

To do justice to this subject, we must examine the sources of our knowledge.

What *do* we know about the Civil War, and how do we know it? All the witnesses are dead. We have only the written word and a few thousand photographs.

There are books about the Civil War, many books, thousands of books, probably fifty thousand books. There are hundreds of books about the Battle of Gettysburg alone. In a possibly irreverent attempt to describe this literature, I would state that the books tend to fall into seven different categories, which I have illustrated here with imaginary titles.

1. Memories of famous officers (*Sabres and Saddles—the Recollections of J. B. W. Chalfontville, Major General, CSA*).

2. Regimental histories (*Keystone Comrades: The History of the 240th Regiment of Pennsylvania Volunteers*).

3. Controversy and second-guessing (*What General Snodgrass Should Have Done at Sawtooth Gap*).

4. Technical analyses (*The Suspender Shortage as a Factor at Gettysburg*).

5. General histories such as Shelby Foote's, Bruce Catton's, and Douglas Southall Freeman's monumental works (not imaginary).

6. Collections of letters (*A Boy in Blue Writes Home*).

7. Diaries (*One Step at a Time—Diary of a Rebel Sentry*).

Of these seven categories, only the last two are likely to say much about the earthy or bawdy side of Civil War life. (There are exceptions, of course, such as Bell I. Wiley, Edmund G. Love, and Margaret Leech.) Letters to Mom and Dad were usually pretty tame, so the small fraction of letters written to peers at home can be valuable sources of personal experience. Diaries, too, were often candid. Both diaries and letters, however, before they ever saw the light of public scrutiny, underwent that dread process—editing.

The soldier himself, now a respected citizen and veteran, was quick to blue-pencil the scandalous reality of his past before it reached the public. But even more prone to the censor's wrath were those letters and diaries edited for publication by the (usually) unmarried daughter of the now-deceased veteran, whose hallowed memory was hardly to be defamed by imprudent recollections of whores, clap, dysentery, blasphemy, and farting in the tent. No accurate figure is possible, but probably 90 percent of all sexual information has been deleted from the published record of personal lives.

Two other sources, often valuable, are the newspapers of that time and the surgeon's statistics, both Union and Confederate. The daily press, especially the police reports section, was surprisingly frank in its exposés of madams, houses of prostitution, police cover-ups, and other hanky-panky.

The surgeon's reports of venereal disease were quite accurate, considering the limits of medical knowledge in 1861–65, and the huge Report of the Surgeon General, published at the end of the war, has many pages devoted to the type, incidence, and distribution of the ailments of Venus. But in spite of all these sources, the search for what William Shakespeare called "country matters" during the Civil War is arduous and usually unrewarded.

A careful study of the considerable material still extant will add a dimension until now missing from accounts of that greatest of all American struggles.

The researcher who examines history by computerized content analysis, or other methods demanding large numbers of countable events, will be disappointed here. Experiences that are traditionally private, intensely personal, and intentionally censored and concealed, leave few traces.

As to the issue of the propriety of such a quest, the real question should be: "What right does a historian have to conceal a vital part of history?" An emasculated, neutered, sanitized history may well be best for young children, but grown-ups are entitled to know all the dimensions of life as it was lived, and the historian has a positive obligation to present the full panorama of how real people lived their actual lives, neither devils nor angels, but living, breathing, loving human beings—in brief, our own ancestors.

Chapter One

ॡ

Our Founding Fathers

IN THE SEARCH for matters sexual during the War Between the States, an examination of precedents will inevitably be productive, since warfare—and that spark between lad and lass—existed long before 1861.

In the French and Indian Wars of 1754–64, Gen. Edward Braddock, when setting off for Fort Duquesne, limited his troops to a "maximum of six women per company." The records of the time leave no doubt that these cooks and laundresses had a more primary function as companions to the soldiers. To reduce the female consorts to six per company, Braddock had to send a much larger number back to civilization.

The women who were sent home were the fortunate ones, for after Braddock's defeat by the French, several of the English women were scalped and three were taken prisoner. The French commander kept one woman for himself and sold the other two.

During the Revolution, the British troops coming from England were allowed one woman for each ten men. In the passenger manifests, the officers' wives were on one list, while those of the enlisted men were listed under "baggage," giving rise to an old term for women of low social standing.

While the British may have arrived in America with one woman for each ten men, these numbers soon grew. In 1781, the British forces in New York were 23,000 men and 7,000 women and children. By the end of the war, there was one woman for every four soldiers. Daniel Wier, the commissary officer for the British, wrote, "The women and children of every regiment are indeed very numerous beyond any idea of imagination."

In 1776, when Gen. William Howe evacuated Boston, he loaded 8,900 soldiers, 900 women camp followers, and 1,100 Loyalists on ships and sailed for Halifax. Two years later, when Gen. Henry Clinton evacuated

11

Philadelphia, 15,000 soldiers, 1,500 women, and 1,500 children, along with their supplies, formed a wagon train 12 miles long.

The women of the British enlisted men traveled on foot, and they performed useful services such as cooking and sewing in addition to their amorous activities. Among the officer class, who lived in relative luxury, were some notorious instances of poor example and lax discipline.

Gen. William Howe's dalliance with Mrs. Loring, an American, was made more notorious by the bribe he presented to her husband: Joshua Loring was made commissary general of prisoners. In this post, Loring stole so much that hundreds of Yankee prisoners died of starvation. Howe's enemies skewered him in a ditty, popular at the time:

> Sir William, he, snug as a flea,
> Lay all this time asnoring,
> Nor dreamed of harm,
> As he lay warm,
> In bed with Mrs. Loring.

The mercenaries—the Hessians, Brunswickers, and Anspachers—had their own followers. Hessian general Friedrich von Wurmb said, "This corps has more women and children than men."

The American Revolutionary forces of George Washington were also followed by women, but in much fewer numbers, and many of these women were there for honorable reasons as their homes were occupied or burned, and they traveled to cook and sew for their husbands. The women also formed the nursing corps, as the American forces had little provision for tending the wounded.

General Washington did his best to stem the flood of women who followed his troops. In June 1777, he issued an order, "A return is to be made tomorrow, to the Adjutant General, of all the women belonging to the camp." Several years later, his new order read, "A return of the number of women in the several regiments which compose this army, is to be given to the orderly office the second of January [1783]." In between these two orders, he issued twenty-three others on the subject of women, with requests that included asking for a head count, requesting that they go home if possible, asking that pregnant women not join the march, and demanding that the women be kept off the supply trains.[1]

Washington was not the only person to have women in his entourage. In September 1775 Gen. Benedict Arnold departed Cambridge for a long-distance raid on Quebec. The battalion led by Christopher Green, of Rhode Island, had with it a nineteen-year-old officer, the cocky Aaron Burr. In spite of the hardships of the journey, Burr found time to dally with his young Indian companion, known to the troops as the "Abenaki Queen with Golden Thighs."[2]

Back in New Jersey, Washington showed his realism and compassion in a letter to then Secretary of Finance Robert Morris. Morris had requested that Washington issue only enough rations to feed one woman for each fifteen troops. The American commander replied, "I was obliged to give provision to the extra women in the Regiments or lose by Desertion some of the oldest and best soldiers in the service. The New Yorkers have fled their homes and have no means of subsistence. The cries of these women, the suffering of their children, and the complaints of their husbands would admit of no alternative."

He chafed at directives from bureaucrats safe at headquarters, far from the scene of the action: "but if from misinformation or a partial investigation, my business is taken up by others at a distance of 150 miles, it is easy to conceive the confusion which must ensue."

It is obvious that hundreds of women, the original daughters of the American Revolution, followed the American troops, and that their activities included not only cooking, sewing, and nursing, but also participating in those physical bonds that have drawn men and women together for millennia.[3]

In 1826, fifty years after George Washington took the field, the U.S. Navy, in the form of the sex-starved crew of the USS *Dolphin,* demonstrated the power of lust during the long-forgotten Battle of Honolulu. This conflict has a unique history.

The Hawaiian Islands in the early 1800s were in a state of violent social and political change. The aristocracy and the priesthood had ruled for centuries through a complex system of social class structure and taboo. The usual penalty for any infraction was death. When the first whites arrived, they challenged the taboos and were not struck dead, either by the gods or by the aristocracy. (Captain Cook was an unlucky exception.)

When the general population saw that the white sailors did as they pleased, the sailors were accorded status as aristocracy, almost demigods. These seafarers, whether from whaling ships or merchant vessels, were largely illiterate, hard-living, working-class men, used to bad pay, worse food, violent discipline, and low status. They were understandably delighted to be suddenly accepted into the top ranks of society, with unlimited access to women and power. The Hawaiians had a very open view of sexual behavior (in vivid contrast to early Victorian-age New England), which the sailors took as loose morals and an opportunity for exploitation.

Parallel with this influx of opportunists was the continuing epidemic, now waxing, now waning, of venereal disease. The British had landed on Kauai in 1778; within two years, venereal disease had spread to the southern tip of the big island of Hawaii, nearly 200 miles away. Each ship brought fresh inoculations of those diseases that plague the generative organs, as well as deadly epidemics of measles and smallpox.

Thus two cultures were on a fatal collision course. The Hawaiians had lost all faith in their gods; their new king, the young Liholiho, had declared the old religion dead. Since the aristocracy and the old priesthood were mutually supportive, the mandate for governance was gone. The whites, mostly renegade sailors turned economic and sexual exploiters, were gaining power and land (and owned the best weapons). With the old culture dead and the new culture a mixture of anarchy, greed, and societal collapse, there seemed no future for the Hawaiians.

At this propitious moment, in 1820, an alternative arrived aboard the ship *Thaddeus:* the first of the American missionaries. The Hawaiians, desperate from the loss of their own belief system, willingly embraced this new world view. There was an almost-instantaneous mass conversion to Christianity. From the aristocracy downward, the new teaching took hold. And almost the first stricture was the new taboo: no more indiscriminate sexual intercourse.

A U.S. Navy ship, the *Dolphin,* Lt. John Percival commanding, arrived in Hawaii in 1826. The *Dolphin's* crew, like all mariners then, had long heard of the friendliness of women in the South Seas, and after many months away from land they were eager to match their ardor with the legendary sexual charms of the wahine. The men were enraged to learn that times had changed; the women were forbidden to all forms of promiscuity. The crew petitioned their commander (known to history as "Mad Jack" Percival) for relief.

Percival, in turn, demanded an audience with Prime Minister Kalanimoku and the Dowager Queen (and regent) Kaahumanu. In his message, Percival asserted that denying women to his crew was an insult to the American flag.

The Queen replied, in a letter, that she had a right to control her own subjects; that in punishing her offending subjects she had done no injustice to other nations and that she sought only to save her own nation from vice and ruin. She further reminded Percival that strangers in a new country are expected to follow the laws and customs of their hosts.

The governor of Oahu delivered this message. Mad Jack, in a frenzy of rage, replied that he would not write the Queen again but would visit her in person, and if the leader of the missionaries appeared, he would shoot him.

An audience was arranged. Percival demanded that the Queen release her women: "It is not good to taboo the women. It is not so in America! Why do you deny women to us when you gave them to the British?"

The Queen replied, "In former times, before the Word of God arrived here, we were dark-minded, lewd and murderous; at the present time we are seeking a better way." She added, "Had you brought American women with you, and we had tabooed them, you might then justly be displeased with us."[4]

There was more such discussion, with no change of opinion. Mad Jack clenched his fists in rage and said that the next day he would give his men rum and send them ashore, where, if they were still denied women, they would pull down the houses of the missionaries and take the women they wanted.

The next day was the Sabbath. In the afternoon, as the royal family gathered in the prime minister's home for divine services, 150 drunken sailors (merchant seamen had joined the navy men) arrived, repeated their demands for women, made loud threats, and then smashed seventy windowpanes. A contingent proceeded on to the home of Hiram Bingham, the leader of the missionaries. Mrs. Bingham locked the front door, and the sailors proceeded to smash in her windows.

Then the mob found Bingham himself, surrounded him, cursed him loudly, and menaced him with clubs and knives. A group of Hawaiian men, Christian converts, stood calmly by; they told Bingham no harm would come to him.

When the first American sailor actually struck a blow at Bingham, the riot was over. The Hawaiians clubbed the ringleaders unconscious and disarmed the remainder. The sailors still able to walk were sent back to the ships, their arms bound tightly.

Another group, which had returned to Bingham's home and was attempting to break down the door, was interrupted by the ship's officers and beaten off with canes.

In the late afternoon, Percival reappeared, grudgingly admitted that his men had gone too far, and repeated his demands for women. In fact, he said that the *Dolphin* would not leave Honolulu until his men were satisfied.

The Hawaiians, intimidated by the threats of further violence, reluctantly agreed to a lifting of the taboo. Soon the shouts and laughter from canoes filled with willing women were heard over the waters of the harbor. Percival, in a small concession to his Hawaiian hosts, put the two most violent sailors in irons and arranged for the repair of the damaged homes. Thus ended the first visit of the U.S. Navy to Honolulu.[5]

Chapter Two

ॐ

The Birds and the Bees

IN 1860, WHAT DID PEOPLE BELIEVE about sexual matters, and further, how did they conduct themselves in their actual moments of physical intimacy? The truth of the matter is that though oceans of ink have been spilled on both subjects, we know precious little about either.

We do know a great deal, however, about what people in 1860 were told to do, as dozens of popular books and pamphlets have survived from that era, and we do have a substantial lode of medical articles that doctors wrote for their colleagues. As to actual behavior, though, we are mostly, but not entirely, in the dark.

Alfred Kinsey, in the era from 1940 to 1950, interviewed tens of thousands of men and women about their sexual habits, using very thoughtful questions and skilled interviewing techniques. Research of this quality never existed before, has not been repeated since, and probably will never take place again, so we must do the best we can with what history has left us, censored by the modesty of the participants themselves and by the prudery of their heirs.

In our search for the facts of life in the mid–nineteenth century, let us consider the subjects of religion and sexuality, the utopian reformers, masturbation, menstruation, premarital pregnancy, and the self-help books of the early Victorian times, as well as review the few glimmers of factual information available from those years.

The largest religious contingent to make their way to the New World were the Anabaptists, but they came not for sexual freedom but for freedom to practice their own brand of pietistic perfection. They wanted the New Jerusalem, not Merry Olde England.

While the frontier and parts of the South embraced a more liberal stance, the core of New England puritanism held to sexual asceticism, to the church as the agent of social control. Although New England discipline was relatively lenient by the standard of the times, it was firm enough and sufficiently all-encompassing to claim jurisdiction over nearly every civil matter. The war against the natural instincts produced the usual tension between impulse and society and the usual blend of repression and hypocrisy.

Even in a society as tightly controlled as pre-Revolutionary New England, human tendencies were hard to totally suppress. In Boston between 1670 and 1680, eleven cases of prostitution were prosecuted. The Society of Friends exercised tight control in Philadelphia, so the prostitutes set up camp in caves outside the city limits. William Penn found them so offensive that in 1685 he ordered the caves closed.

Boston, no doubt because of its role as a major seaport, led the colonies as a center of prostitution, and the citizens reacted with indignation and vigilante committees. In 1734 and 1737, mobs attacked and damaged two whorehouses, causing the inmates to flee. The Boston merchants, noting that the growing population of unmarried women formed a recruiting pool for prostitution, saw that putting them to work would suppress vice while at the same time producing the additional benefit of increasing the labor supply. One of the job fairs sponsored by the burghers saw 300 unmarried women on Boston Common, bent over their spinning wheels.

As the new century dawned, the French turned to legalized and regulated prostitution, but the Americans, like the British, have never been able to stomach the notion of openly accepting the oldest profession. Instead, our forefathers fought this evil through the Sunday School societies, handing out thousands of pamphlets. The Boston Society for the Moral and Religious Instruction of the Poor distributed booklets urging the poor to work harder and save their money, with the secondary purpose of removing the economic advantages of prostitution.

The unspoken message in all of this, of course, was that sexuality outside of marriage was evil and that religious duty prescribed that every effort be made to rescue fallen women, and if they insisted on remaining fallen, they should be made to change their ways, either by police enforcement or by direct action (paralleling the antisaloon crusaders who took axes to the furniture and mirrors of the offending taverns).

A cosmopolitan traveler once observed that, "France is a nation of one religion and fifty sauces, while America is just the opposite." Leaving aside the merits of the liquid half of biscuits and gravy, there is no doubt that America has been a fertile ground for new denominations, especially in the sixty years between 1800 and the Civil War.[1]

Alexander Campbell founded the Disciples of Christ. Joseph Smith founded the Church of Jesus Christ of Latter-day Saints. William Miller helped create the Seventh Day Adventist Church, and Mary Baker Eddy expounded the doctrines of Christian Science. Religious revival was in the air.

One of the most remarkable figures in this time of spiritual adventurers was John Humphrey Noyes, whose founding of the Oneida Colony marked a startling fusion of religious and sexual doctrine. Noyes, born in 1811, graduated from Dartmouth at age nineteen and pursued his religious studies at the Yale School of Divinity, where he was heavily influenced by the Perfectionists, who believed that mortal man could attain a state of perfect love between himself and God. At age twenty-three, he announced that he had become Perfect; he was asked to leave Yale and his license to preach was revoked.

After spending several years in a state of spiritual turmoil, during which he lived as an itinerant preacher and his family worried that he might be deranged, he founded a Perfectionist community at Putney, Vermont, with money inherited from his father; six years later, in 1847, he was asked to leave town because of allegations of group sex, a misinterpretation of what Noyes called Complex Marriage. The following year, he founded the Oneida Colony, which persists today as a successful silverware manufacturing company. Complex Marriage was abandoned in 1879, and the original commune was dissolved in 1880.

Just what were the practices that so excited Noyes's neighbors? His two basic beliefs may be summarized as follows: First, the Second Coming of Christ had already happened, in A.D. 70, at the time of the destruction of Jerusalem, thus all promised things are possible; and, second, citing Matthew 22:30, "in the resurrection, they neither marry nor are given in marriage, but are like angels in heaven," leading to the conclusion that heavenly marriage is possible right here on earth for Perfect people. Such marriage precludes monogamy, because all are one flesh.

This doctrine seems to have been revealed to Noyes around May 1846, when he found himself very attracted to a member of the community, Mrs. Mary E. Cragin. Not only did she return his feelings, but her husband, George Cragin, and Mrs. Noyes discovered that they, too, were very attracted to each other. After earnest prayer and prolonged discussion, it became clear that it was God's will for them to exchange sexual partners. Within a few months, two more couples became disciples of Complex Marriage. By the end of the year, the group had written down the principles of their "social union," which included an absolute community of property—not only furniture and land, but also their bodies—and a recognition of the ultimate authority of God, who manifested Himself through the will of John Noyes, "the father and overseer whom the Holy Ghost has set over the family thus constituted."

Lest this community be confused with the free-love hippie communes of the 1960s, an examination of the details of life in a Perfect community will show some important differences.

At the time of the Civil War, the sexual doctrines of the Oneida Colony prohibited both love and monogamy, as these activities militated against the community as a whole. If a male member of the community felt attracted to one of the women, he approached her through a intermediary, usually one of the older women. If she approved, and the object of his attention agreed, the couple retired to a private room for their sexual meeting. Coitus reservatus was required; in this technique, the man refrained from ejaculation, but the woman was not limited in her orgasms. The usual encounter lasted for an hour. Afterward, the couple was required to return to their own separate rooms, as pillow talk and couple-bonding detracted from the community.

How did the man avoid ejaculation? By attending Noyes's lectures on male continence, in which Noyes compared the technique to "rowing near a waterfall. Too near, and you will go over the edge." It must have been successful, as the birth rate in the colony was very low.

Another feature of Complex Marriage was the concept of mixing ages, in the belief that the older and more spiritually developed would teach the younger, in bed as well as out. In a typical month, each community member would have five different partners. Noyes explained to his flock that sexual pleasure was a divine gift; since coitus reservatus gave the woman opportunity for multiple orgasms, and the men reported "satiation" after an hour of coitus, Noyes found relatively little quarrel with his pupils.

Conceiving a child was a different matter. Approval of the entire community was needed, but most of all the blessing of Noyes himself, whose ideas had turned to the next generation of Perfect community members. Heavily influenced in the 1860s by Darwin's *Origin of the Species,* Noyes wrote against "involuntary and random procreation." Galton's term "eugenics" lay in the future, but Noyes was ever creative; his program would be called "stirpiculture," from the Latin *stirps,* meaning root or stem. As the 1860s came to a close, the young men of the community presented Noyes with a written testament of their loyalty. "The undersigned desire that you may feel that we most heartily sympathize with your purposes in regards to scientific propagation, and offer ourselves to be used in forming any combination that might seem to you desirable. We claim no rights. We ask no privileges . . . with a prayer that the grace of God will help us in this resolution, we are your true soldiers."

The young women of the community signed a similar manifesto, which opened with the ringing words, "we do not belong to ourselves in any respect, but that we do belong first to God, and second to Mr. Noyes as God's true representative."

While this might seem repugnant to today's feminists, it is well to remember that the usual lot of women 130 years ago was to be celibate or to have a dozen offspring and perhaps finally die in childbirth. Many men in those times wore out three or more wives.

In actual practice, stirpiculture was a partial success. In the years 1869–79, forty-eight live children were born at the community. Thirty-five were intentionally conceived, and thirteen were "accidents." Most women had only one child; twelve women had two children, and two women had three children, most of whom were accidentally conceived.

Noyes was a strict believer that heredity could be improved by changing the individual, the view also held by Lamarck and Lysenko, now long discredited. Chromosomes lay in the distant future. Perfectionists believed that spiritually advanced sires would father better children. Noyes believed sincerely in his own Perfection and was the father of ten of the "stirpicults," while Noyes's eldest son, Theodore, fathered three more.

Naturally, these ideas, magnified by rumor and gossip, created a sensation in the outside community, and there were many curious visitors to Oneida, both ordinary citizens and members of the press seeking a juicy story. All were disappointed. They came to see orgies, but what they found was neatness, prosperity, Christian discussion, and excellent food. The children appeared healthier than anywhere else in the country.

As to participating in the Civil War, the Perfectionists took the view that slavery was evil, but that no national problems could be solved until the nation as a whole turned to Christ. No one in the Community was drafted, but they did send cash to raise volunteers in the nearby communities.[2]

Another giant of utopian reform in the 1860s was Sylvester Graham. Now known only for the cracker that bears his name, he was a household word a century ago, a combination of Billy Graham, Benjamin Spock, and Linus Pauling.

Graham was born in Connecticut in 1794, as modernization was changing the patriarchal puritan theocracies into Yankee capitalist communities. The sense of lost roots, of a bygone age of clarity and stability, was pervasive. Graham was descended from preachers; his grandfather, a graduate of the University of Glasgow, held several New England pulpits. His father graduated from Yale and was an ardent supporter of the New Lights in the Great Awakening, a revivalist movement of the 1750s. Sylvester's father held the same pulpit in West Suffield, Connecticut, for fifty years. When his father died at age seventy-four, young Sylvester was only two years old.

The venerable preacher had been married twice. The ten children by his first wife grew to be prosperous businessmen or to marry prosperous businessmen. His second wife, Ruth, was overwhelmed at becoming a widow and having to raise her seven children alone. Her younger children were removed by the Probate Court because she was "in a deranged state of mind." When Sylvester was twenty-three, his mother moved to New Jersey, and Sylvester went with her, as he had no marketable job skills. His new neighbors remembered him as "an eccentric and wayward genius," who ran a small country store and spent his leisure time acting in amateur theatricals and pursuing hopeless love affairs.

At age twenty-nine, he entered the prep school run by Amherst College, but left after only one semester, a victim of bullies who disliked his arrogant personality. He then moved to Compton, Rhode Island, where he had a nervous breakdown and soon married one of the women who had nursed him back to health. He was thirty, and about to change his life.

Seized with the desire to become a minister, but not wanting to attend college, he apprenticed himself to the man who had officiated at his own wedding and, two years later, was licensed as an evangelist by the Mendon Association. He spent nearly a year as the pastor of a small Presbyterian congregation, and at age thirty-four was hired as a lecturer by the Pennsylvania Society for Discouraging the Use of Ardent Spirits. He spent a year in Philadelphia, then the center of American medicine, where he vastly increased his knowledge of both theology and physiology and created a new identity for himself—he became a professional reformer. In this uniquely American occupation, he launched an attack on the evils of diet and sex.

His views on the former are actually quite consistent with current ideas of nutrition. In the years of 1790–1830, Americans lived on alcohol, grease, salt, and white flour. The average American drank twenty-four quarts of whiskey a year and fried his food in lard. Land was cheap and transport was expensive; it was easy to grow corn but costly to send it to market. The most economic way to ship corn was in the form of whiskey and pork. Per capita meat consumption was 180 pounds a year, mostly bacon and ham.

Graham's dietary recommendations would raise no eyebrows today: drink water, not whiskey. Eat vegetables, grains, and whole wheat flour. Eat less fat and more fruit.

It was his ideas on sexual matters that are of greater concern to us, since he launched his career with the famous *Lectures to Young Men,* which in book form went through ten editions in fifteen years and kindled the conflagration of antimasturbation mania. Before Graham, minor attention had been focused on "self-abuse," but after 1834, all that changed.

Graham thundered, "Among the hapless inmates of the lunatic asylum, none is more incorrigible nor more incurable than the wretched victim of this odious vice! What of the fragments of his shattered reason he is still capable of gathering up from the sexual wreck, he craftily exercises in devising means and securing opportunities to elude the vigilance of his keepers and to indulge his despotic lust."

On and on, page after page, Sylvester Graham warned of the horrid results of self-stimulation: debasement of the mind, destruction of the moral faculties, self-loathing, physical decay, insanity, and finally, suicide. Graham was joined in his crusade by the leading psychiatrists of the day, who confirmed his warnings by creating the term "masturbatory insanity." The superintendent of the State Lunatic Hospital at Worcester, Massachusetts, claimed that 30 percent of the patients were insane because of their masturbation, and similar claims were made by many other psychiatric specialists. Still other writers warned that the loss of sperm permanently removed vital energies from the body. Graham was not concerned just with the solitary vice, however. He believed that the discharge of sperm in marital coitus was also debilitating. He urged marriage, not to legitimize sex, but to reduce it, believing that as spouses become bored with each other, they would have less sexual desire. On no condition should couples have intercourse more than twelve times a year.

Encouraged by the success of his book on self-abuse, he published a thick volume on diet and morality. Both long and boring, it sold poorly. He then tried the same ideas on the lecture circuit, but found little enthusiasm in his audiences. By 1838, he was deep in a second nervous breakdown, from which he never fully recovered. After twelve years of writing poems of despondency and wandering his hometown in a bathrobe, muttering incoherently, he died in 1851, certain that his work had been forgotten.[3]

He need not have worried. Forty-five years later, the crusade was still in full swing, as we see from the twenty-first edition of F. C. Fowler's *Life: How to Enjoy and How to Prolong It*. The author, a self-anointed physiognomist and anthropologist, described masturbation as a "brutal and brutalizing habit, a crime most monstrous, odious to extremity, absolutely ruinous, extinguishing the hope of posterity." Professor Fowler continued, saying that a single ejaculation is as harmful as the loss of 2 ounces of blood, that mental hospitals are full of the victims of masturbation, and that 90 percent of the deaths from tuberculosis were actually the result of sexual excess. His book is illustrated with pictures of pale, hollow-eyed demented boys who practiced the unnatural art.[4]

Most adults' association with the name Kellogg has to do with cornflakes and the box tops they once mailed off in exchange for various toys, but a century ago, one of the Kellogg brothers had much to say to America's youth about sex and diet.

Both brothers were raised as Seventh Day Adventists. Will Keith Kellogg, whose signature appears on the breakfast cereal boxes, was a pioneer in the technology of converting rolled corn mush into tasty, crunchy flakes. John Harvey Kellogg was a highly skilled surgeon, whose sexual ideas, expressed in his 1888 book, *Plain Facts for Old and Young People,* were less scientific than his work with a scalpel. Those who commit the "sin of self-pollution" were "below the meanest brute that breathes," worse than "the most loathsome reptile," and "ought to be ashamed to look into the eyes of an honest dog."[5]

We have no way of knowing how America's youth was influenced by such dire warnings about the disasters that allegedly befell one from the practice of self-stimulation. Did they react like Mark Twain in his famous speech before the Stomach Club in 1879, when he said to his audience, "I will . . . caution you against that species of recreation called 'self-abuse,' to which I see you are much addicted"? Twain went on to state that Homer, in the *Iliad,* said, "Give me masturbation or give me death," and that Julius Caesar asserted, "To the lonely it is company; to the forsaken it is a friend; to the aged and to the impotent it is a benefactor; they that are penniless are yet rich, in that they still have this majestic diversion."[6]

Or did they lack that rich sense of the absurd that enabled Twain to make light of the whole subject? Did they, instead, labor under the weight of guilt and shame, struggling against the impulse, yielding furtively and then anxiously awaiting the prophesied degeneration? No one knows for sure, but army records attribute some cases of death and debility to onanism.

William Hampton of Company M, 2d Nebraska Cavalry, had been a farmer. When he enlisted at age twenty-three, he had dark hair and gray eyes. Three months later, he died at Camp Cook, Dakota Territory; the cause: "Mania from Masturbation." We will never know, in modern medical terms, what killed him.

Pvt. Ehler Wilking of Company I, 76th Illinois Volunteers, a German-born farmer, enlisted at age twenty-two. Eight months later, at Vicksburg, he contracted "Spinal Meningitis" with dilation of the pupils and convulsions. He was described as "Crazy—Almost Insanity." After surviving this episode, he was transferred, six months later, to the Second Division hospital, where one doctor noted, "suffering from the symptoms of self abuse," and another diagnosed, "Masturbation, inveterate, accompanied by obvious loss of mental and physical vigor and epileptiform convulsions about once a week. Is not a case for a pension." Today, the unfortunate Wilking would probably be diagnosed as a postmeningitic Kluever-Bucy Syndrome and treated more sympathetically. His masturbation was, of course, a symptom, not a cause.

Even the intimation of self-stimulation was enough to cause great hardship for Pvt. James Hadsall of Battery K, 2d Pennsylvania Artillery. Dr. H. J. Borland and his wife were in their buggy, headed for Fort Simmons, near Washington, D.C. As they passed a column of marching soldiers, the doctor testified, Hadsall "turned around facing me and placed himself in the position of masturbation; he went through the motions of self-pollution until I drove past." Hadsall got six months at hard labor with a 24-pound iron ball on his ankle.[7]

A contemporary student of anti-onanist psychology has clarified the motivations of physicians who supported the polemics against self-abuse. In the Middle Ages, disease was seen to originate in sin, and the priest supplied the explanation for the mysteries of pain and sickness. In the secular era of 1800 to 1880, the clergy was no longer the authority on the origins of illness, but doctors were just as ignorant of the causes of diseases as any minister.

In all crises, *something* must be blamed. The mind craves explanation. Masturbation became the medical equivalent of sin. The victim could confess his self-abuse, the doctor would confirm its harmful effects and would then prescribe a penance: cold baths, nauseating medicines, painful chastity belts, agonizing dilation of the urethra, or (in the case of female masturbation) amputation of the clitoris. If the patient recovered, it "proved" the thesis; if he or she remained sick or died, it proved that the patient had arrived too late. The alleged harm of masturbation made sense of a confusing world.[8]

Physicians struggled with their own ignorance and preconceptions in more than one area of sexual functioning. Menstruation proved almost as perplexing to doctors as masturbation. Some doctors believed that the moon controlled women's cycles; others believed the fetus formed from menstrual blood. Some medical opinion held that menstruation was a disease, citing Adam and Eve, who allegedly reproduced without sex; it seems likely that the doctor was unfamiliar with Genesis 4:1. Ten years after the Civil War, Dr. A. F. A. King, in the *American Journal of Obstetrics*, claimed that women ovulated during their menses and should avoid coitus then, because menstrual blood caused gonorrhea. Further, Edward H. Clarke, a professor at Harvard, stated that the intellectual work of college was more harmful to girls than factory labor and that by 1910 American women would be completely infertile from overeducation.[9]

The quality of advice published in 1861 related to physiology and solitary sexual activity was certainly fraught with scientific inaccuracies and unfounded, terrifying admonitions. What advice was offered for men and women in the privacy of their own bedrooms? Dozens of marriage manuals survive in library collections. The salient points of a few will illustrate the genre.

Elizabeth Willard, in 1867, advised couples to have intercourse only twelve times a year. James C. Jackson, in his 1861 book, *The Sexual Organism,* identified female masturbators by a peculiar wiggle of the hips as they walked, and warned couples that "excessive" coitus would cause infertility. William Alcott, in his 1858 marriage manual, warned that masturbation was more dangerous than childbirth and that intercourse at night was harmful. Edward Foote, a "medical and electrical therapeutist" of Saratoga Springs, recommended that episodes of intercourse be spaced days or weeks apart to "render chemical electricity active in copulation."

An unknown author in the 1700s produced what was usually titled *Aristotle's Masterpiece,* though it was also called *The Works of Aristotle the Famous Philosopher.* It went through many printings, many editions, and many revisions, becoming the widest-read sexual advice book before 1850. As a sampling, the unknown author described the clitoris as "a sinewy and hard part of the womb, replete with spongy and black matter within." While the author recognized that the clitoris produced pleasure, being "the seat of lust," he asserted that unless the clitoris became erect, both pleasure and conception were impossible. (Imagine the confusion of an innocent bridegroom trying to comprehend his new wife's anatomy, after having read that the clitoris is part of the uterus.)

Even the most blockbuster authors today cannot claim a book that has gone through five hundred editions, but such was the success of Frederick Hollick, whose 1850 *Marriage Guide,* in its more positive moments, acknowledged that women have sexual feelings, that the clitoris can provide sexual pleasure, and that vaginal organisms can be perceived as "deeper" than clitoral ones. On the negative side, by today's standards, were his assertions that masturbation causes more sickness than all other sources combined, and that women "addicted" to the solitary vice should undergo amputation of the clitoris.

Another mixture of negative and positive is seen in Seth Pancoast's 1859 *The Ladies' Medical Guide and Marriage Friend.* Much of it was beauty advice, but as he turned to the subject of the clitoris, he waxed eloquent for pages on "the thrill or voluptuous sensation" to be found there. He blamed women's problems on excessive childbearing rather than masturbation, and recommended against abstinence. After denouncing lesbianism ("this revolting vice"), he advocated educational and professional opportunities for women, but drew the line at giving women the vote.

The Lover's Marriage Lighthouse, Harmon Root's 1858 guide for the perplexed, is yet another hodgepodge of progressivism and reaction. In its 511 pages, Root advocated easy divorce as well as sex before marriage for women, so that they can choose a compatible partner. On the other hand, his polemic against masturbation included not only the usual cautions, but also a warning against the use of dildos. Further, he believed that conception begins with "spiritual impregnation," in which the wife fertilizes the husband with her eyes, a novel concept called "spirit mating."

And, finally, an article showing the sexual dangers of being a working woman appeared in the *New Orleans Medical and Surgical Journal* in 1867. Sewing machines then were operated by a foot pedal. If the operator pressed her thighs together and pedaled rapidly the friction could produce an orgasm. The author warned shop foremen to listen for "runaway sewing machines," thus removing one of the few fringe benefits provided by sweatshop work.[10]

Returning now to the issue of what people *actually did* years ago, there are two studies of some relevance. Daniel Smith reasoned that in a society without reliable birth control, premarital sex could best be measured by counting pregnant brides, and studied two New England towns that have kept records since the year 1650. The results are striking.

In 1650, about 8 percent of brides were pregnant. This rose to 15 percent by 1700 and peaked at 35 percent in 1760. Then there was a steep decline until, in 1840, the rate was only 10 percent. By the end of the Civil War, the rate had more than doubled, to 25 percent. Times of turmoil were associated with increased premarital sex.[11]

The other study is by Clelia D. Mosher, who was a physician at Stanford University in the early years of this century. After her death in 1940, there were found the results of a questionnaire completed by forty-five women, mostly women who had married before 1900.[12] While the survey is not up to modern research standards, it is the only Kinsey-type study from this era.

Dr. Mosher found that most of the women entered marriage ignorant of sexual matters, but after a few years, 35 percent "usually" or "always" experienced orgasm doing coitus with their husbands. Some continued to find the entire activity distasteful, several waxed rhapsodic about the spiritual oneness in sexual delight, and the rest were scattered across the spectrum in between.

From the little that we know, in spite of the advisors warning that sexual activity was loathsome or dangerous, a substantial minority of American women found the sexual part of their lives to be pleasant, or even enjoyable.[13]

Chapter Three

&

I Take Pen in Hand . . .

IN THE WAR BETWEEN THE STATES, so many soldiers wrote letters that it contributed to a nationwide paper shortage. The mail carried millions of epistles. A substantial but lesser number of men and women kept diaries. Many of these have been published, but in the four generations since the war, the heirs, editors, and descendants of those writers and diarists have expurgated, purified, bowdlerized, amputated, and gelded the surviving material. Precious little has escaped the censor. But here and there enough has survived that we can reconstruct a history of the earthy side of the war, as a paleontologist may describe an extinct animal from a single bone.

Take the diary of John B. Fletcher. He was headed north by steamboat in 1863 but was delayed in Memphis. For six long days he promised himself that he would start home immediately, but he apparently was having too much fun to continue his travels. His journal tells the story.

> December 14th. Dwight and myself went to the theatre last night. Had a good time. I hardly know when I shall start up the river.
> December 15th. It's a pleasant kind of day. Indeed I must start up today or tomorrow without fail.
> December 16. I'm still with Dwight. I am enjoying myself very much.
> December 17th. A very cold kind of a morning. Dwight and myself went to the theatre last night. Had a first-rate time. I should go up the river in two or three days.
> December 18th. It's a very pleasant morning. I intend to leave here tomorrow without fail. Had an introduction to Miss Annie Renney.

December 19th. I have not gone yet. Shall go on the first
boat. Spent the afternoon with Annie Renney. FXXXK
Good. Had a first-rate time.
December 20th. I had a first-rate time last night with Annie.
FXXXK good. I do hope there will be a boat going up today.
I am very anxious to get north.[1]

Robert Waitt has unearthed a remarkable collection of contemporary
writing about this aspect of the war. Harris Levin of Company L, 2d Virginia Reserves, wrote in late 1864 from Drewry's Bluff, "Several nights a
week our lonely post is visited by two sisters who are rentable for riding.
They visit the boys at Brooks and Semmes also, as they lived at Hatcher's.
Amanda is about 15 and my favorite. She has never asked for more of me
than good poking, but does of the others, but her sister, Carrie, will ask
pay for her accommodations to me, so you know which I choose. Sometimes they bring a nigger with them and the gentlemen prefer her, but I
have never had wealth enough to acquire such tastes."

A musician in the 14th North Carolina Regimental band reported
from Carlisle, Pennsylvania. There, on June 27, 1863, they had captured
a large supply of Yankee whiskey. "Some of the Pennsylvania women,
hearing the noise of the revel and the music, dared to come near us. Soon
they had formed the center of attention and joined the spirit of the doings.
After much whiskey and dancing, they shed most of their garments and
offered to us their bottoms. Each took on dozens of us, squealing in delight.
For me it was hard come, easy go."

In March 1885, a Union scouting party, after chasing a group of
Confederate pickets from White's Tavern on Charles City Road, "found
we had interrupted a party in the side room. Our little Ernestine was left
in bed, ready, paid, but unused—we were too much of the gentlemen to
leave a 'lady' in so distressing a condition."

Out west, things were not much different. Several days after the
Battle of Valverde (New Mexico), a soldier in Capt. James "Paddy"
Graydon's Spy Company wrote in his diary, "My scout party met up with
four titless half-breed girls who had been well used by the rebels. They
were so lived up from their battles they offered us their favors at prices
unheard of by the girls at Fort Craig. After much pleasuring, we found
that the invaders had paid them off in Rebel money. This we bought.
Back in our camp, we sold it as souvenirs so dear that we had our pleasure
and a lot of money for more pleasure."

City Point, Virginia, seems to have been the flagship of moral dissolution. A young worker in the Sanitary Commission wrote to his father in late 1864:

> But now to the evils of this place. There is a whole city of whores. Yes, father, a whole city. They have laid out a village to the east of where the railroad bends to the docks. Streets, signs and even corduroy sidewalks with drain gutters. Of course, it was all built with Army supplies and by the very men for free that they have extracted their sinful wages from. These whores do pay the Negroes fair wages for whatever work they do, but so much more than we can that the blacks prefer to work for them to us. Our older workers here say that I must accept this evil. They fear it is here yet to the end. I found that my conscience would not let it go unchallenged from me. I determined to see the place for myself, and to protest to General Grant in person. There were three parallel streets about four blocks each long. Each block there are about ten structures on either side. They are for the most part one-storied, northern log or clapboard make. The number of rooms are different. How many, I am not sure, since I have not been in any. For the most part, they do not cook inside but have tents with Negroes behind or on the side of them, with pine or evergreen boughs covering. They, like the rebels, seem to separate the officers from the men. They will not do double duty. To each their own. Most of the officers ones have fine horses, saddles, furniture, et cetera, all from our supply houses. The [enlisted] men ones have things in equality from the storehouse. At pay time, the lines before these houses are appalling and men often fight each other for a place. The average charge is three dollars and on paydays some make as much as $250 to $300. Though between pay periods, it is said that they will take their time and do many special things and charge accordingly. Some of these hussies, during their indisposed periods, sell their services to the men to write letters for them to their loved ones back home. How foul. A mother, wife or sweetheart receiving a mistle penned by these soiled hands. I have not yet been able to reach Grant to protest these matters. Though he has ordered our men not to rape the rebel women, under penalty of death, two have been so executed since I have been here. I have talked with Bowers and he tries to defend the village as necessary in view of that order. Think of it, Father, he implies our devoted soldiers would become rapers and satyrs if not for these creatures.[2]

Bell I. Wiley, in a book on Confederate soldiers, unearthed many comments that had escaped the censor's wrath. J. M. Jordan wrote, with obvious embarrassment, to his wife, on February 8, 1864:

> We have a good spring of water and the health of our regiment is good, except some disease that I feel a delicacy in spelling them out to you as you are a female person but however I reckon you can't blush at little things these times. It is the Pocks and the Clap. The cases of this complaint is numerous, especially among the officers, and by the by Company A has got one officer toillin with the Pock and one private with the Clap. I now drop the subject as I have no interest it will interest you to be reading about that.[3]

Israel Gibbons, a soldier and reporter for the New Orleans *Daily Crescent,* published these comments on the January 8, 1862, issue. "It is really curious to observe how well and how strictly the three classes of women in camp keep aloof from each other." Gibbons went on to describe these social distinctions. "The wives and daughters of Colonels, Captains and other officers constitute the first class. The rough cooks and washers who have their husbands along form the second class." With obvious distaste he continued about the final group: "The third and last class is happily the smallest; here and there a female of elegant appearance and unexceptionable manners; truly wife-like in their tented seclusion, but lacking that great and only voucher of respectability for females in camp—the marriage tie."

In March 1863, a group of Confederate soldiers quartered near Fredericksburg put on an all-male burlesque show. One of the numbers featured a man, totally nude. The audience had many civilians, including some women. W. C. McClellan wrote to his sister the next day that he was not concerned about the possibility of shocking the visitors, as "they ware dresses but there is about them not much of the lady."

A young North Carolinian wrote to a male friend in 1863, "About two weeks ago there was a woman come from Petersburg and stoped about 200 yards from our camp. Several of the boys went up and had lots of fun with her. It was about drill time and one of the boys missed drill and they put him on double duty."

Sgt. A. L. P. Vairin wrote in his diary two days after Christmas, 1862, near Weldon, North Carolina, "This section of the country seems to abound in very bad women." Pvt. Orville Bumpass was equally unimpressed by the women of the piney woods of northern Alabama. He wrote to his wife, "The state of morals is quite as low as the soil, almost all the women are given to whoredom and the ugliest, sallow-faced, shaggy-headed, barefooted, dirty wretches you ever saw."[4]

Things were not much different in the North, as noted by Wiley in a book about Yankee soldiers. The universal penchant for cursing was noted by John B. Cuzner of the 16th Regiment, Connecticut Volunteers, in an 1863 letter to his sweetheart: "Mother wanted to come down and see me she wrote and asked me what I thought of it but the camp is no place for Women there is so much vulgar talk I thought I had got toughened to it, but last night one of the boys got tight and his swearing made my hair stand straight up."

Eli Veazie, a Massachusetts soldier stationed in Virginia in April 1863, wrote to a friend about a visit to Washington, D.C. "I had a gay old time I tell you. Lager Beer and a horse and buggy and in the evening Horizontal Refreshments or in Plainer words Riding a Dutch Gal—had a good time generally I tell you. I can take care of two correspondents for some time. . . . I see . . . any quantity women around a Plenty Whores . . . a little Toten don't go bad."

Frank Lyman, a New Hampshire soldier stationed at City Point, complained in a letter home, "We cannot get anything here but fucking and that is plenty." Samuel Jarret, a Pennsylvanian with the occupying forces in Savannah, Georgia, wrote about his sentry duty: "I am on duty every other day; but the reason of it is because there are so many hore houses in town which must have a Sentinel at each door for to keep them Straight." [5]

Another book by Wiley, about the struggling secessionist states, contains a letter from a Mississippi woman, who wrote her husband about the moral collapse of her female neighbors saying, "I am not astonished to hear of General Sherman saying he could buy the chastity of any Southern woman for a few pounds of coffee—[though] there are still many virtuous women in the Confederacy."

From Spring Hill, Tennessee, a young soldier wrote his wife: "This is a most beautiful region of country here but I am sorry I cannot say much for the morals of it from the way I hear the boys speaking of going out to see the women. I fear the standard of virtue is not very high." [6]

Another persistent searcher for the earthy and human is James I. Robertson, Jr., C. P. Miles professor of history at Virginia Polytechnic Institute. Robertson, the most illustrious protégé of the immortal Bell I. Wiley, was executive director of the U.S. Civil War Commission, and these duties plus his academic work brought him in contact with hundreds of additional primary sources, which tell us even more of everyday soldier life.

Rape was severely punished in that era. In June 1864, three Union men were shot by firing squad for a rape committed near Memphis. In August of the same year, two teamsters with a New York regiment were hanged for rape, and 10,000 soldiers were ranked around the scaffold to enforce the lesson.

Part of the lesson seems to be that a man would be a fool to commit rape when so many willing women could be found. James Greenalch of the 1st Michigan Engineers (with whom the author's great-grandfather served) wrote to his wife on December 26, 1864, from Savannah, Georgia: "some of the women . . . have been convinced that the Yankees have hornes but not horns on top of the head. I should have hesitated to of believed that men or those pretend to be men would become so demoralized and void of all decency or respect."

Cyrus F. Boyd of the 15th Iowa noted in an 1862 diary entry: "Corinth [Mississippi] is full of 'fast womin' who have come in within a few days and are demoralizing many of the men and with the help of bad whiskey will lay many of them out." David Beem of the 14th Indiana wrote his wife of a visit to our nation's Capital: "They wanted me to go to a performance called the 'Varieties,' but I very respectfully declined, as I knew the performances consisted mostly of dancing by ladies who, although they may be good looking, yet exhibit too many charms to suit modest eyes, and you know how *very modest* I am."

E. H. C. Cavins of the same Indiana regiment wrote to his wife on August 17, 1863, from his camp near Alexandria, Virginia: "I would rather be farther off from town. It is said that one house of every ten is a bawdy house—it is a perfect Sodom. The result will be that in a week or two, there will be an increase of sickness in camp. . . . Women pass along the bank of the Potomac and look at the men while they are bathing."

In August 1864, the commander of Camp McClellan Hospital, near Davenport, Iowa, grew annoyed at the women of easy virtue, who were "trifling" with his convalescent soldiers. The Davenport *Gazette* reported that the Cyprians were "treated to a cold bath in the Mississippi River."

The problem of "laundresses" was as acute in the East as it was at the frontier forts. Bernt Olmanson, a Norwegian lad serving in a Minnesota regiment, wrote home in November 1861: "We have about forty women in the regiment, some of them make lots of money natures' way. One of them had a bill today against a soldier for forty dollars." Another soldier, James Phillips of the 92d Illinois, wrote to his wife from Lexington, Kentucky, that "I have seen wenches here that would weight one to four hundred pounds. they are great greecy looking things. . . . they strut around here to day with there hoops and shakers on and plaid dresses. our boys have plenty of fun with them. . . . The Boys are having great times with the wenches here to day ketching them and squeesing them. They are all dressed to fit."

Jesse Reid of the 4th South Carolina wrote to his wife in June 1861 about the prostitutes visiting his camp: "If you could be here on those occasions you would think that there was not a married man in the regiment but me. A great many of them are married men, but they are obliged to say so." Henry C. Bear of the 116th Illinois described his lieutenant, who kept a woman, Kate, dressed in soldier's clothes. "There is a few in our Company that would like to have such rips as her in camp. . . . You could hardly tell her from a man."

Kate was certainly not the only woman in soldier's clothes. Mary and Mollie Bell (apparently sisters) spent two years in one of Jubal Early's regiments as Tom Parker and Bob Morgan. The Richmond *Enquirer* reported on October 31, 1864, that the Bells were imprisoned for "aiding in the demoralization of General Early's veterans." They had apparently been busy with activities other than shooting Yankees.

It didn't take long for some soldiers to be demoralized. In June 1861, a few months after the outbreak of war, Perry Mayo of the 2d Michigan wrote home to his wife about his comrades made sick by "imprudence." A friend had been "caught in bad company and is so bad off he has not been on duty since we have been here and stands a good chance to be discharged."

While most Civil War correspondence between husband and wife was quite formal and proper, a few revealed the sender's feelings about personal matters. James Greenalch, who had earlier complained of his colleagues "horns," wrote to his wife Fidelia about his concerns regarding women left alone at home. "I have herd men when they are talking about old men being guilty of such [a] thing that the older the Back the stifer the horn and the women, some of them, appear to have the same disease. I hope you won't ketch it." One hopes that the openness and directness that was shared by James and Fidelia was an effective vaccination against infidelity.

Another couple, Elnathan and Jane Keeler, also committed to paper the kind of lighthearted intimacy that is seen in happy couples. While Elnathan was stationed with the 16th New York at Petersburg, Virginia, in 1864, Jane sent him a box of food with a note that included this thought: "don't let that horseradish make you horney for I am not there you know and I don't believe them blacks taste good unless it is in the dark." A few months later, he wrote to Jane advising her to get another man if he were killed. She replied that she would prefer to keep his remains at home, stuffed with straw, rather than remarry.[7]

A soldier of the Second Regiment of Maryland Volunteers wrote home of a little adventure in October of 1863:

> The Colonel was out in the woods one fine evening and noticed several soldiers dodging him and apparently wishing to be unobserved. Massa Geems [the enlisted men's nickname for their colonel] thought something was going on wrong, so after going

a circuitous route he approached the same spot . . . unseen.
He discovered to his astonishment two individuals [of the
sable hue] in petticoats and crinoline. Well, these two femmes
were carrying on quite a lucrative trade and the Colonel stood
and watched long enough to satisfy his curiosity, when he
dodged and caught a fellow by the arm just going to camp
through the bushes. "Well, sir," said the Colonel, "Where have
you been and what have you been doing?" The fellow stam-
mered a little, but with remarkable presence of mind replied,
"Why, you see, Colonel, I have got a bad cold and have been
out here to get some Sassafras Root to cure it." "Ah," said the
Colonel, "Sassafras Root, indeed! I have never heard it called by
that name before! Report yourself to the officer of the sword."
The next morning, it leaked out; on the report book of prisoners was the fellow's name, charged with Hunting for Sassafras
Root. The fellow has since been nicknamed Sassafras.[8]

Another letter, this from Falls Church, Virginia, addressed from "Ebb."
to F. A. Burnham, warns his friend at home to beware of "Grass Widows"
who know how to cure "all your aches and panes." The writer continues
with local news: "I will tell you how our boys do things. About a mile
from camp lives a woman by the name of Scott, and she has two girls.
One had been too near a trouser serpent and got bit. The other was brave
and not afraid of snakes. Thursday some boys went over there. The old
woman was sick. The oldest girl having a child, and while one of the boys
diddled, the other boys shot all the chickens for Thanksgiving dinner. I
call this rather Bileous, yes decidedly so. Boys should not be held account-
able for what they do soldiering. Pat Cummings has started for home,
being discharged from reason of a stiff finger from a cut. Now keep mum,
his fingers were cut by a woman Pat was trying to bamboosle and not by
an ax as he tells."[9]

Julia Higgins of Mill Springs wrote to her "dear and intended Husband" on November 25, 1863, suggesting that when he met some Yankees
he could whip two or three of them easily. "If you fetch one home we
can keep him to milk the cows. When we get married, he can sleep with
your ugly black girl. Send the best looking one you can."

Julia soon abandoned the theme of the Yankee milker and expressed
her yearning for her fiancé: "I love you with all my heart and with all my
mind and long to see you Dear Jim. My mind dwells on the treasures we
will have when you come back, embracing each other on the sofa and
bed. I never felt so good as I did the first time I laid on the sofa. I wish it
would last—always it is my daily thought to think of you and the good

feelings we will have when you come home. You must not let anyone see this letter. Lay it next to your heart."

The writer then turned to the pregnancy of a mutual friend: "She said she felt good enough when making it. If it felt as good as it did to me the first time you put it in the full length, it struck bottom, that is sure." Julia next vented her resentment against the abolitionists, but closed the letter with a fresh burst of affection for Jim: "I love you with all my heart and body . . . and will keep it closed for you. When you come home to break it open again it will be as tight as the first time you tried it."[10]

One young soldier displayed both splendid penmanship and a single-minded interest in erotic opportunity: Henry Schelling of Company F, 64th Illinois Volunteers. On November 21, 1863, he wrote to "Friend William," from Giles County, Tennessee, starting with the story of a march through the mud, which they enlivened in a traditional way: "the boys got hold of some corn liquid and about a dozen of them got slightly inebriated, I myself among the number . . . we enlisted a new recruit on the way at Eastport. The boys all took a notion to him. On examination, he proved to have a Cunt so he was discharged. I was sorry for it, for I wanted him for a Bedfellow." On a march from the Tennessee River to Balls Factory, "We passed a Woolen factory where there was about a hundred girls working. They came out on the road. I seen a few I would like to take on my staff for a few minutes . . . boys taking lassies on their cocks." At Pulaski, Tennessee, Henry noted, "There is some nice girls here but they are all secesh. I tried to get me [one] but she said she had a little secesh she would give for a Dozen yankees." After discussing the military situation and his commanding general, Henry closed his letter with these thoughts: "I hope you will be in Charleston when this letter reaches you. You will have lots of nigger fucking I hope and I will try and get a little white skin. There is four whorehouses here where a man can get a single jump for 3 dollars, five dollars for all night in Tennessee money. You may think I am a hard case, but I am as pious as you can find in the Army."[11]

Politics and sex were mixed in the February 20, 1864, letter of Cyrus Beamenderfer, who was stationed in Washington, D.C., at the headquarters of the 2d Division. He described with pride to his friend Daniel Musser that his whole brigade was Copperheads. Cyrus was not a Lincoln man, nor an abolitionist. "They call the loyal Democrats Copperheads . . . my tent fellow is a Copperhead. George B. McClellan is the man for the Army and I suppose for the North, the best man that ever drew a sword. Now you tell me what you are. If you are one of them niger fuggers, let me know, but I hope you are a loyal Democrat, same as

I am." His letter concludes with a promise to describe all the battles he has seen, and assures his correspondent of continuing friendship no matter what conflicts politics might bring.[12]

On a different aspect of sexuality, Abraham Lincoln received a letter on the subject of rape. B. E. Harrison of Leesburg, Virginia, wrote on July 28, 1862, asking to be exempt from General Pope's Order No. 11, citing the needs of a paralyzed wife and his own advanced age of seventy-seven, and that he had suffered from Yankee soldiers taking all of his horses, most of his bacon and poultry, and forcing him to cook dinner for forty of the invaders. His major concern lay elsewhere, however: "A squad of Federal soldiers entered my premises. . . . a servant girl happened to be about 150 yards from the house and one of the soldiers went after her and as she saw him approaching her she ran, but he caught her and forced her to a Brutal act, in full view of my dwelling and Wife and two of her nieces. . . . this act caused her to appeal to me to send her . . . to some other place where she might be safe from such outrage as had been imposed upon the colored girl." Mr. Harrison concluded, "For my Veracity I refer you to the Hon. John S. Carlile of Virginia."[13]

George, Albert, and Charles Hopkins, all of the 72d Illinois Infantry, were determined writers, and 229 of their letters are preserved, including ones they had received. One of the brothers received a missive mailed from Jefferson, Illinois, on May 3, 1863, by Lawrence Kavanagh, still a civilian. He described his wages ($14 a month), their mutual friend, Peter Freeman, who had been sentenced to five years for "impotur, bigmus, and dseter," and concluded with a request to "tell Fred I want to know he get any nigger wench firking."

Charles Hopkins was stationed at "Head Qt 17th A.C." near Cairo, Illinois, in April 1864 and wrote to a brother, "we ar having a good time hear, only one post to stand and sleep with a girl every knight." A few weeks later he wrote to George about the weather: "mud up to a mans ass hear."

Later, just before the fall of Atlanta, Charles wrote again, describing the hard fighting and long campaign, summed up with a crude drawing of a hog being violated by a human finger. He asked George to send him some money ("if you have some that troubles your pocket") and concludes, "tell Fred to suck my as."[14]

Alex Hamilton, of the 72d Ohio Infantry, wrote a friend, complaining of the generalship that caused his brigade to lose 600 men, and then turned to more personal matters: "you say that you don't see Tom once a week. I guess it as you say he has drove the pin too far into the damsel and got stuck there. If he ever gets that pepper box of his into her he will make her squeal for six months. The last letter I got from him he was not well yet. He has had a serious time of it. I don't think he will play stink finger with Jack's gals any more."[15]

Amos Brenneman of the 203d Pennsylvania Volunteers wrote from camp near Richmond on November 27, 1864, "I have not much to tell you more than there was a man shot on the 25th. I was about twenty steps away from him. It was a hard sight. There were thousands upon thousands of soldiers in the field and there will be two more shot before long for fucking a negro. I did not receive the box. . . . I would like to have it, for my shoes are bad when it rains. I get wet feet and that I don't like. I would sooner have a wet cock. . . . I screwed a white woman the other day & my cock raised his head. We see once and a while a woman but of the charcoal complection and my cock don't raise at them."[16]

In late December 1862, Oren A. Hammer of the 26th North Carolina wrote his friend John Harrington of his unhappiness with the denial of a furlough request, but then turned to more cheerful topics: "You ought to have been with me on Christmas. I together with several other officers went over to Petersburg, got drunk and f——ked out. We staid two days and nights, you ought to have seen me going to bed with a gal. I tell you it is a heap better than sleeping with a man. I have a notion of taking one to myself provided I can find one fool enough to have me."

In February of the following year, Harrington heard from his friend Hugh D. Cameron of the 3d North Carolina Cavalry. Cameron described his success at catching deserters, but complained that "the scarcest thing here is cunt—the d——med negros will not give a fellow a bite. I have not got but three tastes since I have been in Va. and that I run up with the great city of Petersburg and I got that from two fine looking women. I tell you the three gals cost me but eleven dollars. Tom Lane got some with me twice from the same gal. He says it is some better than the widow [illegible]. . . . John I expect you to give them old Hoars fits in Raleigh. They come nigh getting all your subsistence."[17]

One of the most touching epistles surviving from the Civil War is the long and impassioned letter of Jane Goodwin, written to her husband, James, who had been away from home almost a year. She speaks at first of the pangs of those widowed and orphaned by the war, and then of the loneliness of wives:

> I have many reasons for speaking in this way, only known by the warm and sympathetic hearts of those who have enjoyed the inexpressible glory and happiness of the honey moon, which makes life feel like a stream of eternal bliss. . . . do you ever suffer your mind to scan the scenes of love and pleasure

of the first night's transactions, which was only witnessed and enjoyed by ourselves. Often when night throws her sable over our land and I am consigned to the sweet embrace of Morpheus, I meet there in the fairy fields of dreamland, and drink in the cup of wedded life, think, James, my dear husband, [of] the night we first retired to the midnight couch, one by one to enjoy the highest streams of pleasure that the soul and body ever knows. [Our wedding chamber] was vacated by my lady friends. . . . I was left alone only to imagine the happy results of the coming night, which when realized were glorious beyond the conception of those who have refused to participate in the great cause of women's rights and man's delight. Soon did I feel my delicate form embraced by his gigantic and robust one for a pillow and the other fondling with anxiety over my small but firm breastworks . . . you becoming more adventurous inclined your right downward *you know where* . . . better to ascertain the position and strength of my noble and generous battery, which so often has given you relief and pleasure. Your remarks [at that moment] so singular as a Quaker: Jane, hoist thy linen, spread thy thighs abroad and receive the seed of Jacob in the name of the Lord. James . . . procure a furlough. . . . I think a certain portion of it is necessary to life. . . . You would find only one difficulty in charging my battery—your ammunition might give out. . . . you need not fear . . . reinforcements could be brought up every twelve hours. . . . You have charged many times satisfactory to both of us without even the amputation of a limb. . . . write soon. . . .[18]

A less romantic view of life is reflected in the diary of Charles B. Haydon. On May 25, 1861, he noted that some very pretty ladies had visited the camp looking for "brothers" or "cousins." "They are pretty sure to find them but the boys are so hard up for money that in most cases, unless love is more powerful than avarice, the meetings terminate unsatisfactory." On September 19, 1861, he was amused by the first corporal, who had been cursing men infected with venereal disease. "Since then one of them induced him to trade drawers and in this way gave the 1st Corpl. the clap." Two months later, he remarked after a visit to the Capital that there seemed to be three types of persons in Washington, D.C.: The first group was soldiers, while "the other two great classes are politicians and prostitutes, both very numerous and about equal in numbers, honesty and morality."[19]

In April 1865, H. P. Hennon of Company H, 87th Pennsylvania, wrote a friend asking for postage stamps, commenting that Lincoln had no business going to theaters, and describing "some fun in Farmsville," in which, near a pontoon bridge, his comrades found "an old wench" behind a pile of tobacco. "So they all began to pitch in keen. Tom Michael held the light and she received about 60 big schlorgers one after another. I nearly killed myself laughing. The darned old bitch could hardly stand." R. C. Wagner of Company B, 2d District of Columbia Volunteers, wrote to his cousin Edman Shriver about an Erie County Court case, in which a Mr. Ryemiller had raped his hired girl, while the pregnant Mrs. Ryemiller held the girl's legs. Later, Wagner wrote to his cousin again, congratulating him on Edman's recent sketches: "These pictures are very well done for such a little boy as you. They are just the kind the boys like to look at." Commenting on Edman's social life, Wagner suggested, "You must try Lilly again perhaps and she will take the cock then. There are plenty of whores around here. Nearly all have the pox [syphilis]."[20]

J. D. James was a draft dodger who was working as a miner in Virginia City, Nevada. On January 3, 1865, he wrote to his friend John Wilson about the price of horses and the issues of abolition, and concluded with social notes: "You spoke of some marriages. It does me good to hear of weddings if I can't get to see any of them. It is very seldom you hear of a marriage here, for in fact there aren't any girls in this country except those that is strictly on the fuck for $5 a go. I take a snoot full about once a month."[21]

Whether romantic or cynical, whether written to a friend or a lover, or just to the writer himself, as in a diary, all these communications pulse with the hot blood of real human beings, men and women whose longings and intentions are as clear today as when they put pen to paper long ago.

While these two dozen or so examples cannot hope to represent all the millions of men who fought on both sides (and all the women who loved them), there is a consistency and internal validation about them that places the burden of proof upon those who would claim that sex, licit or illicit, was absent from the Civil War.

Chapter Four

ૐ

Blue with Oaths

THERE IS A TRADITION that our ancestors were given to cursing of an elaborate and inventive nature. In *Old Times on the Mississippi,* Mark Twain described a first mate whose orders were like a blast of lightning, followed by the thunder of "a long reverberating peal of profanity."

John Billings, in *Hardtack and Coffee,* recalled that Civil War "mule drivers, when duly aroused, could produce a deeper cerulean tint in the surrounding atmosphere than any other class of men in the service."[1] But a spoken word is but a passing shadow, an evanescent wisp, leaving no trace or fossil. Verbatim records of first mates, mule drivers, or even common soldiers are almost absent.

Today, the science of cursing is no laughing matter. The interest of linguists and anthropologists in this arcane art is such that a scholarly journal exists: *Maledicta: The International Journal of Verbal Aggression.* But finding Civil War verbal abuse, even for scientific analysis, is difficult; however, at least one repository does exist.

The archive where these words were preserved is in the transcripts of courts-martial, usually as evidence of disrespect to a superior officer. Most of the records reflect moments of violent conflict, in which the oaths were only secondary offenses. There is no case of a soldier being prosecuted for the solitary act of cursing itself.

A review of three dozen court records involving profanity sheds some light upon the realities of innovative oaths in the Union Army.

At Vicksburg, in the spring of 1864, Pvt. G. W. Gribben of Company E of the 32d Ohio was fined two months' pay for being AWOL. Displeased with this decision, he raised his voice to state, "If the officers want to take my pay, they may take it and be God dammed, and shove it up their arses, if they like it. I can stand it, and I'll be God damned if they make anything of it." Later he was convicted of desertion and conduct prejudicial to good order and sentenced to be shot. Lincoln mitigated the sentence to a stay at Dry Tortugas until the end of the war.[2]

In July 1865, Sgt. R. P. Quinn of Company K, 6th Regiment, U.S. Veteran Volunteers, having been placed under guard near Arsenal, Washington, stirred up his fellow prisoners by stating that he "would kill the damned white-livered, red-headed, son of a bitch" and later struck the corporal of the guard, Charles Silliman of the same company, calling him "a damn big mouth son of a bitch." For this, and the previous attempt at incitement to riot, Sergeant Quinn received a dishonorable discharge and was sentenced to wear an iron ball and chain.[3]

Pvt. Elijah Johnson of Company H, 5th Massachusetts Colored Cavalry, escaped from the guardhouse while awaiting court-martial and attempted to shoot Sgt. William Harris. When he missed, he exclaimed, "God damn you, I meant to kill you." Private Johnson got ten years at hard labor.[4] Pvt. James Tuttle, Company K, 152d New York Volunteers, was apparently in a touchy mood when asked by his captain to close up the marching interval. Shouting, "I will do as I damn please," he seized his captain by the throat and threw him to the ground, the result being a dishonorable discharge and eighteen months at hard labor.[5]

Pvt. James Ducy, Company B, 16th New York Cavalry, when reprimanded by his company commander, said, "Lieutenant, you are a damned son of a bitch; you can suck my ass; I'll mash you and you shall pay for it." This was followed by a spell in prison and a $60 fine.[6]

Near Cheeseman's Creek, Virginia, in April 1862, Pvt. Charles Heath of the 2d New Hampshire Volunteers was threatened with arrest if he did not obey orders. Heath's reply: "If you arrest me, I will rip your God damned guts out and scatter them over the parade ground." The court ordered that Heath be "shot to death with musketry," but the sentence was remitted by President Lincoln.[7] Another beneficiary of Lincoln's largesse was Lt. George Lacy of the 2d New York Heavy Artillery. Somewhere near Petersburg, Virginia, Lacy fell into a dispute with Major Hogg, who ordered Lacy to his quarters under arrest. Lacy exclaimed, "I'll be God damned if I will go to quarters for Hogg or any other man. Major Hogg sucks the arse of Major Maguire. I'm a damn sight better man than either one of them, and if they want to fight, I'm the man for them, God damn them." This contretemps was carried on "in earshot of the enlisted men," and resulted in Lacy being dismissed from the service. Lincoln returned him to duty.[8]

In the spring of 1863, Lt. Joseph Brown, adjutant of the 102d Pennsylvania, was drunk, removed his sword, and offered to fight his colonel without weapons, saying, "You are a damned son of a bitch and you may go to hell." Lieutenant Brown was sentenced to be dismissed from the service, but a reviewing board reversed the sentence, since the transcript showed that the colonel and lieutenant had been gambling together.[9] Another touchy young officer was 2d Lt. William Wolfe, who, when ordered to appear before an examining board, said, "I'll be God damned if I came into the army to study tactics, but to fight," and also emitted "other language insulting his commanding officer in the presence of privates." The lieutenant was sentenced to dismissal but was reinstated because of his good conduct at the battle of Fredericksburg.[10]

Artificer Adolph Schramm of Company D, New York Volunteer Engineer Regiment, refused his colonel's order to embark for Tybee Island, Georgia, incited his peers to mutiny, and demonstrated his interest in things mechanical with the following statement: "I can take care of the colonel with my stick, the son of a bitch, and if the stick fails, why his thing ain't very large and I can take it off with a jack knife." Schramm was sentenced to be shot, but his sentence was remitted because of the colonel's well-known history of misconduct on other occasions.[11] A man with apparently fewer redeeming qualities was Pvt. John Larkin of Company G, 8th Maine Volunteers, who kicked his lieutenant, P. G. Ingalls, and said, "You are a damned son of a bitch and you shall bleed for this." Larkin got three years at Dry Tortugas and a dishonorable discharge.[12]

Today's Army Military History Institute is located at Carlisle Barracks, Pennsylvania. At that place in 1865, Pvt. William Smith of the Permanent Company was drunk on duty, threw a rock at his sergeant, and called him "a son of a bitch" and other improper terms. Smith got sixty days at hard labor.[13]

Capt. James E. Eldridge seems to have had a difficult time with Pvt. Daniel Hampton, Company G, 24th Regiment of the Veteran Reserve Corps, who bit the captain's hand and called him "a damned Vermont son of a bitch." Hampton got a year of hard labor with ball and chain.[14] The 44th Company of the 2d Battalion of the Veterans Reserve Corps had a bad day back in September 1865. Corp. George Taylor had been arrested and was "rescued" by Pvt. Walter Chisholm, who attacked the arresting soldiers, threw Surgeon W. F. Norris to the ground "with great violence," and said to his commanding officer, "I will be God damned to hell if I ever do any more duty, and by Jesus Christ you can't make me."[15]

In a similar vein, Pvt. Phillip Johnson of Company C, 24th Ohio Heavy Artillery, called his corporal, Benjamin Aregood, a "God damned red-headed son of a bitch" and lost a month's pay for his efforts.[16] Corp. Richard Anderson of Company M, 5th Pennsylvania Cavalry, was ordered to picket duty, but apparently dissatisfied, told his sergeant, "You are a damned liar and a son of a bitch." Corporal Anderson became Private Anderson and received three months at hard labor.[17]

Pvt. Joshua Blake of Company A, 4th U.S. Colored Troops, was told by his sergeant to take his gun and equipment and report for drill. Blake caused some concern, because he began to load his gun "in a threatening manner" while stating, "I'll be damned if I will and neither you nor the captain can make me." Blake received sixty days at hard labor with a ball and chain attached to his left ankle.[18]

David Ritter, whom the court described as a "good man when sober," was a private with Company B of the 74th Pennsylvania. While not sober, he called his lieutenant "a loafer, a rowdy and a son of a bitch," thus earning fifteen days at hard labor.[19]

Capt. Harrison Herndon of Company I, 136th United States Colored Troops, was also described by his court-martial board as "a good soldier when sober," but the court remarked sadly that he was sober "only when under heavy guard." Captain Herndon was found drunk in the mud in front of his tent, unable to stand, and when approached by Lieutenant Metcalf called him "a damned rascal and a son of a bitch." It would seem officers were in short supply, because Captain Herndon's sentence of dismissal from the service was remitted and he was returned to duty.[20]

Lt. William H. Justice, on duty with Company H of the 11th Illinois Cavalry at Mobile, Alabama, was another man who did not do well with alcohol. According to the court transcript, Justice had a few drinks and "took his company out for dress parade but was too much under the influence of liquor to handle his company, thereby creating laughter and comments from the enlisted men." Having made a hash of his command functions, he then went to a mess tent and created a row with his fellow officers, calling them things such as "son of a bitch, God damned liar and damned dog" and asked a colleague if he "would allow a nigger to shit on him." After than, Lieutenant Justice "became belligerent." He was dismissed from the service and not invited to return.[21]

While drunk and disturbing the peace, Pvt. Oliver Lichty of Company E, 12th Iowa Veteran Volunteer Infantry, was ordered to return to camp by his lieutenant. The trial record states that Lichty spoke "in a disrespectful and abusive manner, to wit, 'You are a damned fool, a son of a bitch and the son of a whore,' or words to that effect." He also offered to cut the lieutenant's "guts out with a knife" and did split the lieutenant's head with a brick. This outburst, followed by punching and kicking the lieutenant, earned Lichty eighteen months at hard labor.[22] Another excessively touchy individual was Pvt. Orisan A. Osgood of Company A, 23d Veteran Reserve Corps Regiment, at Camp Reno, Milwaukee. Osgood had a few drinks, got into an argument with the officer of the day, Captain Lyon, and called him "a damned son of a bitch, a coward and a liar." This was followed by many threats of violence and, later, by a sentence of two years at hard labor, mitigated to two months.[23]

Lt. J. F. Sweetman of Company I, 214th Pennsylvania, was having a bad day near Winchester, Pennsylvania. In drilling his men, he noted that Private Stack seemed slow to learn the maneuvers and ordered him to the Awkward Squad. Stack cursed the lieutenant, and the lieutenant punched Stack in the face with his fist. After Private Stack went about his business, the next awkward person was Pvt. James Kelly, a man who had previously been in the guardhouse several times for other infractions. The lieutenant ordered Kelly out of the ranks for separate instruction; Kelly reversed his weapon, holding his musket by the barrel, and said, "You son of a bitch, I'll knock your head off." Three months at hard labor.[24]

Lt. Colonel Vieral was trying to round up his troops, as his unit had been ordered to depart from St. Louis. Scouting the countryside, he found Pvt. David Storie of Company G, 3d Massachusetts Cavalry Volunteers, wandering about East St. Louis. When ordered to return to his unit, Storie called the officers nearby "sons of bitches" and threatened to kill the guard. He got a month at hard labor.[25]

Pvt. James Sullivan, Company I of the 13th Regiment of Veteran Reserve Corps, apparently had tired of the military life. When ordered to fall in for dress parade, he told his sergeant "Oh, shit, I cannot." The next day at the breakfast table, he was "loud and boisterous," his remarks including, "You are a liar and can go to hell," and, "I don't want any of your lip and will put your head in that kettle." Sullivan received four months in which he could think over his situation.[26] Pvt. Jasper Burtnett, of Company H, 89th Ohio, also took offense at the order to fall in. He replied to his sergeant, "I'll not fall in 'till I damned please, you damned black-headed thief," struck his sergeant with his musket, splitting the sergeant's scalp, and then broke the sergeant's leg. Burtnett lost a month's pay and was reprimanded in front of his regiment.[27]

An intemperate mouth was not restricted to the enlisted ranks. Col. H. W. Barry, 8th U.S. Colored Heavy Artillery, said, "In the presence of officers and citizens 'General Meredith [his commanding officer] is a God damned old liar.'" Colonel Barry was reprimanded.[28]

In modern times, an ocean cruise is said to have a calming effect. This was not true for Pvt. William Hoffman, Company I, 103d New York Volunteers, while on board the transport ship *Leary.* Just before trying to punch his captain, he said, "You, Captain Schmidt, are a God damned son of a bitch." This earned him three years at hard labor.[29] Another reluctant sailor was Pvt. Timothy Noon of the 14th Maine Volunteers. Noon's unit had been ordered onto the steamer *Starlight,* and for reasons unknown took exception to this suggestion. Noon drew his bayonet and said to his colonel, "God damn you, you will tie me up, will you? I am a soldier, God damn you, but you are no soldier." The court sentenced him to be "shot to death by musketry," but Lincoln commuted the sentence to imprisonment during the term of the war.[30]

Pvt. Thomas Clossen of Company A, 82d Pennsylvania, when told by his commanding officer to go to his quarters, raised a stick and said he'd "be God damned if [he] was afraid of any damned officer in the regiment." Clossen received the opportunity to experience a year with a ball and chain attached to his left leg.[31] Another soldier, apparently unfamiliar with the traditions of the service, was Sgt. Patrick Shields of Company B, 62d New York Volunteers, who entered his captain's quarters at Strasburg, Virginia, without permission. When asked to leave, the sergeant said, "You can go to hell; I will stay just as long as I God damned please," and then he punched his captain. This produced three years in prison.[32]

The difficulties of command are further illustrated by Pvt. Allen Williams, Company F, 118th U.S. Colored Troops, and by Pvt. George G. Tucker, 9th Unattached Company, Massachusetts Heavy Artillery. Williams called his captain "a damned son of a bitch" and struck the captain with his musket.[33] Tucker struck his lieutenant and called him "a God damned villain," and then suggested to his sergeant that "God may damn your soul."[34] Williams was sentenced to the firing squad (later commuted by Lincoln) and Tucker to two years of hard labor with a 12-pound ball and a 6-foot length of chain.

Tempers were running high in the 2d Battalion of the Veteran Reserve Corps when Pvt. John Kelly approached his sergeant, carrying a large knife, and said, "I will cut your damned heart out." When approached by the lieutenant, Kelly stated, "You can't put me in the guardhouse, you damned son of a bitch." Kelly received a year at hard labor.[35] A similar situation pitted Pvt. Thomas Ryan, Company D, 1st Connecticut Cavalry, against his sergeant. Ryan drew his saber against the sergeant and called him "a damned diarrhea son of a bitch." This got him six months.[36]

Pvt. James Connoley of Company G, 14th Regiment Veterans Reserve Corps, and Pvt. Phillip Dolan of Company B, 162d New York Volunteers, both punched their superior officers and called them "a God damned son of a bitch." Each man received time at hard labor.[37]

Pvt. George Carr of the 75th Company, 2d Battalion, Veteran Reserve Corps, seems to have been another man tired of military life. Assigned to sentinel duty, he became drunk, deserted his post, struck his superior, one Colonel Gougman, and called him "a Dutch son of a bitch, a whore-master and a Dutch bastard." Private Carr was relieved of his military duties and given a year at hard labor.[38]

An opportunity to go horseback riding apparently did not appeal to Pvt. Lunas June of Company E, 1st District of Columbia Cavalry. Already in difficulty with his superiors, he was ordered to saddle his horse. He not only refused to saddle up, but drawing a razor from his pocket, he said to his lieutenant, "I have cut a better man's throat than yours, you son of a bitch." Three months at hard labor.[39]

Pvt. Mariman Gray, Company D, 116th Ohio, was doing little for the spirit of reconciliation between North and South when, in April 1864, near Back Creek Bridge, Virginia, he got drunk and mistreated a citizen named John Emerson. Not content to confine his activities to physical abuse, Gray then said to Emerson, "Have you any sisters? If you have, I should like to fuck them. That was my business before I came into the service, and now I am fucking for Uncle Sam." Gray had thirty days at hard labor in which to sober up.[40]

A man who seemed to enjoy his work was Capt. W. J. Stewart, 16th U.S. Infantry, on recruiting duty. Having assembled a score of new recruits, he swore them in with the following words, "You do solemnly swear that you will support Old Abe as long as you live and be a good boy, God damn you?" He might have escaped censure for this somewhat informal swearing-in ceremony, but he had made his life more difficult with habitual drunkenness and pocketing the recruiting bonuses offered to the men. Unusual for a commissioned officer, he received two years at hard labor and a dishonorable discharge.[41]

Capt. John Daly of the 104th New York Volunteers was a prisoner of the Confederates, confined with about 200 other Union officers. Their quarters had become "very filthy," and there was some dispute about who was responsible for organizing the cleanup. The trial records indicate that Captain Daly did "without any provocation whatsoever, say to Lieutenant Colonel Homer B. Sprague . . . in a loud and abusive tone and manner the indecent and obscene words following, to wit—'You [meaning Sprague] suck my arse,' and 'you suck my cock,' thereby wilfully intending to insult and abuse the aforesaid Homer B. Sprague, and did make use of other ungentlemanly language toward the said . . . Homer B. Sprague . . . all this in the presence of several other officers . . . in the Confederate Military Prison at Danville, Virginia." Captain Daly was dismissed from the service.[42]

Capt. John H. Behan also had a way with words. In his duties with Company F of the 16th Virginia Volunteers, while supervising the work of Lt. Joseph B. Hamilton, Behan remarked, "There goes our half-assed Adjutant," which a court convened at Hunter's Chapel, Virginia, concluded would "impair and weaken the influence and control over the Company of said lieutenant." Earlier the same day, Captain Behan had ordered his company out at reveille with the words, "Turn out, you lazy sons of bitches, every God damned one of you." Behan was cashiered.[43]

Regional pride was in the voice of Corp. Albert Woodard of Company E, 4th Wisconsin Cavalry, when he was addressed by Lt. Daniel Bowen of the 38th Massachusetts. Woodard replied, "I'll be God damned if any Massachusetts piss pot can clean out this house. We, the 4th Wisconsin boys and the First Indiana boys will run this house in spite of all the Massachusetts piss pots . . . God damn you . . . understand that." He was soon Private Woodard, sent to hard labor on the fortifications on Ship Island.[44]

In reviewing the oaths and curses registered in the transcripts of these courts-martial, it would seem that there is a certain poverty of invention. The elaborate trills and arpeggios, the inventions and variations upon a theme promised by Twain and Billings, seem to be absent. What we hear instead are the meat and potato curses of angry, usually drunken, men, whose contributions to the science of malediction seem sadly lacking.

Chapter Five

ꝫ

And the Flesh
Was Made Word

THE NAUGHTY, THE RIBALD, the salacious, the bawdy, the scatological, and the "tasteless" occupy a unique place in the arts. By age twelve (often earlier) most children have been exposed to a variety of off-color terms, ditties, stories, and graffiti. Since children soon learn to conceal this knowledge from their parents, there arises a situation in which all concerned pretend that such material is not part of our (and most cultures') heritage and daily conversation. Any attempt to openly discuss such matters or use such language, even in the driest style or in the most boring of academic journals, is met with resistance. Witness the career of Vance Randolph.[1]

In the sympathetic study of folkways and folklore, Randolph, who died in 1980, reigned supreme. While not a native of the hills, he lived, by choice, sixty years in the Ozark mountains. He liked the people; they liked him. This mutual trust and respect opened many doors and enabled him to hear the entire range of that culture's repertoire of tales and songs.

But Randolph's attempts to include the bawdy fraction of that corpus in his published professional collections met with almost total defeat. His four-volume *Ozark Folk Songs* included not one "naughty" song (those selections had been omitted by the publisher), thus distorting by omission the actual breadth of that culture. His informants saw the bawdy as simply one aspect of life, not as something separate and apart.

Randolph's belief that the erotic was a normal and natural element in culture helped keep him from university appointments and from the cornucopia of academic grants and fellowships. He died in poverty, outside the charmed circle of academics who defined what could be studied and published.

His collection of bawdy Ozark tales[2] was not off the press until a few years before his death, at a time when he was blind and crippled and unable to savor this final triumph; his collection of off-color Ozark songs appeared in 1992.[3]

(Real cowboy songs suffered a similar fate. The first unexpurgated collection was not published until 110 years after the longhorns came to Dodge City.)[4]

The spontaneous production of works that include that which is usually excluded is authentic, healthy, and natural. It is a part of life. These songs and stories inform us of one aspect of the human condition, in a direct and unsalacious way.

By contrast, intentional pornography is commercial, artificial, fantastic, unlikely, designed with an eye to the marketplace. It is intended to titillate, not to illuminate or to endorse life. Both types of erotica, folk and commercial, were present during the Civil War.

Let us begin with that great invention—song. Words stimulate one part of the brain and the melody and rhythm another. Combined, they touch the heart and soul.[5] Anyone whose musical breadth extends beyond rap and heavy metal will understand the stirring of memories evoked by "Dixie" or "The Battle Hymn of the Republic." Any family who has had a loved one headed for combat will understand such Civil War favorites as "Weeping, Sad and Lonely," "The Vacant Chair," or "Just before the Battle, Mother." "The Bonnie Blue Flag" can still warm the blood of Southerners.

But with "Jeff Davis' Dream," we see a dichotomy. There are two versions: One written in 1863 by Bernard Covert described the Confederate president trembling at the thought of a Yankee noose around his neck, and criticized England and France for aiding the rebels. All the themes are political. Utterly different is the second version, which appears in numerous hand-written editions.[6]

> One night as Jeff lay fast asleep
> With his wife huged to his heart,
> A little closer she did creep,
> And chanced to let a fart.
>
> The fart it smelt so strong,
> And sounded so much louder
> He thought that something wrong must be
> For he smelt the Lincoln powder.
>
> Hark, Hark says he yet unawake,
> How will I show my spunkey?

And reaching down his gun to take
His fingers touched her monkey.

Twas then his courage did appear
He thought he had found a pistol,
He brought his arse up in the air
With his cock as hard as crystal.

"Swab," he cried, "Swab out the gun,
And give old Lincoln thunder—
Oh, now my boys we'll have some fun
And show him his great blunder."

His cock into his monkey went
His arse it went to bobbing—
He let a fart, and then he spent—
Says Jeffrey's wife, "I'm co- co- coming."

"Fine, fine," cried Jeff, "the gun is clean,"
He strained enough to split—
And throwing his arms around his dear
He strained again and shit.

"Oh, oh," cried Jeff, "I'm shot, I'm shot,
"My leg is bleeding—bleeding.
"Help, help, come here to this spot,
"Oh, death is slowly feeding.

"Oh, would that I were loyal now
"I hear old Abe coming,
"He'll hang me, he will, I vow,
"Yes, yes, I hear him drumming."

"You've shit, you fool," Jeff's wife says
As she held him on a level:
"I never saw such rebel strife
You nasty stinking devel."

"Oh, dear," says Jeff, now wide awake,
"What have I done indeed?
Oh, my wife please take my trembling hand
And we will both secede."

Coarse? Yes. Tasteless? Certainly. Good poetry? Not for a moment.

A real part of our culture's history? As real as any other aspect, and certainly not softened by any patina of time or cosmetic bleaching by an editor's hand.

"The Yellow Rose of Texas" is a song revived so often that it is known to almost every generation, but Civil War soldiers knew the version sung by Christy's Minstrels (and perhaps more ribald versions, as well), in which the Rose was "yaller" rather than yellow, a woman of mixed race, and, some say, a bawdy house madam in Galveston.[7]

> She's the sweetest rose of color
> That this darkey ever knew;
> Her eyes as bright as diamonds,
> And they sparkle like the dew.

Another ditty, popular on both sides of the Mason-Dixon line, was based on a real-life event.[8] The Confederate Mining and Nitre Bureau, whose officials included Capt. Jonathan Harrolson, sent tank cars around the Southern cities collecting urine ("chamber lye"), from which ammonium nitrate could be extracted for use in gunpowder. The Southern version of the song commemorating this event was written by Thomas Wetmore and went as follows:

> John Harrolson! John Harrolson!
> You are a wretched creature,
> You've added to this bloody war
> a new and awful feature.
> You'd have us think while every man
> Is bound to be a fighter,
> That ladies, bless the dears,
> should save their pee for nitre.
> John Harrolson! John Harrolson!
> Where did you get the notion,
> To send your barrel 'round the town
> to gather up the lotion?
> We thought the girls had work enough
> making shirts and kissing,
> But you have put the pretty dears
> to patriotic pissing.
> John Harrolson! John Harrolson!
> Do pray invent a neater;
> And somewhat more modest mode
> of making your saltpetre;
> But 'tis an awful idea, John,
> gunpowdery and cranky,

That when a lady lifts her skirts
she's killing off a Yankee![9]

The Northern version of the poem appeared a few months later,
printed in the newspaper of an Ohio infantry regiment and later repub-
lished in an illustrated version by H. De Marsan of New York City.

John Harrolson! John Harrolson!
We've read in song and story
How women's tears through all the years
have moistened fields of glory,
But never was it told before
amid such scenes of slaughter,
Your Southern belles dried their tears
and went to making water.
No wonder that your boys are brave,
who wouldn't be a fighter,
if every time he fired his gun,
he used his sweetheart's nitre:
And vice versa, what would make
a Yankee soldier madder,
Than dodging bullets fired from
a pretty woman's bladder?
They say there was a subtle smell
that lingered in the powder,
And as the smoke grew thicker
and the din of battle louder,
There was found to this compound
one serious objection,
No soldier boy did sniff the stuff
without having an erection!

Tamer ditties circulated in the camps, mostly honoring the foibles
of Yankee generals.[10] Hooker's penchant for fancy dress uniforms appeared
in this form:

Joe Hooker had a nice tin sword;
Jack bent it up one day.
When Halleck heard at Washington,
He wrote, "Come home and stay."

Shortly after Dan Sickles shot Philip Barton Key, his wife's lover,
the aspect of cold-blooded murder was reflected in these lines:

Yankee Sickles came to fight,
And Dan was just a dandy;
Quite quick to shoot when 'tother man
Had nary a pistol handy!

In Vance Randolph's collection of 101 bawdy Ozark tales, there are some whose origins (unknown to the tellers) date back as far as 600 years ago, appearing in Boccaccio's *Decameron* or even earlier. Two of the stories in this collection relate to Civil War themes. The first story is entitled "He Didn't Get No Pension."

One time there was a fellow named Jubal that fought in the Yank army, but they didn't give him no pension. Jubal says he has got all kinds of ailments, and also he is pretty near blind. Finally the government doctor made Jubal undress and examined him all over, but it looked like he is as strong as a horse. There was a card hung up with letters on it, but Jubal says he don't see no letters, and he can't even see the card. They brought a big light to shine in his eyes, but Jubal didn't pay no attention. The government doctor didn't know what to think, but he watched Jubal mighty close.

Pretty soon a girl come in the office and she pulled up her dress to show her legs. That sure is a pretty girl, ain't it? says the doctor. Jubal says he don't see no girl, but he began to sweat. So then the doctor snapped his fingers, and the girl showed a lot more, but Jubal still says he don't see nothing. The doctor made another sign to the girl, and she took off her clothes. There she was, a'prancing around without a stitch on, only her shoes and stockings. Jubal never batted an eye, but the girl busted out laughing. "Look at his pecker, doc," she says. "It's a'standin' up like a tree."

The doctor grinned a little, too. "Your eyesight ain't as bad as you thought it was," says he. Jubal was pretty goddamned mad, but he just put on his clothes and walked out of the office. Jubal ain't the only one that was mad, either, because lots of other old soldiers has been done out of their pension the same way. Them government doctors ain't got much sense, but they sure know how to find out if a man is blind or not.[11]

The original of the next story appeared in a joke book published in 1755. When collected by Vance Randolph, it was told to him by a man who claimed to have heard it around 1895, in Newton County, Arkansas. This story is called "She Grabbed the Saddlehorn."

> One time there was a pretty girl lived out west of Neosho, and young Tom Harper was fetching her home from a dance. You know how they done it in them days. A boy just had one saddle horse, and the girl used to climb on behind him. Sometimes he would make the horse cut up a little, and then she had to put her arms around the boy's waist to keep from getting throwed off.
>
> Tom was a'riding a pretty lively pony that night, and maybe he used the spur a little bit. Him and the girl was both red-faced and panting when they got to her house. The next morning she kept telling the folks about what a wild ride they had through the woods. "I would have fell off sure," she says, "only I throwed my arms around Tom and held onto the saddlehorn."
>
> The girl's old pappy listened at her a'talkin', and after a while he called her out where he was sitting in the front yard. "Daughter," says he, "if I was you, I wouldn't say no more about holding onto the saddlehorn." The pretty girl says that's exactly what happened and surely there ain't no harm in telling the truth. The old man just kind of winked at her. "Daughter," he says, "what you had a'hold of is your own business, and I ain't asking any questions. But everybody knows that Tom Harper rides a McClellan saddle."
>
> The pretty girl turned red as a beet when she heard that, because the McClellan is an old-style Army saddle, and there ain't no horn on it. After while she just grinned a little and went back in the house. She never said another word about that wild ride through the woods with Tom Harper neither.[12]

The world of commercial pornography was a different matter entirely. The provost marshal general of the Army of the Potomac, Marsena Patrick, noted in his diary on June 8, 1863, "Amongst other things, I have seized upon and now hold, large amounts of Bogus jewelry, watches, et cetera, all from the same houses that furnish the vilest of obscene books, of which I have made a great haul lately." Two nights later, he noted: "There has been a bonfire in the rear of my tent, burning up a large quantity of obscene books, taken from the mails."[13]

Col. Lafayette Baker, head of the Secret Service, was upset over the "large numbers of obscene books and prints" that were mailed to soldiers in the Army of the Potomac.[14]

Capt. M. G. Tousley wrote a long letter directly to the president, complaining of the catalogs of obscene material being sent to the troops, and enclosed a sample catalog, thus preserving the material for posterity in the National Archives.[15]

Four of the catalogs have been preserved in a private collection and certainly verify Captain Tousley's assertions, in page after page of detailed offerings.

The flyer from Richards & Roche, 101 Division Street, New York City, features "New Pictures for Bachelors," including a "party of beautiful young girls" bathing in a spring, "mermaids wearing only mist and foam," "The Temptation of St. Anthony," showing the "naked charms" of the evil ones, and "Storming the Enemy's Breastworks" in which a Union soldier makes "an indelicate assault" upon a Southern girl.

The personal effects of Pvt. Edmon Shriver of Company F, 42d Ohio, contained the 1863 catalog of G. S. Hoskins and Co., also of New York City. The book selection contains twenty-three titles, including *Fanny Hill, The Lustful Turk,* and *The Libertine Enchantress* (more on this later). For $1, one could purchase *Matron's Manual of Midwifery, Prostitution in Paris, Male Generative Organs,* or *Aristotle Illustrated.* For only 50¢, one could choose among nine titles, including *Venus in Cloister, The Marriage Bed, Secret Passions,* and *Physiology of Love.*

Hoskins offered other merchandise as well: "spicy" song books, French tobacco boxes (in the shape of "human manure"), marked playing cards, transparent playing cards water-marked with naked women, French ticklers, love powders, false moustaches, dildos, three types of condoms, and stereoscopic pictures at $9 a dozen.

For only $3 a dozen, the soldier could receive, post-paid, *cartes de visite* of "London and Paris voluptuaries," portraying "the mysteries and delights of naked female beauty, male and female together and separate." The pièces de résistance were microscopic photos, set in stickpins, showing, when held close to the eye, "two or more figures photographed from life, engaged in sexual enjoyment."

Another publisher's *Catalogue of Fancy Photographs* featured "Bedroom Photographs for Gentlemen Only," listing eighty-five different views, including "Leda and the Swan," Passion Flower," "Nature's Mirror," and "Coming from the Bath." In addition to the usual selection of condoms, "both skin and India rubber," the catalog offers *The Book of Nature,* which is "not for exhibit to families but to keep under lock and key for private reading." This text is recommended for "every person of marriageable age." A further offering is *The Wedding Night—Advice to Timid Bridegrooms,* which included "Colored Plates, comprising the arts of getting sound and vigorous infants."

A fourth brochure lists the usual offerings, including *Silas Shovewell's Amours with the Nuns, Rose de Amour, The French Courtesan, The Cabinet of Venus Unlocked, Love on the Sly,* and *The Amorous Sketch Book.* Almost a full page is devoted to a listing of books by "Paul de Kock," including *The Secret Amours of Napoleon, Don Juan of France, Monsieur Dupont, Grisettes of Paris, Don Pedro in Search of a Wife,* and *Memoirs of a Man of Pleasure.* In addition, the publisher offered playing cards, marked on both sides, $1.50 a pack or $100 per gross.[16]

Who were the publishers and authors in this business of pornography? As an American industry, it dated back only to 1846. Before that time, the few such books in circulation were limited reprints of European erotic classics. The bestseller in these early years was *Maria Monk,* a rabidly anti-Catholic novel, with wild sex scenes between priests and nuns.

But in 1846, William Haynes, an Irish surgeon, immigrated to New York and quickly made a small fortune by publishing an American edition of *Fannie Hill.* With his new wealth, Haynes founded a firm that published cheap erotic novels. *Confessions of a Lady's Waiting Maid* appeared in 1848. Other titles included *The Merry Order of St. Bridget* (1857) and *Amours of an American Adventurer in the New World and Old* (1865).[17]

In the past 130 years, almost all these books have been destroyed. Only three Civil War–era American erotic novels are known to survive; all three are in the library of the Kinsey Institute at Bloomington, Indiana.

The first, *The Libertine Enchantress,* begins in sweet innocence. Lucinda is an orphan, being raised by her wealthy aunt and uncle in a "great yellow house on the plains." When she is fourteen, a young visitor notices her. Lucinda intercepts his letter to a friend and is thrilled to see herself described in glowing terms: "Although so young, she is dressed with singular taste, wearing a rather short blue silk dress from under which display themselves a couple of robust calves and an ankle that will one day make somebody's heart jump at first sight. She is modest and reserved in the company of her elders, but when she has occasion to speak she does so without *mauvais honte,* and pronounces her words full and distinct with an emphasis peculiar to herself and in a clear silvery voice which is worth a fortune in itself. But you will begin to say that I am in love with this bewitching creature. Not yet, friend of mine, for she is not yet a woman."

But Lucinda's aunt and uncle have already selected a mate for her, a man intended to be her fiancé. Lucinda is not impressed.

"He did not appear beautiful to me. On the contrary, his whole appearance and bearing inspired me with aversion. His long narrow face was very grave when at rest and of a cadaverous line, while his limbs were long and not well-proportioned nor well-handled. His expressions were very commonplace and his mouth had a very unpleasant expression. I thought Mr. Harden a very dull fellow and quite homely."

Through the next eight pages, Lucinda has the usual Victorian dilemma of how to dump the "cadaverous" youth selected for her arranged marriage, while breathing heavily at the thought of meeting John again, for she has formed the warmest affection for John. For eighteen further pages, she grimly ponders the impending marriage. One evening, after she retires to her upstairs room, she hears in the hallway the voice of her aunt and an unknown man. A whispered voice speculates that Lucinda is asleep. Her aunt and the unknown man enter a storage room across the hallway from our heroine's bedchamber; she decides to investigate. Here the book suddenly changes tone.

"I turned back the bolt in the lock without noise and then opened my door. Stepping to the opposite door, I looked through the keyhole, and what I saw caused me, at first, to start back with affright. My aunt was leaning over the end of the bed; her clothes were thrown up over her back and her broad, white buttocks were turned up naked and in full view. Between her thighs . . ."

Now, Lucinda's life accelerates into the style common to most pornography: wild couplings, heavy breathing, innocence violated, strange combinations of lovers, lust let loose. The plot dwindles to a diaphanous thread; the rest is action.[18]

The second fossil of a bygone age of American prurience is *The Secret History of a Votary of Pleasure*. The author launches his narrative in the efflorescent style that flowed so easily from the Victorian pen.

"I am better entitled to be called a 'Votary of Pleasure' than any other man who has yet lived. This last assertion will probably cause some surprise, and even a little incredulity, when I confess, as I do now, that I am neither a lascivious Italian, nor a hot-blooded Spaniard, nor a lewd Frenchman, nor a lustful Turk, (brought up under the loose discipline of the harem), but a New England Yankee, reared in the hotbed of Puritanism, and under the strictest 'blue laws;' institutions that, however contradictory it may seem, most powerfully excite to lechery, and stimulate to an inordinate desire for voluptuousness."

Soon, under the guise of instruction in the history of morality, the author has invoked Cesare Borgia, the Earl of Rochester, Charles II, Aaron Burr, and Margaret of Navarre. He further details his strict hellfire Congregational upbringing, which he believes has sown the seeds of his own lust and perversion. As a child, he reveled in the cruelties portrayed in the Old Testament and, in his attempts to emulate a wrathful God, tortured insects and pulled the wings off baby birds.

He describes running shrieking from his infant brother's funeral, as he visualized the baby in hell, a victim of Calvinistic infant damnation, broiling and crackling like a roasting pig on a spit.

These first thirty pages seem intended to give a redeeming gloss of moral uplift and social values before the author launches into his adolescent sexual experiences.[19]

The third example, a book entitled *The Love Feast,* has no such preamble, no pretense at moral instruction. Instead, the author, without even benefit of paragraphing, launches directly into his narrative:

> The feast was over, the guests were gone
> And youthful Frank was all my own.
> The bridesmaids in my room were met
> To robe the bride *en chemisette.*
> All merrily disposed to haste
> The feast for wanton husband's taste.
> A dish, that daintiest of meats:
> A virgin in a pair of sheets.
> Their wanton words made blushes rise
> And sparkles glitter in my eyes.
> They gave the rein to ardent lust
> And praised my dainty legs and bust;
> While one, more wanton than the rest
> Seized on love's moss-bounded nest.
> And cried, "Poor puss shall have a treat
> For the first time of juicy meat."
> While one my rosy nipples seized,
> And my ripe, rounded boobies squeezed,
> 'til stiff each little rosebud stood,
> Like cuckoo pintles in the bud.
> When quite undressed, the bower of bliss
> Dissolved in one warm rush of piss
> Whose briny jet bedewed the nick,
> Expectant of the luscious prick,
> With a soft sponge, they bathe the lips,
> My buttocks, belly, thighs and hips
> Till ready for a husband's power.
> I'm glowing like a newborn flower,
> The fairest ever Cupid plucked,
> To be caressed and kissed and fucked.

Through the next fifty-eight pages, the unrelenting rhythm persists. No sexual contortion remains unnamed, no body fluid rests undrained. Every orifice is filled, every excretory function is delineated. Both bride and groom, in an unparagraphed one-week marathon of sweat and multiple orgasms, consummate their marriage, leaving no possibility unexplored. *The Love Feast* is not for those who treasure subtlety.[20]

Although each of these books approaches its task of titillation in some different way, they all have size in common. Each is 3 inches wide and 4 inches high, an ideal size for a pocket or knapsack. Bound in dark cloth, they might easily be mistaken for small Bibles. The publishers' market research seems unerring.

Few courses in the history of American literature mention any of these works, but it seems clear that Civil War soldiers could be avid consumers of commercial, explicit sexual works, as well as creators of homespun bawdy songs and stories.

Homemade visual pornography from the Civil War is the rarest of finds. One collection has three sketches by Pvt. Edman Shriver of the 42d Ohio, drawn on the backs of merchants' cards and mailed to friends. All of them have a remarkable resemblance to men's restroom graffiti today. *Plus ça change* . . . The Shriver sketch is a typical male fantasy, a megaphallus admired by a naked woman. The second drawing is of a woman receiving two men simultaneously. The third is more bizarre—a urolagniac (erotic arousal in the presence of urination) scene involving a transparent chamber pot.[21]

Pornographic photographs from the 1860s are rare. It is very unlikely that they were rare during the war itself, however. The daguerreotype was perfected in 1841; it was quickly followed by the calotype, a paper negative from which unlimited numbers of prints could be made. In 1851, the ambrotype, with a glass plate negative, was an enormous commercial success. Prints and enlargements were easy, and the negative plate itself, backed with black velvet, formed an inexpensive positive image. The tintype was a variation on the ambrotype and gave a cheap, lightweight, unbreakable image, ideal for a soldier in the field. By 1861, there were 2,879 photographers in Paris alone and 200 schools teaching photography in London.

To this outpouring was added the *carte de visite,* patented by A. E. Disderi in 1854. A single click of the shutter produced eight photos of the subject. At the height of the *carte* craze, 300 million a year were sold in England alone. Were any of these photographs of nudes? Certainly.[22]

Roger Fenton, the world's first war photographer (Crimea), did nudes. John Watson, whose engravings illustrated *Pilgrim's Progress* and *Robinson Crusoe,* photographed nudes. Parisian photographer Nadar photographed the actress Christine Roux; the same unmistakable body and pose reappears in Ingres's 1856 painting, *La Source*. Lewis Carroll, the creator of *Alice in Wonderland*, spent his leisure hours photographing little girls who were entirely nude.[23]

In the same era, were there "explicit" photos as well as "art" photos? Certainly. The remarkable collection of Gerard Levy has an 1855 print by Moulin of a nude couple embracing; the man's right hand is on the woman's breast, and his left hand is between her legs. He is half tumescent. A hand-tinted stereographic daguerreotype shows a woman staring directly at the camera; her legs are parted and she has no undergarments.[24] In fact, the explicit photo industry had grown so large by 1859, producing mostly stereoscopic photos for tourists, that Baudelaire published a diatribe denouncing the practice.

Was there an American industry of explicit photos? The cities were full of hungry prostitutes; mass-production photography was cheap; millions of young men were bored, away from home, and had money in their pockets. Were there explicit American photos? Almost certainly.

Where are those photos today? Thousands were destroyed to prevent families from seeing them after the war. Hundreds still remain in private collections, known only to an inner circle. The few that have been unearthed in seven years of research are shown here.

After a century and a half of Victorian purging, enough written and graphic material remains to indicate that a large and prosperous pornography industry existed during the Civil War, alongside the amateur production of poetry, songs, and drawings.

Chapter Six

❧

Prostitution: East

THE VICTORIAN WORLD reveled in euphemism. Prostitutes were soiled doves or Cyprians. Doves are white and pure; soiled, they are something less. Cyprian has a classic touch: Aphrodite, the goddess of love, was born on Cyprus.[1]

And were there American Cyprians before the Civil War? In 1858, Dr. William Sanger of the Venereal Disease Hospital on Blackwell's Island, New York, gave the definitive answer: yes. He not only treated thousands of prostitutes, but persuaded 2,000 of them to complete a questionnaire. Eighty-eight percent of the women were under the age of thirty; 40 percent were less than twenty. Most of his group, at follow-up, had died within four years of entering their profession, usually from venereal disease and/or alcoholism.

Sixty-two percent were foreign-born; of these, 57 percent were Irish, 20 percent were German, and 8 percent were English. One out of every 250 immigrants became a prostitute.

Thirty percent of the women had a child; nearly all the children died before reaching school age. From a survey of precinct police captains, Sanger concluded that there were 7,900 prostitutes in New York City, which then had a population of 1.2 million.[2]

In a speech denouncing the evils of the skin trade, New York City bishop Matthew Simpson asked his flock, "Are you aware that there are more prostitutes than Methodists in our city?"[3]

Sanger did not study Washington, D.C., or Richmond, Virginia, but by 1862 he might have found an even worse story than he unfolded in New York.

The tourist visiting Washington, D.C., today is certain to spend time in the city's magnificent museums. Imagine a visitor emerging from the north entrance of the National Museum of American History. Constitution Avenue lies before him, and across its busy surface lies Federal Triangle, with the Customs Service, Internal Revenue Service, and Justice Department buildings directly before his eyes. To his left is the Ellipse and the White House; to his right is the Museum of Natural History and the National Gallery of Art. Grandiose architecture housing the nation's treasures and command posts. If the visitor exits the south door, he will see the white dome of the Capitol and the Washington Monument, and on the grassy expanse of Capitol Mall, he will see the homeless, huddled over the warm air grates that ventilate the Metro subway. In the far distance, he may hear gunshots, as drug dealers murder their rivals as well as innocent bystanders.

Washington is, and always has been, a city of contrasts: rich and poor, splendor and degradation, an ongoing historic experiment in democracy, constantly under assault by entropy, greed, and the forces of violence.

The contrast between the intended and the actual, in our nation's Capital, reached its zenith during the War Between the States. The area now occupied by Federal Triangle was then thirteen blocks of vice, a dense warren of low saloons, boisterous brothels, and hideouts for pimps, thieves, and pickpockets. The land now occupied by the three great museums was an open sewer, the Washington Canal, a 150-foot-wide channel full of foul-smelling human waste and rotting garbage, draining slowly into the Potomac. Reflected in its filthy waters was the half-completed dome of the Capitol, unfinished business just like the Union itself. The history of this small center of Washington contains all the contradictions in American life.

In the preceding decade, the population of Washington had increased by more than 50 percent, reaching 61,000 in 1860. As the Civil War approached, new buildings were springing up and old ones were being renovated. The new House chamber was opened in 1857 and the Senate in 1859, a cause for celebration. Most of the streets were still unpaved, however, and became mud wallows in the winter and emitted clouds of dust in the summer.

As the population grew, the poor and those at the fringes of society began to accumulate in the area between Constitution Avenue (then B Street) and Pennsylvania Avenue. The area was filled with gamblers, thieves, and prostitutes. The ambience inspired several names: Louse Alley, Rum Row, and Murder Bay. The aromas of sweat and outhouses, the stench of the Washington Canal, and the odors of the fish market at 15th and B Streets all combined to offend any person of delicacy.

With the war, the influx of soldiers, opportunists, government workers, camp followers, and escaped slaves gave fresh impetus to the life of Murder Bay.[4]

A *New York Times* correspondent expressed the situation eloquently: "Washington at the time I went there in July, 1862, was a cesspool into which drained all the iniquity and filth of the nation. It was filled with runaway Negroes, contractors, adventurers, office-seekers, gamblers, confidence men, courtesans, uniformed officers shirking their duties, and the riff-raff, the outscourings of all creation."[5]

In the area where 13th and D Streets intersected, dozens of bawdy houses operated in defiance of the law. D Street alone had houses managed by Maggie Murphy, Sally Murphy, Mary Taylor (two houses), Mollie Mason, Joe Horn, Mina Bearing, Miss Nichols, Louie Myers, Louie Hayes, Leota Gaskill, and Maggie Walters (probably assumed names), and these accounted for only a fraction of the prostitution trade in the few blocks between the White House and the Congress.

While the poorer prostitutes congregated in the older Murder Bay area, the younger and more beautiful girls, and the madams who sold them, occupied attractive houses in the better residential areas. Marble Alley, which lay between Pennsylvania and Missouri Avenues, was in a good neighborhood yet contained the sporting houses operated by Sal Austin and Julie Dean.

Yet even the better houses shared in the sordidness inherent in prostitution. The plumbing at Sal Austin's was a privy in the small backyard, and at least one dead newborn baby was fished out of its cesspool. Nearly all the brothels sold liquor (illegally), and a drunken client was just as dangerous whether he was rich or poor, officer or enlisted.

Some Union volunteer officers did little to set an example. Their bored horses spent all night outside the brothels, while the equally bored orderlies tended the horses and waited for their officers to emerge in the light of early dawn.

The fanciful names of the bordellos—Fort Sumter, the Ironclad, Headquarters, U.S.A., the Devil's Own, the Wolf's Den (kept by Mrs. Wolf), Mary Hall's, the Cottage by the Sea, No. 10 Marble Alley, the Haystack (kept by Mrs. Hay), the Blue Goose, Madam Russel's Bake Oven, and Madam Wilton's Private Residence for Ladies—were known to almost every soldier. It was a time when the notorious and the scandalous flourished. The Light family—mother, father, and three daughters—were an outrageous example. They all had long police records; mother acted as the madam for her three prostitute daughters, Kate, Anna, and Matilda. On one occasion, they were all arrested when the Lights had hired an organ grinder (and his monkey) to provide music for a Dance of the Seven Veils, performed by the three Light girls and attended by a large crowd of appreciative soldiers. The soldiers' shouts of encouragement created such a racket that the police were called, and the entire Light family, the organ grinder, and the monkey were all brought before the magistrate.

The three sisters were notoriously quarrelsome and filthy mouthed, so much so that they were unwelcome even in their own sordid world. They were chased from the Island and then from English Hill. Later, they set up a little family brothel in some empty barracks on North Seventh Street, and then moved on to a shanty near Cliffburne Hospital. There, they helped incite a riot between one group of soldiers from the District and a second group from Pennsylvania. The Lights were evicted again, and in their new location they engaged in a free-for-all fight with eighteen soldiers. Back to court they went and onto the streets again.

There were several attempts to curb the epidemics of violence and demoralization. Brig. Gen. Joseph Hooker's division was camped outside the city, and in their off-duty hours his forces found endless mischief in nearly every part of the city. To aid the military police by localizing the problem, Hooker herded many of the prostitutes into the Murder Bay (future Federal Triangle) area. Soon this place of freshly concentrated vice was known as "Hooker's Division" or simply "The Division." The derivation of today's word "hooker" as a designation for prostitute is warmly debated, but no matter what the correct origin, the general's name became linked with this area of vice.[6]

The Civil War usage of "Hooker's Division" is attested in many sources. The *Evening Star,* Washington's more sensational newspaper, noted on March 29, 1865, that a group of sailors had taken on "a full cargo of grog, after which they made their way to Hooker's Division." The same newspaper, on August 24, 1864, referred to a riot as "a lovely night in Hooker's Division," and five days later described a woman as "a boarder in Hooker's Division." On March 2, 1865, the *Star* reported that Lucy Stanwood, accused of stealing $100, "resided in a house of ill repute in Hooker's Division," and on March 31 a woman arrested in boy's clothes, "gave her name as Susan Rider and resides in Hooker's Division."[7]

Whether General Hooker's administrative action in any way decreased the problem with prostitution is unknown, but it linked his name with that industry for more than a century to come.

Three different agencies attempted to stem the flood of crime in wartime Washington: the District of Columbia Metropolitan Police, the military Provost Guard, and Col. Lafayette C. Baker's secret agents.

The police department was formed in 1861, with a force of 150 men, and was overwhelmed from the day of its inception—overwhelmed not only by the 230 miles of streets and 77 miles of alleys in Washington and by the challenge of living on a salary of $1.31 a day, but by the sheer magnitude of the task; 24,000 arrests were made in 1863.[8]

Police Superintendent William B. Webb despaired of his task, because the criminals that he arrested were quickly back on the streets. Bail was easily procured and cases were postponed from term to term. Webb openly stated that the chief obstacle to the control of crime was the judicial system. Even when there was a conviction, there was no jail space: The District Penitentiary had been requisitioned for ammunition storage, the County Jail was in such a state of disrepair that any healthy prisoner could bore a hole through the wall, and the workhouse had no security nor any work to do. Serious cases were sent to the New York State Prison at Albany, but that left hundreds of other prisoners with no clear destination.[9]

The Provost Guard, with its military powers, was welcomed by the ordinary citizen, who was far more concerned about being murdered or robbed than he was about the civil rights of criminals. In its initial foray, the Guard was less than successful: The newspapers reported that in its "raid" in Madam Duprez's whorehouse, the officer of the guard was in bed with one of the inmates, while his squad was celebrating elsewhere in the neighborhood. But these laggards soon were purged, and the Provost Guard came to be feared by the criminal element.[10]

One of its fanatic agents was Lt. W. G. Raymond. In civilian life he had been a clergyman, and he exercised his military duties in an atmosphere of Old Testament wrath. He and his squad stayed up all night, bursting into bordellos, arresting colonels and privates with even-handed fierceness. The madams and their young charges made it a point of honor to obey what they could not avoid. They opened all doors wide and went readily before the magistrates. Whenever possible, the madam brought enough cash to bail out her whole crew, and the next night they would be back in business. Raids on illegal saloons and gambling dens were more successful, as the whiskey could be poured out into the gutter and the roulette tables smashed, but the Cyprians' professional equipment was out of bounds to the enemies of crime.[11]

In 1863, the Provost Guard tried a tactic little used since the Middle Ages: summary roundup of known or supposed criminals and an attempt to publicly humiliate them. Handcuffed, wearing large red signs reading "Pickpocket and Thief," these individuals were marched through the streets to the railroad station, followed by a fife and drum corps playing "The Rogue's March." Once in the train, they were watched until the cars pulled out of the station. Who received them is not recorded. The *Daily Morning Chronicle* for April 4, 1863, reporting on the thieves on parade, noted, "Two girls calling themselves Anna Smith and Sarah Davidson were included in this interesting party, but were taken to the depot under guard in an ambulance. They did not seem to feel much shame at their disgraceful situation and though we could hardly have wished that they should have been exposed as well as the men, we believe that they would have stood the ordeal as well as their male confederates." (By coincidence, the same issue of the paper had an advertisement for a sexual cure: "Manhood: How lost! How restored! Just published in a sealed envelope. Six cents. A lecture on the Nature, Treatment and Radical Cure of Spermatorrhea or Seminal Weakness . . . and Involuntary Emissions . . . by Robert Culverwell, M.D.")

The third agency fighting crime in wartime Washington, D.C., was the Secret Service, organized by Col. Lafayette Curry Baker.

Baker was an American original. He had been an itinerant mechanic whose only police background was brief membership in one of the San Francisco vigilante committees. In 1861, he applied for Federal employment. He was sent on a secret mission to Richmond, Virginia, where he obtained information, was captured, escaped, and returned north. Pyramiding his success as a spy, and his gift of eloquence, he was appointed a detective and soon had a colonel's commission and wide powers.

His undoubted success in unmasking traitors, counterfeiters, bounty jumpers, and fraudulent contractors rested, at least in part, upon a disregard for due process, search warrants, and other fine points of the law. In Washington, D.C., he charged into illegal saloons, gambling halls, and brothels, arresting with fine impartiality both guests and inmates. He was called a tyrant, a liar, and a cheat, but he was never called lazy, and the streets of the city ran with liquor spilled by his detectives. The ordinary citizens were happy to see *someone* with effective law enforcement power.[12]

The *Evening Star* was ever quick to publicize the sensational. On March 5, 1861, Inauguration Day, this paper commented upon the Philadelphia detectives brought to control the inaugural crowds: "A drunken party of them entered a well-known Cyprian establishment on 13th Street, south of the Avenue, last night, pioneered by one of our own police and possibly they quartered for the night. The city, we presume, will foot the bill."

In May 1864, the *Star* reported a drunken brawl at the Admiral House, a saloon on Pennsylvania Avenue, near Third Street East. A soldier and his girl were drinking there and proposed a toast "to the Union." Two of the waitresses, Southern sympathizers, objected. In the fight that followed, the proprietor and his wife also jumped on the visiting couple, one of whom was cut over the eye with a knife. The Guard was summoned, the proprietor was placed in the Guardhouse, and the place, "a resort for women of questionable character," was closed. It had been closed four times previously.

On August 26, 1862, the *Star* ran a long page-one article about the illegal gambling dens. The reporter noted that the best customers were Congressmen and Union officers in full uniform. Most of the customers seemed to be losing money at a great rate.

In July of the following year, there was a long article about a theft at the bordello run by Madam Pauline Meyer on 14th Street near N Street. A soldier lost his silver watch there and was not able to retrieve it. A few days later, the madam had a quarrel with her "boarders" and fired them all. The now out-of-work girls went to the police station and denounced Madam Meyer as a thief. The police retrieved the watch and arrested Meyer and her "husband," August Meyer, on charges of larceny and keeping a bawdy house.

Out on bail, the Meyers were at home when the "boarders," accompanied by friends, returned to retrieve their clothes. In the ensuing brawl and police interruption, Mr. Meyer experienced "the ornament-ing of his forehead with a knot, with various rays extending from the center."

In June 1861, the *Star* warned soldiers against bathing in the Washing-ton Canal, which is "hardly more than a drain for the populous portion of the city, into which all the sewers empty." The paper recommended swimming instead near the Washington Monument, where the water was cleaner, but only at dawn and dusk, when their naked bodies would not offend the local citizens.

The government sent a shipload of Cyprians to the Confederate States of America. It is true that politics makes strange bedfellows. The most ardent secessionists in the nation's Capital were the Episcopalian gentlefolk and the prostitutes. Whether they had other traits in common cannot be answered, but they seemed to agree on states' rights. The pros-titutes were a little more open in their sympathies and when drunk would stand in the streets, cheering for Jeff Davis and singing "The Bonnie Blue Flag."

When the Federal Government announced safe passage to the South for ladies of secessionist inclination, 70 of the 600 applicants were women of the night.

The evening before the bon voyage party, Federal officers searched the luggage looking for contraband items that might aid the rebels: dry goods, shoes, medicines, pins and needles. One young lady offered her favors to an inspector, should he ever come to Richmond, but he was not so easily deflected from his duty.

Three months later, the Confederate exchange agent, Robert Ould, a former Washington attorney, returned two of the more easygoing secessionists to his Union counterpart with a stiff note: "Sir: I send back to you two strumpets." After invoking "holy feelings" and "the purity of a flag of truce," Ould closed with this ominous thought: "If I did not believe you were imposed upon, I would be justified in taking this as a matter of personal affront."[13] Ould's Yankee counterpart wisely sidestepped this invitation to a duel.

The notions of honor and chivalry were tested daily in the streets of Washington in the association between the volunteer officers and the painted ladies. Freed from the narrow bounds of their families and hometowns, and safe from combat, large numbers of officers celebrated by gambling and drinking all night, and consorting openly with women who were unmistakably prostitutes. One of the officers attended the Campbell Minstrel Show with a harlot on each arm. On every clear day, carriages paraded Pennsylvania Avenue, filled with officers in full uniform, laughing with their gaudy courtesans. The *Star* complained of two army officers, returning from the races in an open barouche, who sat out the traffic jam by hugging and kissing their "fair but frail" girls in full view of a regiment on parade.[14]

In the same racetrack crowd were two carriages full of painted ladies, who enjoyed a professional rivalry. As Sal Austin's carriage drew abreast of one occupied by courtesans Fannie Lee and Fannie Dennis, they exchanged friendly remarks and one of them pronounced Sal to be a "tub of guts." Madam Austin called the police, who hauled the Fannies before a justice. Each was fined $2.50.[15]

The extent of the courtesan problem may be seen in the provost marshal's records, which show 450 registered bawdy houses in 1862. In 1863, the *Star* estimated that there were 5,000 prostitutes in Washington, D.C., along with another 2,500 in Georgetown and Alexandria. This did not include kept women of all sorts. In 1864, the provost marshal (as shown in the table on pages 73–75) listed seventy-three bawdy houses with white inmates and a dozen "coloured" bawdy houses, each identified as to location, number of inmates, and level of quality.[16] It could hardly be said that prostitution was a secret in our nation's Capital.

One of the keenest observers of Washington life was Pvt. Alfred Bellard, who was on military police duty in 1863 with the Veteran Reserve Corps. His twenty-four-man squad, headed by a commissioned officer, made a daily patrol through the cross streets off Pennsylvania Avenue, "visiting the houses of ill fame on the look out for officers and soldiers who were not provided with passes." The group also visited the Island, that part of the city southwest of the Washington Canal, an area that contained "the worst places in the city." They patrolled Tin Cup Alley, a sort of courtyard entered through an unnamed alley, where the houses were "occupied by black and white, all mixed together . . . you pays your money takes your choice." At Castle Thunder, a large brick house that the police visited only in groups, Bellard observed a man relieving himself on the main staircase. At another "notorious den," he was sent to the back to prevent escape during a raid. There were no shutters, and a man and woman continued their activities, untroubled by his presence. The worst bordello he saw was called the Hospital and was near the Capitol grounds; even out on the street the stench was overpowering. Later, Bellard noted in his diary, "I had a little experience on the Island myself, that might have been a serious thing for me." The next page was carefully cut.[17]

Peace did not bring an exodus of the painted ladies. Although the troops had marched home, the size of the Federal administration continued to grow and there was no shortage of customers.

Hooker's Division continued to be a neighborhood of working-class men, manufacturing firms, saloons, and brothels, all within convenient walking distance of the Capitol and the business district.

During the second administration of Grover Cleveland (1893–97), a reform group published a map titled "Within Sight of the White House," showing every saloon and bordello between Ohio and Pennsylvania Avenues. The unknown author of this map asserted that in this area there were 109 houses of prostitution, as well as numerous houses of assignation. In the single block bounded by C, D, 13th, and 13½ Streets, there were thirty-one bawdy houses.[18]

Little changed in Hooker's Division until 1914, when the Congress made ownership of a house for purposes of prostitution a legal nuisance. Today, the canal, the saloons, and the bordellos of Hooker's Division are gone. They are remembered chiefly by the small flocks of archaeologists who, like cattle egrets gleaning a disturbed field, walk behind the bulldozers of urban renewal.

But instead of the frogs and crickets prized by egrets, the archaeologists find little treasures of the heart and mind, faint echoes of the women, who, long ago, tried to make a house a home. Old Hooker's Division yields up cosmetic bottles, fancy buttons, and toys . . . palpable shadows of the women (and their children) who lived there and formed part of the unofficial history, the earthy side, of our nation's Capital.[19]

RICHMOND

The Confederate capital had its own story. When the center of the Rebel government was moved from Montgomery, Alabama, to Richmond, one of the crowded trains was occupied by a reporter, Charles Stuart. He described the many officials and place-seekers and noted that, with "the connivance of a few War Department officials, one of the cars had smuggled into it some 'fair ones' whom a good brother would not introduce to his sister."[20]

By every means of transportation, more "fair ones" arrived in Richmond. One writer estimated that wartime Richmond had more harlots than New Orleans and Paris combined.[21] The center of Richmond's social life was in the four blocks southwest of Capitol Square. The prime hotels for the sporting life were the Ballard and the Exchange. The former was at 1400–1406 East Franklin Street; the latter was across the street, at 1403 Franklin. They were joined by a pedestrian bridge over the street.[22]

Scattered throughout the neighborhood were forty major gambling establishments, which served the best food in town; one spent $10,000 a day on edibles. The furniture was luxurious; the finest whiskey and champagne were sold at the bars. Senators, generals, and the well-connected filled these gambling halls and attracted a raft of hangers-on, low-life thieves, confidence men, contractors, and fraudulent officers whose title of "Colonel" had been bestowed in the brothels.[23]

The high-class harlots lived upstairs, above the gambling dens, and along Locust Alley, a narrow street that ran from Main to Franklin, in the block bounded by 14th and 15th Streets. Locust Alley was populated almost entirely by courtesans, such as the legendary Clara A., whose diary entries appear in chapter 14.

Of course, there were more privates than generals, and far from the chandeliers and champagne of the elegant clubs were hundreds of low-class dives and disreputable saloons that served the less aristocratic.

West out Broad Street was the suburb of Screamersville, named after the shouting men tormented by the hallucinations of delirium tremens. Sallow-faced, dope-drugged, booze-sotted harlots of the most desperate sort served a clientele little better than themselves. The rawest rotgut, tangle-foot whiskey, took the place of the sparkling wine of the clubs.[24]

Running a mile east of downtown, along Main and Cary Streets, was another rowdy area of illegal liquor sales, alcoholic whores, pickpockets, and cutthroats. Drunkenness and fighting were normal; love and good manners were not even on the agenda. Back on Capitol Square, there was a perennial shortage of cabs, as most were on permanent hire to the courtesans for their assignations.[25] A reader wrote to the *Enquirer,* suggesting that harlots be horse-whipped, but did not offer to do the work himself.

The *Daily Dispatch* reported a flood of prostitutes of both sexes and complained that these newcomers "have been disporting themselves extensively on the sidewalks, and in hacks and open carriages . . . (with) smirks and smiles, winks and . . . remarks not of a choice kind in a loud voice."[26]

Well-known hookers such as Margaret Phelin, Margaret Lynch, Mary Moose, and Teeny Kidd were frequently in the police courts for keeping "disorderly houses" (and some were, indeed, quite disorderly). They paid their fines and went back to work.[27]

The *Daily Whig* mentioned the arrests or trials of Lizzy Winn, Cecillia Smith, Elizabeth Hardeman, Mary Driscoll, Susan Pendergrast, Mary Waldron, Ann Thomas, Alice Ashley, Anna Thompson, and Mary Stevens, all on charges of prostitution. In the case of Anna Thompson, ten additional women were listed, all employees at the Thompson bordello.[28]

The Young Men's Christian Association operated a home for convalescent soldiers on South Tenth Street. An enterprising madam opened a bawdy house just across the way, behind Duval's Drug Store. The women appeared at the windows of their house and, by various states of undress and suggestive gestures, lured many of the men into activities sufficiently vigorous to slow their recuperation.[29]

Some of the pimps had permanent tables at the best saloon bars, whence they steered clientele to their women. An editorial in the September 4, 1862, *Examiner* deplored the large number of pimps walking the streets and criticized their fine silk shirts, imported woolens, and custom-made shoes. These pimps clearly did not feel the shortages that other Southerners suffered as a result of the blockade.[30]

Many Confederate records have been lost, but in the "Rebel Archives" now housed in Washington, D.C., there is the report of J. H. Carrington, who was asked to investigate five women sent under arrest to Richmond from Culpeper Court House. They were Sarah Gibbs and the four Fletcher sisters: Lucy, Livy, Joanna, and Betty. All were described as "women of loose morals." When interviewed, Sarah stated that her husband had been in the 17th Georgia and died in action near Richmond. Lucy said her husband was killed at Gettysburg. Carrington's report concluded: "They are abandoned [i.e., loose] women who were sent from Culpeper C. H. and in default of another receptacle, seem to have been consigned to Richmond, as the [illegible] for all characters whose presence is undesirable elsewhere. I see no reason why they, more than any other Cyprians, be confined and I therefor recommend their discharge."[31]

(No one seems to have suggested that they might really be war widows, in need of assistance.)

Sgt. Ira Matthews seems to have had an undeniable attraction towards Cyprians. Stationed in Richmond in the spring of 1865, with Company J, 14th U.S. Infantry, he was charged with visiting "a house filled with the most degraded and loathsome of their sex . . . prostitutes very badly diseased, so much so that they were considered by the Medical Department as unfit to be allowed to remain in the city." Matthews said he didn't know his visit was forbidden. Bvt. Maj. I. J. Miller testified that Matthews had been instructed to avoid the women "except when sent there on business." The court was not inclined to believe the sergeant's story.[32]

In both capitals, in addition to the ordinary romantic connections between men and women, there were clearly extensive industries of commercial sex during the Civil War.

The following register of Washington, D.C., bawdy houses was assembled by the provost marshal in 1864–65. The "Inmates" column lists the number of women in each house. In the evaluations of "Class," 1 is best, 2 is fair, 3 is poor, and "low" is bad. "Island" refers to the area bounded by the canal and the Potomac River. The original is handwritten and often hard to read. The file number is Vol. 298, RG 393, Provost Marshal, 22nd Army Corps, National Archives. Courtesy of James O. Hall.

Provost Marshal's Register

Bawdy Houses & Addresses	Inmates	Class
1. Miss Lucy Hart *21 Pa. Av.*	4	1
2. Madam Miller *51 Pa. Av.*	6	1
3. Mrs. Catharine Campbell *138 24th St.*	5	2
4. Madam Bennett *148 F St.*	7	?
5. Mrs. Louise Turner *446 19th St. (?)*	5	1
6. Lizzie Miller Co *18th & E St.*	6	2
7. Mollie Turner *62 C St.*	3	1
8. Hattie Farwell *28 13½ St.*	2	2
9. Ellen Wolfe *494 13½ St.*	4	3
10. Miss Mina Bowers *478 13½ St.*	6	3
11. Mrs. Sarah Duncan *474 13½ St.*	2	2
12. Miss Maggie Murphy *282 D St.*	6	1
13. Sallie Murphy *286 D St.*	6	1
14. Mary Taylor *298 D St.*	6	low
15. Mollie Mason *287 D St.*	7	1
16. Miss Joe Horn *291 D St.*	7	2
17. Mrs. Mary Taylor *305 D St.*	9	3
18. Mina Bearing *309 D St.*	6	3
19. Miss Nichols *591 12th St.*	5	1
20. Louie Myers *533 12th St.*	4	2
21. Mrs. Louie Hays *537 12th St.*	5	3
22. Miss Leote Gaskill *541 12th St.*	6	1
23. Mrs. Louisa Koener *540 12th St.*	5	3
24. Mrs. Maggie Walters *532 12th St.*	14	1
25. Mrs. Louise South *252 C St.*	6	2
26. John Sputsvists *313 D St.*	6	low
27. Eliza Gibson *531 11th St.*	House of Assignation	
28. Miss Mollie Florence *533 11th St.*	3	2
29. Miss Kate Walters *595 11th St.*	3	2
30. Miss Mary Miller *597 11th St.*	6	3
31. Mrs. Elizabeth Harrison *284 C St.*	House of Assignation	
32. Miss Annie Wilson *510 10th St.*	4	1
33. Miss Sophie Hoffman *484 10th St.*	6	3
34. Mrs. E. M. Post *487 10th St.*	6	1
35. Miss Nellie Gwinn, *348 E. St.*	4	1
36. Miss Jane Ross *348 E St. back*	4	2
37. Sallie Austin *500 6th St.*	9	1
38. Miss Julia Deen *12 Marble Alley*	8	2
39. Miss Nellie Mathews *10 Marble Alley*	6	2

Provost Marshal's Register (continued)

Bawdy Houses & Addresses	Inmates	Class
40. Mrs. Elizabeth Harris *33 Maine Av. Island*	9	2
41. Laura Tompkins *225 B St., Island*	2	3
42. Mrs. J. Rhoades *474 Maryland, Island*	6	very low
43. Mrs. E.M. Mark *473 Maryland, Island*	2	very low
44. Mary Hall *459 Maryland, Island*	18	1
45. Elizabeth Harley *4 Maryland, Island*	3	1
46. Hattie Mills *2nd near Maryland, Island*	3	3
47. Ann Benton *Tin Cup Alley, Island*	5	3
48. Mary Hessler *513 3rd St., Island*	5	3
49. Mary Murrey *493 3rd St., Island*	6	very low
50. Miss Mary Donnelly *339 C St., Island*	3	very low
51. Sarah Brown *rear of 339 C St., Island*	5	very low
52. Margaret Wilson *rear of 339 C St., Island*	3	very low
53. Mrs. Roland *250 F St., Island*	4	4
54. Margaret Hanks *Fighting Alley, Island*	6	low
55. Matilda Wade *Fighting Alley, Island*	6	low
56. Mrs. Johnson *640 7th St.*	3	low
57. Ellen Hall *434 Virginia Ave., Island*	6	1
58. Mary Tolson *G St. nr. 1st St., Island*	3	very low
59. Catharine Dinkloker *4th @ N, nr. Navy Yard*	6	3
60. Rachel Rappider *574 9th St. nr. H St.*	5	very low
61. Mary Conklin *95 Pa. Ave nr 10th St.*	5	very low
62. Julia Fleet *444 3rd St. Fox Hospital*	6	very low
63. Emaline Bateman *N St. tween 11th & 12th*	2	2
64. Margaret Venerable *249 10th St.*	4	4
65. Louisa Sanford Co *3rd & L Sts.*	4	1
66. Eliza Foster *rear N.J. Av & C St.*	1	3
67. Mary Jacobs *rear N.J. Av & C St.*	1	3
68. Emma Howard *rear N.J. Av & C St.*	5	3
69. Philamena Preston *331 G. St.*	3	3
70. Mrs. Weldon *497 10th St. bt. G & H*	2	1
71. Mrs. Wiggons *Cor 1st & B St., Island*	6	very low
72. John Muntz *512 N.J. Ave.*	(not recorded)	
73. Annie Jones *195 Pa. Av. nr. 10th*	5	very low

Coloured Bawdy Houses

Name and Address	Inmates	Class
1. Julia Thomas *480 13th St.*	4	3
2. Two Houses *rear of 348 E St.*	4	4
3. Misses Seal & Brown *13 Marble Alley*	6	low
4. Theadosia Herbert *Tin Cup Alley*	5	1
5. Rebecca Gaunt *Tin Cup Alley*	4	2
6. Sarah Wallace *Tin Cup Alley*	5	2
7. Sophia Harbour *489 3rd St.*	2	1
8. Selia Higgins *rear of 339 C St.*	5	2
9. Josaphine Webster *Fighting Alley*	12	low
10. Biloy Becket *243 E St. nr 3rd*	5	low
11. Levinia Pergins *352 Virginia Av.*	3	2
12. Emily Brown *H St. nr 20th St.*	6	low

Chapter Seven

≈

Prostitution: West

NASHVILLE

THE AUTUMN OF 1860 was a splendid season in the Cumberland Valley. The weather had been perfect, the crops abundant, and the barns and warehouses were full at all the farms around Nashville. The trees were flaming yellow and red as the farmers drove into town to spend some of nature's largesse. The merchants were pleased by their renewed prosperity and with all the progress they saw around them.

Just that year, a new suspension bridge had linked the city with the lands northward. Railroads now converged on Nashville from four directions, and the new telegraph brought news in seconds that had taken weeks before.

Annual commerce was over $25 million, remarkable for a population of 14,000 nonslave residents, but Nashville's wealth from its rich farms and its hundred steamboats was rivaled by three industries of the mind: education, publishing, and religion.

A major university, a medical school, and an excellent system of high schools and academies attracted scholars from all over the South. More than thirty publishers and journals made their homes in Nashville, and their products enhanced the prosperity and prestige of the city on the Cumberland.

There were eight Methodist churches, three Presbyterian, and a wide representation of other denominations: Baptist, Catholic, Episcopal, and Lutheran.

The crowning glory of this thriving city was the state capitol, just completed five years earlier. Patterned after an Ionic Greek temple, it floated above the city on one of the highest hills. Its classic beauty and the intellectual arts that flourished on the hills around it earned Nashville its title of the Athens of the South.

Down the hill from the Greek temple, closer to the river, lay another district, Smokey Row, an area two blocks wide and four blocks long, where a different industry thrived: eight full blocks of prostitution. For three-quarters of a mile on either side of Spring (now Church) Street, every shack or building along Front, Market, College, and Cherry (now First, Second, Third, and Fourth) Streets was a house of ill fame.

During June of 1860, the Nashville marshals for the federal census had been unusually diligent. Their efforts identified 207 women who listed their occupation as "prostitute." (There were probably many others, who listed themselves as seamstresses, waitresses, and the like.) Of those 207, we know a remarkable amount: 198 were white and 9 were mulatto. Eighty-seven were totally illiterate and eight could read but not write. Twenty were widowed. The youngest was age fifteen, the oldest fifty-nine; mean age was twenty-three.

Most were natives: 113 were born in Tennessee. Twelve each were born in Kentucky and Alabama, and the others hailed from ten additional states, Ireland (three), and Canada (one).

Judged by their names (which may be fictitious), they were largely Anglo-Saxon. The most common last name was Brown, followed by Scott and Richardson. Their first names were usual for the time: Mary, Elizabeth, Nancy, Martha, and Eliza accounted for eighty-three of the women.

There were a few luxurious houses, but many poorer ones. The flagship of the Nashville bordello trade was operated by Rebecca and Eliza Higgins at 101–103 North Front Street. The house was valued at $24,000, a very great sum in 1860, and it was occupied by twenty-eight people. There were seventeen prostitutes, six schoolchildren, two preschool children, a carpenter, a brick mason, and a twenty-two-year-old black man named Tom Trimble.

The next largest bawdy house was operated by Mag Seats, who seemed to specialize in providing adolescent sex. Six of the eleven girls were in their teens, and the oldest was only twenty-four.

Martha Reeder, the thirty-one-year-old Tennessee-born madam of 72 North Front Street, owned $15,000 of personal property, putting her among Nashville's wealthiest citizens. Such prosperity was the exception, however. The typical Nashville Cyprian, in this year before the outbreak of war, was around age thirty, widowed with small children, and lived and worked in a two-room "crib," one step from total poverty.

If the weather was warm, women of Smokey Row could be seen in every state of undress. The busy river commerce and the affluence of city trade supported, as we have seen, at least 200 ladies of the night in 1860.[1]

The autumns of the next four years would see a very different Nashville. In April 1861, Fort Sumter was bombarded and the war began. On February 16, 1862, Fort Donelson fell, which opened the Yankee path to Nashville. The city officially surrendered nine days later. On March 12, 1862, Andrew Johnson arrived as military governor of Tennessee. He was not a popular governor: Shortly after he arrived, he arrested the city council for treason and jailed seven ministers for refusing a loyalty oath.

Some of the women were Southern sympathizers, perhaps, but not all. The residents of Smokey Row, and their sisters who flocked from all over the Union to join them, were more than happy to see the Yankee dollars. Soon there was the inevitable spread of venereal disease to both military and civilian population.[2]

The newspapers reflected the problem in their advertisements. On North Cherry Street, Dr. Coleman opened his Dispensary for Private Diseases and Dr. A. Richard Jones on Deaderick Street also offered his services for the relief of "private diseases."[3]

The first major attempt to control wartime prostitution was described by Capt. Ephraim Wilson: "During the winter of 1862–1863, the Army had a social enemy to contend with which seriously threatened its very existence . . . the women of the town." Wilson continued, ". . . fifteen hundred of them at a single time were gathered up and placed aboard a train and were compelled to leave and conducted under guard to Louisville. Louisville at first objected to receiving such a formidable array of unwelcome guests, but finally consented to do so, and Nashville was afterward all the happier and better off for their conspicuous absence."[4] The 30,000 Union soldiers in the area may have felt the loss more than did Captain Wilson.

It would seem that the women sent to Louisville did not like being deported, and swarmed back. Soon the problem was as bad as before. In the words of the *Medical and Surgical History*, "Brigadier General R. S. Granger, in command at Nashville in June, 1863, was 'daily and almost hourly beset' by the commanders of regiments and their surgeons to devise some way to rid the city of the diseased prostitutes infesting it. The matter was referred to the provost marshal, Lt. Col. George Spalding, of the 18th Michigan, who, by means of the police force and provost guard under his command, succeeded in placing on board a steamer which he had chartered, all the [white] women of the city publicly known to be of vile character." The vicissitudes of this attempt at steamboat therapy are described in another chapter, but here it is sufficient to say that by August 3, they were all back at Nashville.[5]

Something that Colonel Spalding may have overlooked was the law of supply and demand. During the month that the white prostitutes were embarked on their river cruise, their places back at Nashville were filled by their black colleagues. The Nashville newspapers thundered, "So bare-faced are these black prostitutes becoming that they parade the streets and even public squares by day and night."[6]

A few days later, on July 9, 1863, another paper complained that "Unless the aggravated curse of lechery as it exists among the Negresses of the town is destroyed by rigid military or civil mandates, or the indiscriminate expulsion of the guilty sex, the ejectment of the white class will turn out to have been productive of the sin it was intended to eradicate."[7]

Colonel Spalding, faced now with his original white prostitute population to which had been added the influx of black ones, proposed a system of licensed prostitution. His memorandum outlined the details:

1. That a license be issued to each prostitute, a record of which shall be kept at this office, together with the number and street of her residence.
2. That one skillful surgeon be appointed as a Board of Examination, whose duty it shall be to examine personally, every week, each licensed prostitute, giving certificates of soundness to those who are healthy and ordering into hospital those who are in the slightest degree diseased.
3. That a building suitable for a hospital for the invalids be taken for that purpose, and that a weekly tax of 50 cents be levied on each prostitute for the purposes of defraying the expenses of said hospital.
4. That all public women found plying their vocation without license and certificate be at once arrested and incarcerated in the workhouse for a period of not less than 30 days.[8]

This first American exercise in legalized prostitution seems to have had some benefit. As of April 30, 1864, 352 women were licensed, and 92 infected women had been treated in the new facility created for this problem. (In the early summer of 1864, the licensing and examination procedures were extended to cover "colored prostitutes.")[9]

The surgeon general noted, "Under these regulations, a marked improvement was speedily noticed in the manner and appearance of the women. When the inspections were first enforced, many were exceedingly filthy in their person and apparel, and obscene and coarse in their language, but this soon gave way to cleanliness and propriety." There seems to have been an actual increase in the number of prostitutes in the city, since "many of the better class of prostitutes had been drawn to Nashville from Northern cities by the comparative protection from venereal disease which its license system afforded."[10]

Another factor that may have made the program more attractive to the women was the attention given to their comfort. In Dr. Chambers's report of January 31, 1865, he describes, "a proper place for conducting the examination was a house in a secluded part of town with upper rooms in view of obtaining a good light. The women to be examined enter a reception room which is comfortably furnished and in cold or disagreeable weather well heated. They pass in time from this apartment into an adjoining examination room in which there are a bed, a table and all the necessary appliances for examining them."

The examinations were required every fourteen days, later shortened to every ten days. Those who passed were issued a certificate. Those who failed were sent to the hospital.[11]

The provost marshal's report for the week ending August 22, 1863, showed that 123 women were examined and gives their names, residences, and the results of the examination. For instance, Mary Little of 159 College Street was examined and given a certificate of health. Thirty-seven of the women lived on College Street, thirteen lived in Smokey Row, seven on Cherry Street, and the remainder elsewhere. As in the 1860 census, the average age of the prostitutes was twenty-three. The youngest was fifteen.[12]

During the war, Nashville had twenty-three different hospitals operated by the military. Hospital Number Eleven, to which the infected prostitutes were referred, was housed in the former residence of the Catholic bishop on Market Street, just north of Locust Street. (Other sources place it on University Pike.) Hospital Number Eleven is designated in some reports as the "Pest House" and in others as the "Female Venereal Hospital."[13]

Dr. Chambers's 1865 report describes the facility as the "hospital for prostitutes," gives its locality as being "on the western verge of the city, in a healthy locality," and states that the building was previously a smallpox hospital. The facility had a living room (furnished from funds collected as examination fees), a treatment room, and two wards with ten beds each. "The Matron, Nurse and cook are colored women. One colored man is hired to do the laboring work." The doctor assigned to the hospital for prostitutes was Surgeon R. Fletcher, of the U.S. Volunteers.[14]

The provost marshal furnished guards for the hospital, and they were under orders to admit no one, under any pretext, unless that person

was accompanied by Dr. Fletcher himself. The guards also enforced the rule prohibiting profane language; offenders were given solitary confinement. Patients were not allowed to leave until "perfectly cured."

As of January 31, 1865, 207 women were treated in this hospital. Of these, 40 had gonorrhea, 137 had "primary syphilis," and 30 had "soft chancre," combined with secondary syphilis. The primary syphilis cases stayed an average of eleven days, the secondary cases thirty-eight days, and the ones with gonorrhea ten days. Two women died, one of tuberculosis and one of smallpox.[15]

Wallace, describing the hospital for prostitutes and the hospital for infected soldiers, said, "The object of the former is to diminish the number of patients in the latter." He noted that when the women were cured they were "returned to duty."[16]

In a photograph taken during the war, labeled simply, "Nashville Hospital laundry yard, July, 1863," a dozen white women stand next to clotheslines filled with sheets. At that time and place, white women did not do laundry. James A. Hoobler suggests that the date is wrong and that these women are patients at the hospital for prostitutes.[17] If so, this is the only known photograph of that facility.

The final word on the hospital for women is seen in Dr. Fletcher's letter, dated August 15, 1864.

It is not to be supposed that a system hastily devised, established for the first time on this continent, and certain to encounter all the obstacles that vicious interests or pious ignorance could put forth, should be other than imperfect. We have here no Parisian "Bureau des Moeurs" [morals], with its vigilant police, its careful scrutiny of the mode of conduct of houses of prostitution, and its general care of the public welfare, both morally and in its sanitary consideration. This much, however, is to be claimed, that after the attempt to reduce disease by the forcible expulsion of the prostitutes had, as it always has, utterly failed, the more philosophic plan of recognizing and controlling an ineradicable evil has met with undoubted success.

Among the difficulties to be overcome was the opposition of the public women. This has so effectually disappeared that I believe they are now earnest advocates of a system which protects their health and delivers them from the extortion of quacks and charlatans. They gladly exhibit to their visitors the "certificate" when it is asked for, a demand, I am informed, not unfrequently made. The majority of the patients in the hospital are not sent from the inspection room, but consists of women who, suspecting their malady, have voluntarily come for examination and treatment.

That a vast amount of venereal disease still exists in this army is incontestable, but from careful inquiries made of the men, when opportunity served, and from the reports of surgeons of regiments, the origin of the evil has been but to a small extent traceable to this city. When a soldier of the post forces is infected it is not uncommon for his captain to report the case, with the name of the suspected woman, who is immediately arrested and examined.[18]

The male equivalent of the Nashville Women's Pest House was Hospital Number Fifteen, the "Soldier's Syphilitic Hospital." The Hynes High School, on Line Street near Summer Street, was the three-story brick building completed just four years before the war. Commandeered by the military government, it made an ideal hospital.[19]

The physician in charge of this 140-bed facility for soldiers with venereal disease was Dr. William M. Chambers (1814–92), surgeon of volunteers. He was a native of Kentucky, and after the war, he returned to his adopted home and his practice in Charleston, Illinois.

As of December 31, 1864, 2,330 men had been admitted to the Soldier's Syphilitic Hospital. It is a tribute to Dr. Fletcher's efforts that of the first 999 men admitted, only 30 had contracted their disease in Nashville.[20]

Dr. Chambers noted that when large numbers of reenlisted Union veterans returning from home entered Nashville, the number of infected patients entering both the men's and the women's syphilitic hospitals, "greatly and astonishingly increased." It is clear that the efforts to control venereal disease in other areas were a failure, and this also raises the specter of an epidemic of sexual disease brought home by the veterans.

Officers were not immune to these diseases. Chambers noted in early 1863 that he always had from ten to twenty officers under treatment at any given time, but after the inception of regulated prostitution this number dropped to one officer per month.

Not all officers were discreet about their relationships with the *filles de joie*. The Nashville *Daily Press* noted that officers were frequently seen in open carriages with known prostitutes. One young Cyprian rode out with her officer friend into the downtown "nude from the waist heavenward," which caused considerable disturbance.[21]

Dr. Chambers also made house calls. At the direction of the provost marshal, he visited and examined "kept women" and whorehouse madams at their homes. The fee for the house visit was an additional dollar.

Hospital Number Eleven, the "Female Venereal Hospital," was located on Market Street near Locust Street in Nashville, Tennessee. Historian James Hoobler notes that since white women seem to be doing the laundry, they are likely to be prostitutes detained for treatment. The hospital had a black matron, nurse, cook, and maintenance man. During the summer of 1864 the hospital began admitting black prostitutes, an early venture in desegregated medical care. *National Archives negative 165-B-2499.*

Hospital Number Fifteen, for soldiers with venereal diseases, sat on the corner of Line and Summer Streets in Nashville, Tennessee. It had been Hynes High School, opened just before the war as the city's most prestigious secondary school. The building no longer exists. *National Archives negative 165-C-922.*

WHO'S BEEN HERE SINCE I'SE BEEN GONE.

This humorous drawing shows a long-absent soldier wondering about the parentage of the newborn child in his home. The original, about two by three inches, has no publisher's mark and is badly worn, doubtless from being passed around the campfire. *Author's collection.*

The daguerreotype photograph was widely available by 1850, eleven years before the Civil War, and yielded fine detail and rich tones of black and gray. This young woman had her image recorded by an unknown American around 1855. *Collection of Herb Peck, Jr., Nashville, Tennessee.*

A peep-show box, probably displaying a nude photo, attracts Federal soldiers at Culpeper Court House in Virginia. This sketch by Edwin Forbes appeared in the January 8, 1864, issue of *Frank Leslie's Magazine. Library of Congress negative LC-USZ62-12805.*

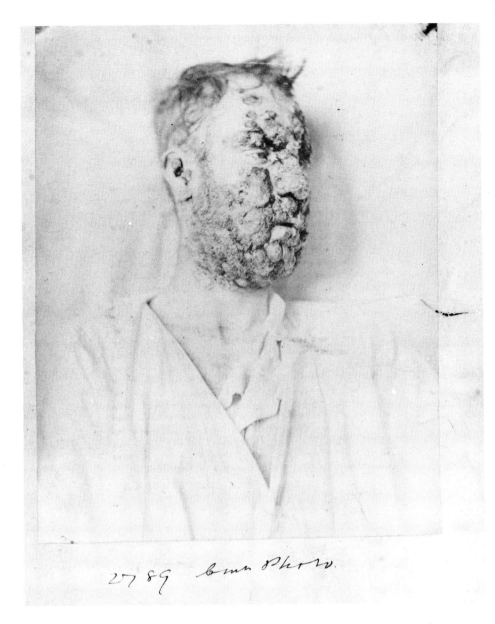

27 89 _own Photo._

No antibiotics were available to help this unfortunate soldier with the scabs and blisters characteristic of the rupia-type lesions of third-stage syphilis. The remedy for syphilis in 1865 was salts of mercury, giving rise to the pun, "A night with Venus, a lifetime with Mercury." *Otis Historical Archives, National Museum of Health and Medicine, CP# 2789.*

The *carte de visite* was a photo print glued on cardboard. This format, widely available after 1854, was so popular and so easily mass produced that in England alone more than 200 million were produced in a single year. The usual *carte* was a formal portrait, to be given to friends. The studio's name was printed on the cardboard backing. In this pornographic pose there is no publisher's imprint, in order to evade prosecution. The mount of this *carte* is thin, square-cornered cardboard with a gold border, dating it to the mid- or late 1860s. *Collection of Carl Mautz, Oregon House, California.*

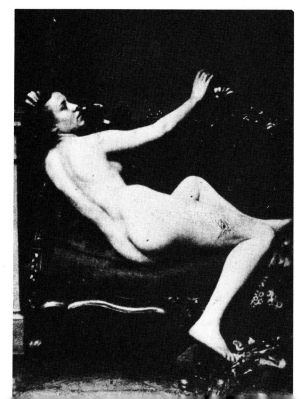

In 1859, the international trade in erotic photos was so great that Charles Baudelaire published an essay in the *Revue Française* denouncing the trade as a vulgarization of art. This *carte*, also without a publisher's imprint, was produced in France in the mid-1860s. The original is about two by three inches. *Author's collection.*

No. 16

Office of Provost Marshal,
MEDICAL DEPARTMENT,
Nashville, Tenn. Dec. 20 1863

I Certify *that I have made a personal examination of* Bettie Duncan,
and find her free from contagious venereal diseases.

Bay. C. Depot.

W. M. Chambers
Surgeon U. S, Vols,

PROVOST MARSHAL'S OFFICE,

NASHVILLE, TENN., _____, 1863.

Provost Orders, No. 21:

All Public Women in the City of Nashville are hereby ordered to report at the Provost Marshal's Office before the 20th day of August, 1863.

On presentation of Surgeon's Certificate and payment of Five Dollars [$ 5:00] they will receive License for the practice of their profession.

All such Women found doing business after the 20th day of August, inst.. without such Certificate and License, will be arrested and incarcerated in the Work House for a period not less than Thirty Days.

By command of

Brig. Gen. R. S. GRANGER.

GEO. SPAULDING, Lieut. Col. and Provost Marshal.

(*Top*) Prostitute Bettie Duncan was issued this Weekly Certificate of Health on December 30, 1863, by the U.S. Army, signed by Dr. William M. Chambers. (*Bottom*) All Nashville prostitutes were notified that they must register and be examined or face thirty days' confinement. *National Archives, courtesy of Michael Musick.*

The buildings in the middle distance are part of "Hooker's Division," a whole neighborhood of brothels and low saloons, as seen from the south porch of the Treasury Building in 1862. In the left background can be seen the Smithsonian Building. On this same Treasury porch, the deranged Reverend James C. Richmond pressed obscene drawings and verses into the hands of his unwilling love object. *Collection of the Smithsonian Institution, negative 18603.*

Maj. Gen. Joseph ("Fighting Joe") Hooker, a tall, handsome man, whose name became associated with the red-light district of Washington, D.C. Charles Francis Adams, Jr., described Hooker's Army of the Potomac headquarters as a combination "barroom and brothel." *National Archives negative 111-B-3320.*

MADAME RESTELL.

☞FEMALE PHYSICIAN, is happy in complying with the solicitations of the numerous importunities of those who have tested the efficacy and success of her medicines, as being so especially adapted to female complaints.

Their known celebrity in the Female Hospitals of Vienna and Paris, where they have been altogether adopted as well as their adoption in this country, to the xclusion of the many and deleterious compounds hereto re palmed upon their notice, is ample evidence of the e imation in which they are held to make any lengthened advertisements superfluous; it is sufficient to say that her celel ated 'FEMALE MONTHLY PILLS,' now acknowledged by the medical fraternity to be the only safe, mild and efficient remedy to be depended upon in long standing cases of Suppression, irregularity or stoppage of those functions of nature, the neglect of which is the source of such deplorable defects on the female frame, dizziness in the head, disturbed sleep, sallow complexion, and the innumerable frightful effects which sooner or later terminate in incurable consumption.

The married, it is desired necessary to state, must under some circumstances abstain from their use, for reasons contained in the full directions when and how to be used accompanying each box. Price $1.

Females laboring under weakness, debility, fluor al bus, often so destructive and undermining to the health, will obtain instant relief by the use of these Pills.

PREVENTIVE POWDERS, for married ladies in delicate health, the adoption of which has been the means of preserving many an affectionate wife and fond mother from an early and premature grave. Price $5,00 a package. Their nature is most fully explained in a pamphlet entitled 'Suggestion to the Married.' which can be obtained free of expense, at the office, where ladies will find one of their own sex, conversant with their indisposition, in attendance.

FEMALE MEDICAL OFFICE, No. 7 Essex street, Boston. Office hours from 8 A.M. to 8 P.M.

Philadelphia Office, No. 7 South Seventh street.

Principal Office, No 148 Greenwhich street New York.

ol   tfo

This advertisement appeared in the January 2, 1845, Boston *Daily Times*. Madame Restell not only sold abortion pills but also for thirty-three years ran a lucrative abortion clinic in New York City. When Anthony Comstock closed her clinic in 1878, she committed suicide. The journal *Puck* published a cartoon entitled "Fifth Avenue Four Years After Madame Restell's Death," showing the street clogged with pregnant women and small children. *From Abortion in America, by James C. Mohr (New York: Oxford University Press, 1978).*

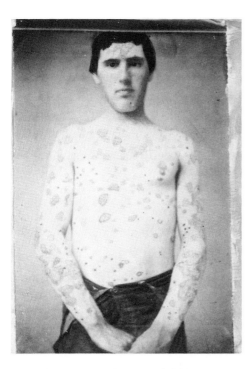

With rampant prostitution in the Civil War, there came epidemics of venereal disease. This photo shows a young man, probably a Union soldier, with an acute skin eruption identified as secondary syphilis. The photo was in the collection of Dr. A. Lippe when acquired by the Army Medical Department. *Otis Historical Archives, National Museum of Health and Medicine, CP# 1896.*

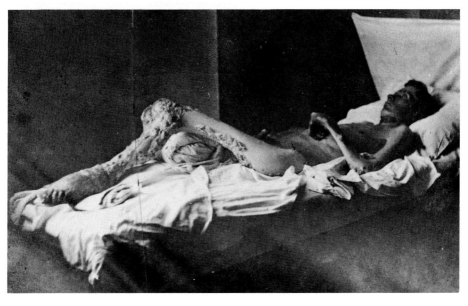

73,382 white Union soldiers were diagnosed with syphilis during the Civil War. The treatments of that era had not helped this young man, whose massive leg ulcerations mark the terminal stage of his disease. *Otis Historical Archives, National Museum of Health and Medicine, CP# 2141.*

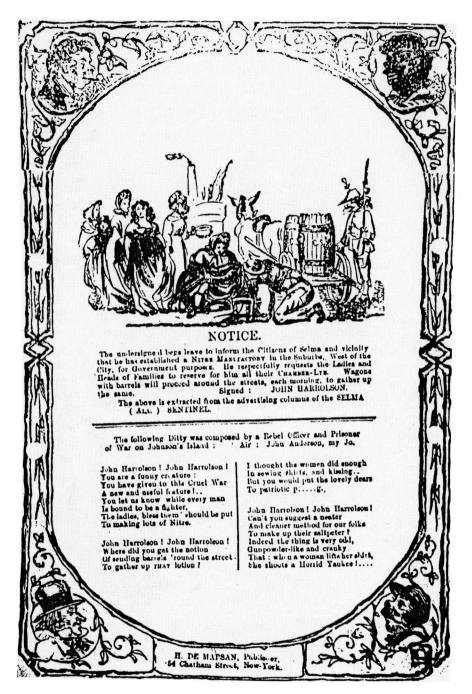

NOTICE.

The undersigned begs leave to inform the Citizens of Selma and vicinity that he has established a NITRE MANUFACTORY in the Suburbs, West of the City, for Government purposes. He respectfully requests the Ladies and Heads of Families to reserve for him all their CHAMBER-LYE. Wagons with barrels will proceed around the streets, each morning, to gather up the same.　　　　　Signed :　　JOHN HARROLSON.

　　The above is extracted from the advertising columns of the SELMA
　　(ALA.) SENTINEL.

　　The following Ditty was composed by a Rebel Officer and Prisoner of War on Johnson's Island :　　' Air : John Anderson, my Jo.

John Harrolson ! John Harrolson !
You are a funny creature :
You have given to this Cruel War
A new and useful feature !..
You let us know while every man
Is bound to be a fighter,
The ladies, bless them' should be put
To making lots of Nitre.

John Harrolson ! John Harrolson !
Where did you get the notion
Of sending barrels 'round the street.
To gather up THAT lotion ?

I thought the women did enough
In sewing shirts, and kissing..
But you would put the lovely dears
To patriotic p.....g.,

John Harrolson ! John Harrolson !
Can't you suggest a neater
And cleaner method for our folks
To make up their saltpeter ?
Indeed the thing is very odd,
Gunpowder-like and cranky,
That : when a woman lifts her shirt,
She shoots a Horrid Yankee !....

H. DE MARSAN, Publisher,
54 Chatham Street, New-York.

A popular broadside verse parodies Confederate efforts to collect urine for making gunpowder. A version published several months later (see page 52) was more ribald and suggested that the battlefield smoke from such powder would cause mass erections. *Published in New York by H. DeMarsan. Bell I. Wiley papers, Emory University.*

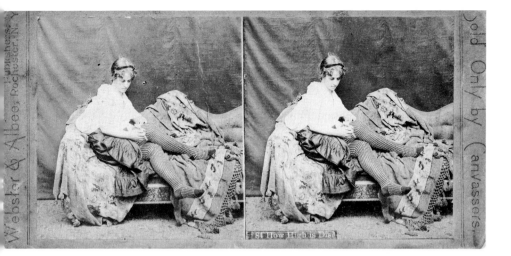

Almost every Victorian-era American parlor contained a stereopticon, with a box of stereo photos, usually of travel or religious scenes. For a racier audience, this woman reveals her ample thighs, highlighted by patterned stockings. Her provocative query suggests that she might lift her skirts higher. *Published by Webster & Albee, Rochester, New York. Author's collection.*

Anna Johnson carried this prostitute license issued by the U.S. Army in Nashville, Tennessee. Her license was signed by Provost Marshal Lt. Col. George Spalding. *National Archives, courtesy of Michael Musick.*

James C. Richmond, the prurient priest, in his robes of office. In 1863
he became infatuated with Rosa Bielaski, a young copyist in the
Treasury Building, and showered her with obscene love notes. *Library
of Congress, negative LC-USZ62-108021.*

Page two of the infamous April 4, 1863, letter the Reverend James C. Richmond sent to Rosa Bielaski. (See page 160 for a transcript of the letter.) The same week he penned these thoughts, Richmond met with Abraham Lincoln and assured the president, "I am driving the devil out of Washington." However, it was Richmond who was obliged to leave the capital, branded "lewd and wicked" by a fellow Army chaplain. *National Archives, courtesy of Michael Musick and Howard Madaus.*

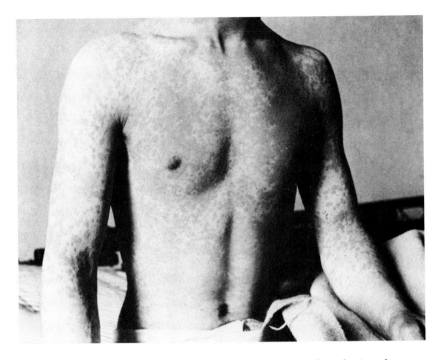

More than 100,000 Union soldiers contracted gonorrhea during the Civil War. Pvt. W. C. of the 4th Artillery, Fort Monroe, Virginia, developed this Roetheln-type (measles-like) rash in 1887 while under treatment for acute gonorrhea. The surgeon was Dr. P. Brooke. *Otis Historical Archives, National Museum of Health and Medicine, CP# 1860.*

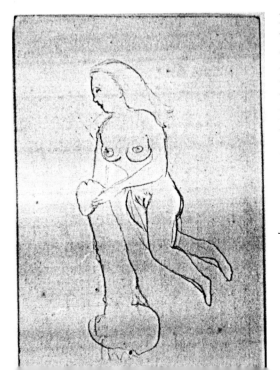

Pvt. Edman Shriver of the 42nd Ohio made this erotic sketch (and several others) and mailed them to his cousin Pvt. R. C. Wagner of Co. B, 2nd Regt. D.C. Volunteers, who replied, "Ed, these pictures are very well done for such a little boy as you. They are just the kind the boys like to look at." *Collection of James C. Frasca, Croton, Ohio.*

FRENCH PERIODICAL PILLS.

Warranted to have the desired effect in all cases.

THESE Pills contain a portion of the only article in the whole meteria medica, which can regulate the system and produce the monthly turns of females that can be taken, without hazarding life, and this article is not to be found in any of the pills or nostrums which are pictured forth so largely in the papers of the day. It has frequently occurred that the unhappy patient has by the use of these pills and nostrums given nature such a shock that they have never since enjoyed health, and they never can. It seems that they are got up and advertised merely for the object of making money, regardless of the consequences, and the venders are usually considered beneath responsibility, by all who know them.

The French Periodical Pills are the result of the combined knowledge and experience of some of the oldest and most distinguished physicians of Europe, and have been used by females embracing the gentility and most of the nobility of France, for the last twenty-three years. To eulogize their virtues would not add to their merits. We will only say TRY THEM. and if they do not prove to be what they are here represented to be, your money shall be refunded.

They contain no medicine detrimental to the constitution, but restore all debilitated constitutions to their wonted energy and healthfulness by removing from the system every impurity.

The only precaution necessary to be observed is ladies married should not take them if they have reason to believe they are en ciente, as they are sure to produce a miscarriage, almost without the knowledge of the patient, so gentle yet active are they.

All letters to be directed to DR. L. MONROE, U. S. Agent and Importer, No 58 Union street, Boston.

N. B. The above Pills can only be obtained at 58 Union street, all sold elsewhere in Boston, are counterfeit, and only calculated to deceive.

N. B Full directions accompanying the Pills.

1 m*   J3

Dr. L. Monroe advertised these abortion pills in the Boston *Daily Times*, January 23, 1845, claiming their use by "most of the nobility of France." The doctor warned that they should not be taken during pregnancy "as they are sure to produce a miscarriage." *From* Abortion in America, *by James C. Mohr (New York: Oxford University Press, 1978).*

Col. Lafayette C. Baker, head of the U.S. Secret Service in 1864, had no previous police experience other than brief membership in a San Francisco vigilante committee. His energy, ambition, and lack of attentions to legal niceties made him effective in raids on Washington's brothels and in burning obscene literature seized from the mails. *National Archives, negative 111-B-1116.*

Sarah Edmonds disguised herself in men's clothing and served as Pvt. Franklin Thompson, Co. F, 2nd Michigan. She worked as a male nurse near Washington, D.C., and later as a mail carrier, soldier, ambulance worker, orderly to Gen. Philip Kearny, and spy. After the war she married and raised five children. *State Archives of Michigan, negative 02254.*

Dr. Chambers's closing remark in his January 31, 1865, report, indicates that as the war ended and soldiers left Nashville, "These women are rapidly leaving in all directions. Some profess to be going home, while others are looking out for situations where more money can be obtained wherewith to bedeck and bedizzen themselves."[22]

But not all the Yankees left. Encouraged as much by Cupid as by Eros, 174 Northerners of all ranks married Nashville women. At least thirteen high-ranking Union officers chose local brides and settled at Nashville.[23]

In the realm of unmarried sex, Nashville remains America's first experiment with legalized, regulated prostitution. Even with the primitive medical treatment available then, it seems to have been a remarkable success.

MEMPHIS

Nashville lies on the banks of the Cumberland, a substantial river, but Memphis is on the Father of Waters, the Mighty Mississippi himself.

Memphis is shaped by the river. As an example, for thirty-one years the only hospital in town for poor people was restricted to caring for boat crews and transients. The long-term residents of Memphis, who were not wealthy, had to wait until 1860 before there was a hospital for the citizens of the town itself.

The river had brought trade, new people, prosperity, excitement, news, and manufactured goods—everything the city needed. On June 6, 1862, the river brought Yankees. Following a one-sided gunboat battle on the river, the town formally surrendered to Union naval officers. After several brief administrations by other military governors, William Tecumseh Sherman took over the command of Memphis from late July until December 8, 1862.

In his memoirs, Sherman remarked, "When we first entered Memphis, July 21, 1862, I found the place dead: no business doing, the stores closed, churches, schools and everything shut up. . . . I caused all the stores to be opened, churches, schools, theaters and places of amusement to be re-established. . . ."

But these positive actions did not seem to modify Southern sentiment. Sherman noted further, "The people were all more or less in sympathy with our enemies . . . all in the south are enemies of all in the north. There is not a garrison in Tennessee where a man can go beyond the sight of the flagstaff without being shot or captured."[24]

In this hostile environment, the Union military government undertook, successfully, the second American experiment in the regulation of prostitution.

In the year since Memphis had been captured, thousands of Union troops passed through or were quartered there. Ladies of the night flocked to Memphis from all over the country to provide their services. Throughout the city, but especially on the north side of Beale Street, the demimode reigned supreme.[25]

The Yankee soldiers were happy to see white women, but they seemed positively fascinated by black women. One soldier stationed at Memphis wrote home that the black prostitutes "felt loving toward us because they thought we were bringing them freedom and they would not charge us a cent." John N. Williams of the 7th Tennessee Regiment noted in his February 23, 1863, diary entry that not all Southern black women were charmed by the Union soldiers: "Heard from home. The Yankees has been through there. Seem to be their object to commit rape on every Negro woman they can find."[26]

The Memphis *Daily Bulletin* for April 30, 1863, wrote, "It is a fact too obvious that our city at the present time is a perfect beehive of women of ill fame. The importation of lewd women from the North is at high tide. Steamboats bring these women down where they consort with civil and military officers in broad daylight."[27]

Offensive as "consorting" might be morally, the army was even more concerned with the practical problems of having hundreds of soldiers off duty, sick with gonorrhea or syphilis. In 1863–64, Gen. Cadwaller C. Washburn commanded the Department of West Tennessee, with his headquarters in Memphis. Washburn was no novice at politics or administration. He had already made a fortune in banking, railroading, and real estate, and he had served three times in the United States Congress. (After the war, he organized what is now General Mills and made a second fortune.) When it was clear that attempts to suppress prostitution in Memphis through police action were a failure, Washburn took action.

In July and August 1864, several strokes of the pen changed the city. Memphis was placed under martial law. The entire municipal government was suspended. Lt. Col. Thomas H. Harris was appointed mayor. (Later, Capt. Richard Channing filled that office.) Dr. L. L. Coxe, an agent with the U.S. Sanitary Commission, submitted to General Washburn a written elaboration of the Nashville regulations, based upon Coxe's visit to Nashville and study of that program for the control of venereal disease.[28]

Washburn approved the plan. A few days later, the new regulations were endorsed by the surgeon general in Washington, D.C.

On September 30, a printed proclamation was circulated to the women of Memphis. In its details, and in its special provisions ("This circular . . . must not be shown or given to men"), it was a most unusual document.

From the city medical inspection department, Mayor's office, Memphis, Tennessee, September 30, 1864:

All women of the town [a term excluding respectable women, such as housewives] of the City of Memphis and vicinity, whether living in boarding houses, singly or as kept mistresses, are notified that they must hereafter be registered and take out weekly certificates. Women who can show that they are living privately with a responsible citizen of good character will be exempted from the weekly medical inspection by calling weekly between 2:00 and 5:00 o'clock p.m. at the Mayor's office and paying the regular hospital fee. No woman residing in a boarding house will be registered as a kept woman.

All other such kept women, whether practicing prostitution regularly or occasionally, are ordered to call on the City Medical Inspector at the private office, second story over the Confectionery Store on the corner of Main and Union Streets, entrance through the store, or at No. 21 Union Street, on any afternoon between 2:00 and 4:00 o'clock before the tenth of October, and receive a medical certificate, for which $2.50 will be charged.

Or women can receive the medical certificate at their homes by requesting the Medical Inspectors to visit them and paying a $1.00 extra for the visit. A note directed to Lock Box 201, Post Office, giving the street and number will be attended to. On receiving the medical certificate, a ticket of registry must be called for personally at the Mayor's Office, for which $10.00 will be charged.

The money received goes to the support of the private female wards in the new City Hospital, on the corner of Exchange Street and Front Row, into which registered women are admitted at any time for any disease upon showing their weekly certificate, are afforded all the privacy and comfort of a home, and nursed by an experienced matron and female nurses, free from any cost or charge whatever.

"Streetwalking," soliciting, stopping or talking with men on the streets; buggy or horseback riding for pleasure through the city in daylight; wearing a showy, flash or immodest dress in public; any language or conduct in public which attracts attention; visiting the public squares, the New Memphis Theater, or other resorts of LADIES are prohibited and forbidden.

Good conduct will insure relief from detective or police visits, exposure or loss, and a violation of the order will inevitably incur punishment. Any woman of the town, public or private, found in the city or vicinity after the tenth day of October,

1864, without her certificate or registry and her medical exemption certificate, will be arrested by the police and punished.

This circular is intended for the information of women only and must not be shown or given to men.[29]

In the five months that followed the order, 134 prostitutes registered; 13 percent were "housekeepers," 4 percent were "kept women," and 84 percent were "boarders."[30]

A special women's wing was opened in the City Hospital. Thirty-four women were admitted for treatment of venereal disease there between October and February. Unlike most public health programs, it made a profit: $6,429 was collected in fees from the prostitutes and only $2,535 was spent on expenses.

Was the program successful? In the February 11, 1865, report of the provisional mayor, who evidently disliked his connection with prostitution, there is grudging praise for the medical, as opposed to the police, approach: "Any connection with such a department is extremely unpleasant. But I shall certainly regret the abandonment of the system, for the result of my own observation has been favorable to it." Mayor Channing concluded his report by noting that credit for a successful operation is "entirely due to Mr. J. C. Heazlett, who is charged with the registration, and to Dr. A. Gregg, the City Physician who conducts the medical examinations and treatment of the women."[31]

A few months later, Memphis returned to civilian control and the program of legalized and regulated prostitution was abolished. The great experiment was over.

Vignettes from two other cities suggest that no Civil War–era municipalities were free of the flocks of soiled doves. The Vicksburg *Herald* for September 7, 1864, contained a letter to the editor regarding the neighborhood between Main and Jackson Streets, near Walnut Street, where, according to the writer, there were "a large number of Negroes, the majority of whom have no visible means of support, i.e., in the daytime, except quarreling, fighting, throwing bricks, etc." He mentions several women of an "abandoned character, who have no sense of decency or decorum, either in language or actions." Two days later, under "Local Items," the reporter notes that six of these women "were yesterday sent over the river." The writer concluded, "We cannot too highly commend the authorities for the promptitude displayed in purging the city of disreputable and unworthy characters."

In Detroit, Pvt. James Collins of the Michigan Provost Guard was stationed as a sentinel at Post No. 9. The court-martial proceedings note that he "abandoned his post and knowingly permitted a public prostitute to enter the camp and pass his beat on post and hold conversation with her and then and there have illicit intercourse with such prostitute at Detroit Barracks, May 1, 1863." Private Collins received ten days on bread and water and the prostitute was jailed for one year.[32]

Until the advent of legalized prostitution in the state of Nevada, wartime Nashville and Memphis were America's only experiments in legalized and government-regulated prostitution. Under the systems at Nashville and Memphis, public order was improved, disease was reduced, and both the prostitutes and their clients appear to have benefited, at little cost. Today, research has shown that in the legalized houses of prostitution in Nevada, there has not been a single case of AIDS. The same certainly can not be said for the streetwalkers of great American cities. It is hard to escape the conclusion that there is a lesson here.

Chapter Eight

ૐ

Bred upon the Waters

THINK OF STEAMBOATS today and you think of romance. Pick up a travel magazine, and there is the *Delta Queen* or a sister ship, the white superstructure outlined against a bank of magnolias. In the evenings, the savory smell of a lavish supper beckons from the main saloon. The sound of music over the water enlivens the soft Southern air; a couple by the rail is silhouetted against the moon's reflected path, dancing over the river waters.

Perhaps it is the soft sighs of the water against the hull, perhaps it is the insistent vibration of the huge paddlewheel, perhaps it is the recurrent pulsing throb of the gigantic steam pistons, but few passengers escape an animal stirring, a wish to be close.

In the antebellum days, 75 percent of the passengers were male. Few of them wanted to find romance with another man, so many steamboats had an arrangement for remedying the lack of female companionship—for a price. Such boats allowed a small number of the better-class courtesans to travel on each trip. Although they paid full fare, these women were restricted to certain parts of the deck, assigned to staterooms abaft the sidewheels and made to dine by themselves.

These were small enough restrictions when offered a chance at the most prosperous clientele on the Mississippi. These river-borne nymphs were well behaved, because being disorderly meant being dumped at the next landing, ticket or no. Many "respectable" families traveling the great rivers never knew that some of their well-dressed, well-mannered fellow passengers were Cyprians.

Some religious captains would not tolerate prostitutes on their steamboats, but the bawds soon discovered which were "open" boats and which were "closed."[1]

In 1863, a strange sight was seen on the great waterways: a steamboat in which all the passengers were whores. The boat was the *Idahoe,* just built at Cincinnati. The captain, John Newcomb (who was also one of the owners), had chartered his boat to the U.S. Army. Suddenly he found himself as a principal in a drama not to his liking.

Newcomb was given a cargo of Nashville's most disruptive citizens; his request for guards and food was refused, and he was sent down the Cumberland River, where every town had been alerted as to his mission of deportation. At each place, the authorities refused disembarkation, while the local men tried to climb on board, encouraged by the women passengers. The actual documents of the time tell the story.

> July 6, 1863. Special Order No. 29. Lt. Col. [George] Spalding, Provost Marshal, is hereby directed without loss of time to seize and transport to Louisville all prostitutes found in this city or known to be here . . . the prevalence of venereal disease at this Post has elicited the notice of the General Commanding Department who has ordered a pre-emptory remedy. By command of Brig. Gen. J. D. Morgan.
>
> July 8, 1863. To the captain of the steamer *Idahoe.* You are hereby directed to proceed to Louisville, Kentucky, with the 100 passengers put on board your steamer today, allowing none to leave the Boat before reaching Louisville. Signed, George Spalding, Lt. Col. and Provost Marshal.[2]

The Nashville *Dispatch* for July 8, 1863, reported under the headline of "Cyprians," the following: "We learn that General Granger has given notice to a large number of women of the town that they must prepare to leave Nashville. It is said they are demoralizing the army and that their removal is a military necessity. They are to be sent north."[3]

The next day, the same paper stated, under the headline "Departure of the Cyprians," that "Yesterday a large number of women of ill fame were transported northward. The number has been previously estimated at from 1,000 to 1,400—probably 500 or 600 would be nearer the mark. Where they are consigned to, we are not advised, but suspect the authorities of the city to which they are landed will feel proud of such an acquisition to their population." The more conservative *Daily Press* of the same date told of the lack of gentleness in the operation: "Squads of soldiers were engaged in . . . heaping furniture out of the various dens, and then tumbling their disconsolate owners after. . . . some respectable ladies were unceremoniously marched off. . . . a boat was chartered by the government for the especial service of deporting the 'sinful fair' to a point where they can exert less mischief, and about 40 of them took passage."[4]

July 10, the *Dispatch* published a retraction. "Our estimate of the number of women sent off Wednesday was slightly exaggerated; but in these days, exaggeration being the rule rather than the exception, we will of course be pardoned for supposing 150 parcels of frail humanity, done up in dry goods and crinoline, presented an appearance as formidable as half a regiment. . . . wayward sisters, go in peace."[5]

After five difficult days, on July 15, the *Idahoe* arrived at Louisville, where the *Daily Journal* reported, "The *Idahoe* arrived at Portland yesterday evening, with prostitutes sent from Nashville. A few of the girls escaped."[6] (Actually, several of them had obtained a writ of habeas corpus.) But Captain Newcomb was not to be so easily relieved of the rest of his burden. Neither the citizens of Louisville nor the U.S. Army wanted anything to do with the girls aboard his ship. The commanding general at Louisville flatly refused the cargo consigned to his care. He placed a military guard aboard the *Idahoe* and ordered Captain Newcomb to sail on to Cincinnati and to await further orders at that location.

Meanwhile, the women who had managed to escape the boat in Louisville had not fared well in their return to Nashville. The Nashville *Dispatch* of July 26 noted, "We are informed that a dozen of our Cyprians who were sent to Louisville a few days ago, were cast into prison on their arrival there, and on Friday morning furnished with a free passage back to Nashville, arriving here Friday evening on the train."[7]

July 17, the Cincinnati *Daily Gazette* reported, "The *Idahoe* came up, bringing a cargo of 150 of the frail sisterhood of Nashville, who had been sent north under military orders. There does not seem to be much desire on the part of our authorities to welcome such a large addition to the already-overflowing numbers engaged in their peculiar profession, and . . . the poor girls are still kept on board." The following day, the same paper reported that, "The *Idahoe* still lies at Newport with its living cargo still on board, the municipal authorities of Cincinnati, Covington and Newport continuing to be too sternly virtuous to allow them to land."[8]

The long-suffering Captain Newcomb (and his equally long-suffering passengers) lay at anchor in the Ohio River, opposite Cincinnati, for thirteen days. Then orders came telling him to take his precious cargo back to Nashville. Still with his army guard, headed by a young lieutenant, the *Idahoe* steamed down the Ohio River and back up the Cumberland, arriving in Nashville on August 5, 1863. The *Dispatch* noted her arrival: "The monotony of the river was yesterday varied by the arrival of the *Idahoe* with her cargo of 150 women just returned from Louisville. A large number of spectators visited the lower landing for the purpose of looking at the steamer which carried out and brought back the precious freight. The *Idahoe* has now become famous."⁹

Upon landing, Captain Newcomb proceeded to the provost marshal's office to be reimbursed for the damage to his steamer and for the expense of feeding 150 women for a month. He was referred to a different office, which in turn referred him onward again. Weeks passed. He was sent to higher authority in Cincinnati. The authorities there said they were unable to help him. Two years later, Captain Newcomb had still not been paid the $5,000 (a small fortune then) that was owed him. He made a special trip to Washington, D.C., where he met with Secretary of War Edwin Stanton and presented the following letter:

> I most respectfully beg leave to draw your attention to the following statement of facts in relation to my claim for subsisting 111 prostitutes from Nashville, Tennessee, to Cincinnati, Ohio, and back to Nashville on board of my steamer *Idahoe*.
>
> On the 8th July, 1863, while my boat was under charter by U.S. and in service at Nashville, these prostitutes were put on board of her by a detachment of soldiers who were ordered to do so by Lt. Col. L.T. Spaulding [sic], Asst. Pro. Mar. and Capt. Stubbs, Asst. Quartermaster, who were acting under orders of General Morgan. I protested against their putting these women on my boat, she being a new boat, only three months built, her furniture new, and a fine passenger boat. I told them it would forever ruin her reputation as a passenger boat if they were put on her, (It has done so—she is now since known as the Floating Whorehouse) and pointed out to them old boats that were in service at the time, which would have answered the purpose as well as mine. . . . on the same day that they were put on board, I was ordered to start with them to Louisville.
>
> I asked Captain Stubbs how these women were to be subsisted, he told me I would have to see General Morgan about that. I saw General Morgan and he told me to subsist them myself. I entreated of him to let the government subsist them that it could do so for much less than I could, he reply was, "You subsist them." When I found General Morgan determined that I should subsist them I had to buy meat and vegetables at enormously high prices from store boats along the river and in addition at many places to buy ice and medicines, these women being diseased and more than one-half of them sick in bed. I applied to the commissaries along the route for commissary stores to feed these women but at each place was refused

by the officers in charge, and the Civil as well as the Military authorities would not allow my boat to land, and put guards along the shore to prevent me from doing so.

When leaving Nashville I applied for a guard to be put on board, General Morgan told me I did not need any but to take charge of them myself. Having no guard I could not keep men along the route from coming on board to these women, when at anchor and being angered because I strove to drive them away both themselves and these bad women destroyed and damaged my boat, and her furniture to a great extent.

When I arrived at Louisville I stated my grievances to General Boyle and he gave me a guard and ordered me to proceed to Cincinnati and await further orders there. I remained in the stream opposite Cincinnati, Ohio because I would not be allowed to land for 13 days, when I was ordered to Nashville again, with my cargo of prostitutes.

I wish to say to your honor that I was compelled to subsist these women, that it cost me all that I have made a charge for, to do so, that this claim is merely a reimbursement of my money which I had to expend while complying with the orders of the Officers of the United States Government. . . . I had to leave my business and travel from Cincinnati to this place to see if I could collect it, it being over two years due me. I am here now one week going from one office to another, to see to get my papers, and to effect a settlement, which I have not yet done, nor a likelihood to have done, unless your honor will please direct payment of this account so justly due me and for so long a time.[10]

Two months later, Captain Newcomb received a letter from L. S. Bradenbury, clerk in the Treasury Department, Third Auditors Office. Without apology or comment, the clerk enclosed a draft for $1,000 "for damages to the staterooms, furniture, bedding, cabin furniture, tableware, etc." and a draft for $4,316 "for subsistence and medicines furnished to 111 prostitutes on board the steamboat *Idahoe* . . . at the rate of $1.50 per day for each."[11]

By the time Captain Newcomb received his money, he had long since sold his interest in the *Idahoe* and she had steamed south to be based at New Orleans under new owners. The *Idahoe* was wrecked and lost on January 10, 1869, on the Ouachita River near Columbia, Louisiana.[12]

Chapter Nine

ॐ

French Letters and American Morals

ALMOST AS SOON as humans grasped the connection between coitus and conception, there sprang up an interest in contraception.

There have always been intense feelings about the subject. Church authorities denounced it as a violation of natural law. Hitler opposed contraception because he wanted troops for the Reich. The American Comstock laws deemed contraception obscene and prescribed time in federal prison for mailing even information about contraception. On the other side are the Malthusians, who warn of overpopulation, Margaret Sanger, who devoted her life to the availability of birth control, and, of course, the millions or billions of women and men who feel that conception should be within their own control.

What was known and available at the time of the Civil War? There were six major techniques of birth control at that time: coitus interruptus, coitus reservatus, condoms, douches, sponges, and abortion.

Coitus interruptus, withdrawal before ejaculation, is described in the thirty-eighth book of Genesis. Onan spilled his seed and avoided his duty to impregnate his wife. Coitus reservatus, termed Karezza by A. B. Stockholm, was publicized by John Noyes, founder of the Oneida Colony. In his technique, there is prolonged coitus with no ejaculation.

The use of condoms goes back three centuries.[1] In 1671, Madame du Sevigne described in a letter, "a sheath made of gold-beater's skin." In the 1700s the English called condoms "French letters," while the French termed them "English caps." Casanova, in a 1753 diary entry, noted buying condoms by the dozen.

Daniel Turner, writing in 1717, said "The condum being the best, if not the only preservative our Libertines have found out at present, and yet by reason of its blunting the sensation, I have heard some of them acknowledge that they had often choose to risk a Clap, rather than engage with spears thus sheathed."[2]

Francis Grose, in his 1785 *Classical Dictionary of the Vulgar Tongue,* has this entry, "cundum, the dried gut of a sheep, worn by men in the act of coition, to prevent venereal infection."

This handbill was given to prospective customers on the streets of London in the late 1700s: "Mrs. Philips, of Number Five Orange Court, near Leicester Fields" states that "It is well known to the public that she has 35 years experience in the business of making and selling machines, commonly called implements of safety. . . . she has likewise great choice of skins and bladders where apothecaries, druggists, et cetera, may be supplied with any quantity of the best sort." She concluded her advertisement with this bit of doggerel:

> To guard yourself from shame or fear
> Votaries to Venus, hasten here;
> None in my wares e're found a flaw,
> Self-preservation's nature's law.[3]

Civil War newspapers frequently carried advertisements for condoms. The process of vulcanizing rubber was invented by Goodyear and Hancock in 1843, but it was not until 1876 that the first rubber condoms were officially introduced, at the Philadelphia World Exposition. (The tons of "obscene mail" seized by Army authorities in the war contained many ads for condoms, both "skins" and "India rubber." The "skins" were lamb caecums, still sold today, but less popular because of cost and failure to impede viruses.) Certainly, condoms were no secret to the boys in blue and gray.[4]

Douching is also an ancient—if not very effective—technique of birth control. Dr. Charles Knowlton, a respected Fellow of the Massachusetts Medical Society, published his *Fruits of Philosophy* in 1833, and advocated postcoital douches made with alum, zinc sulfate, vinegar, or baking soda as the most practical methods of contraception.

Forty years later, a London publisher, who issued an illustrated version of Knowlton's book, was given two years at hard labor for publishing obscenity. The publicity from the trial generated the sale of 277,000 copies.[5]

Sponges that were inserted deep in the vagina and removed postcoitally were advocated in 1797 by the English philosopher Jeremy Bentham. The pioneer birth control advocate, Francis Place, in his 1823 pamphlet,

To the Married of Both Sexes of the Working People, advocated early marriage and sponge tampons as the "true Christian" answer to urban poverty. Forty years later, Yankee women trying to use his advice were frustrated by a sponge shortage, since the major sponge fisheries were in Florida.[6]

Robert D. Owen's 1830 book, *Moral Physiology,* sold 75,000 copies. On the subject of contraception, he recommended coitus interruptus as the best technique. In 1847, Owen received the compliment of plagiarism: Dr. A. M. Mariceau, a leading New York City gynecologist, stole liberally from Owen in the preparation of his *Married Woman's Private Medical Companion.*

Yet another voice was that of Dr. J. Soule of Cincinnati, in his *Science of Reproduction and Reproduction Control.* In this 1856 volume, he made the usual suggestions of coitus interruptus, condoms, and douching, as well as taking a swipe at the "frightful evils of masturbation."[7]

Abortion played a major role in family limitation at the time of the Civil War. Even as early as 1810, home medical guides referred to treatment for "obstructed menses" (a euphemism for early unwanted pregnancy). William Buchan's *Domestic Medicine* prescribed bloodletting, hot baths, mixtures of iron and quinine, tincture of black hellebore (a violent laxative), exercise, lifting heavy weights, jumping from heights, and blows to the belly.[8]

Samuel K. Jennings's *The Married Ladies' Companion* (1808) recommended bleeding, with doses of calomel and aloes, as treatment for "taking the cold," a term common then for missed periods. *The Female Medical Repository,* published in 1810 by Joseph Brevitt, recommended savin as an abortifacient. While he also suggested hellebore and aloes, these latter were expensive, imported European products. Savin, on the other hand, could be extracted from the juniper bushes that grew wild all over the United States. His advice was widely used; in the following eighty years, many cases of savin-induced abortion and accidental deaths from savin overdoses were reported.[9] (In 1807, the Austrian government had forbidden the planting of juniper because of its wide use as an abortifacient.)[10]

Thomas Ewell, a surgeon at Navy Hospital in Washington, D.C., in his 1817 *Letter to Ladies,* urged the usual hot sitz baths, aloes, horseback riding, and jumping, with the addition of douches of very hot water, strong brandy, wine, vinegar, and concentrated brine.[11]

Herbal healers were also active in the treatment of "catamenial obstruction." Peter Smith, in his 1813 brochure *The Indian Doctor's Dispensary,* recommended "Dr. Reeder's chalybeate," a mixture of myrrh, aloes, whiskey, sugar, vinegar, iron dust, ivy, and seneca snakeroot. While this mixture would create a commotion in any system, it was probably the snakeroot that stimulated uterine contractions. Black cohosh, otherwise known as rattleweed or squawroot, was also used to induce abortion.

The availability of such remedies was hardly a secret, as the daily papers frequently carried advertisements for them. The New York *Sun* of March 3, 1846, described "Madame Restell's Female Monthly Pills," which "require but a few days to effect a perfect cure."[12]

The January 8, 1845, Boston *Daily Times* described "Madame Drunette's French Lunar Pills." Eighteen days later, the same paper told the public the virtues of both "Dr. Monroe's French Periodical Pills" and "Dr. Peters' French Renovating Pills." Dr. Ely van de Warker, of Syracuse, New York, studied the abortifacient industry. He estimated the annual consumption in his city to be 9,000 pills per 50,000 adult women.

Other substances used to induce abortion included oil of tansy and oil of rue. Ergot, still in use today as a uterine stimulant, has been known for centuries for these qualities. The French name translates as "uterine powder." The German term is *Kindesmord,* "infant's death." The therapeutic dose of ergot is very close to the lethal dose, a serious problem in any home remedy.[13]

An abortifacient of Southern origin is cottonroot. In 1840, several physicians published reports of its use by slave women. By 1858, it was widely sold in New England pharmacies, and in 1871, a wholesaler noted a 400 percent increase in cottonroot sales since the soldiers had returned home from the war.

In addition to herbal remedies, there was direct physical dilation of the cervix, a technique known to many physicians at that time. In the 1860s, with increasing anatomic knowledge available to the general public, many women mastered the technique of dilating their own cervices to induce abortion (a tribute to desperation). Goose quills were commonly used in this procedure. There was sufficient demand for dilating devices that Parke-Davis marketed "Chamberlain's Utero-Vaginal Syringe," while the Davol Manufacturing Company also offered a line of auto-abortive instruments.[14]

For those reluctant to operate on their own bodies, a wide variety of abortion clinics offered their services. Mrs. W. H. Maxwell, whose women's clinic at Six Greene Street, New York City, operated at the same location for twenty years, was straightforward in her newspaper ads: "She treats all diseases peculiar to women, or, which they may unfortunately have incurred through . . . the wanton unfaithfulness of husbands . . . or through the need to resort to premature delivery."

Doctors Hotaling and Cleveland of Boston, who proclaimed their credentials as "Eclectic and Clairvoyant Physicians" in their handbill, treated "female irregularities" and emphasized their "Private Entrance for Ladies," located on a side street. In many large cities, any woman who did not read a daily newspaper, and thereby missed the ads from abortion clinics, was likely to have pamphlets from these sources thrust into her hand as she walked the sidewalks on her daily errands.[15]

Women who missed information about the existence of abortion from advertisements might learn of it from the frequent news stories of women who had died because of physician- or self-induced abortions and of physicians prosecuted because of botched abortions or for large numbers of successful abortions.

Yankee ingenuity, that muse of inventors, was not lacking in the world of abortion. Dr. Sunot's suction device, which was to be attached to the "lower body," was so powerful that, in the words of its brochure, "It can hardly fail!" Several other devices employed the newly popular mode of electricity. One used electrodes over the belly and lower back to stimulate uterine contractions. Another, the "galvanic bougie," dilated the cervix with an electrically charged probe, while the "McIntosh Combined Galvanic and Faradic Battery" came equipped with an intrauterine attachment and insulated handles to protect the operator. The effect on the patient, who was the recipient of these internal jolts, is not hard to imagine. (While anesthesia had been invented, there is little record of its use during the abortion process.)[16]

A remedy for unwanted pregnancy still in use today is the enlarging bougie, a pencil-like cylinder of dried seaweed. When inserted into the cervix and left overnight, it absorbs moisture, swells, and gradually dilates the cervical canal. The usual seaweed used is the *Laminaria digitata.*

Was the abortion activity of 1840–70 actually reflected in any significant effect on birth rates? The answer appears to be a definite *yes!* By most reasonable estimates, in 1840 there was one abortion for every thirty live births. In 1870, the figure is closer to one abortion for every five live births. Public health statistics as we know them today did not exist, but the physicians who had the greatest access to women's secrets were quick to publish their estimates.[17]

Dr. Edwin M. Hale of Chicago, in his 1860 *On the Homeopathic Treatment of Abortion,* stated that at least 10 percent of married women had had an abortion and that 20 percent of all pregnancies ended in intentional abortion. In his 1866 book, he revised his estimate upward to 25 percent.

In 1868, Dr. Horatio Storer, a former Harvard professor of obstetrics, published *Criminal Abortion.* With his coauthor, Boston attorney Franklin Heard, he concluded that in New York City fully 20 percent of all conceptions ended in abortion. These conclusions were based only upon reported abortions; the actual incidence must have been higher. It is remarkable that Hale, a champion of abortion, and Storer, a violent opponent, agreed so closely on their figures. A third study done just after the Civil War by Dr. J. C. Stone of Iowa also concluded that 20 percent of all pregnancies ended in abortion.

Reports from state medical societies in the early 1870s gave the following estimates: Maine, 16 percent; Illinois, 20 percent; Wisconsin, 30 percent; and Michigan, 34 percent.

These figures shed some light on the extraordinary changes in birth rate in America. At the turn of the century, this country had a higher birth rate than any European country. In 1800, the average American woman gave birth to 7.04 children; in 1900, the figure was 3.56. The steepest drop in this long decline came around 1850. Since there is nothing to suggest a decrease in the incidence of coitus over that century, the best explanation for halving the birth rate is the use of contraception and abortion on a wide and consistent scale.

There is abundant evidence that during the years of the Civil War, both abortion and contraception were widely known and widely used.

Chapter Ten

ॐ

The Ailments of Venus

TO UNDERSTAND THE ROLE of venereal disease in the Civil War, it is necessary to describe the condition of medical knowledge in general in 1861. The Civil War came at a peculiar time in history. In some areas, there had been great technological change, while in others, knowledge lagged far behind.

The steamboat, the locomotive, the telegraph, the camera, and the printing press had revolutionized communication. The rifled cannon, the rifled musket, and the iron-clad gunboat had revolutionized warfare (although tactics still lagged behind).

But in the field of medicine, the revolution lay just over the horizon, too late for most of the sick and wounded among the blue and gray.

Think what we expect from medicine these days. When we turn on the kitchen faucet, we assume (in fact, we do not even think about the subject) that the public health officer and his staff have filtered and chlorinated the water. We assume, and rightly, that our drinking water will not give us typhoid, hepatitis, giardia, or amebic dysentery.

When we take our children for their "shots," we assume that they will become immune to diphtheria, pertussis (whooping cough), tetanus, polio, and measles.

If we become feverish and sweaty and begin to cough up blood, we assume, usually correctly, that antibiotics will cure our pneumonia. We assume that if our ill fortune or bad judgment leaves us with a syphilitic chancre or a gonorrheal drip, these will be curable, and we will almost always be correct.

We assume that if we are hit by an automobile and the broken bones protrude through the flesh, the bones will be set and the contaminated wound made sterile. We assume that after any surgery, the wound will not fill with pus. If we have appendicitis, we assume that we will be asleep,

99

painfree, during the surgery and that we will survive the operation. Of all these assumptions, none would have been true in 1861.

Anesthesia had been discovered about fifteen years before the shots at Fort Sumter, and a few doctors were skilled in its use. Though controversy exists as to who really was first with anesthesia, it is clear that in the mid-1840s, William Morton demonstrated the use of ether and Crawford Long did the same with nitrous oxide. Chloroform, too, was known as a powerful anesthetic.[1]

But in the Civil War, hardly any doctors had been properly trained in their use, and the Union blockade meant that Confederate patients had only whiskey to deaden the agony of amputation.

The causes of contagious diseases were almost totally unknown. Although a Dutchman had first seen bacteria under the microscope in 1665, Harvard Medical School did not even own a microscope until 1869! (In fact, Harvard did not even own a stethoscope until 1868, thirty years after its invention.) And Harvard was one of the good medical schools.[2]

Doctors were helpless because they were ignorant of the most fundamental causes of disease. The little beasties that van Leeuwenhoek had seen under his primitive microscope two centuries earlier were not known to be the causes of illness.

Louis Pasteur, four years before the Civil War, had clarified the roles of yeast and bacteria in winemaking and had made the first connection between specific bacteria and specific diseases.

Joseph Lister, an English surgeon, utilized Pasteur's ideas to reduce operative infection, and in 1867, he published a method to save patients with compound fractures, which had previously been fatal unless there was amputation. Lister sterilized the wounds with carbolic acid solution. Pasteur and Lister were unknown to most Civil War doctors, however, and the new bacterial knowledge played no part in the medical work of the blue and gray.[3]

It was not until 1878 that Robert Koch, a German bacteriologist, demonstrated the role played by bacteria in wound infections. Koch's brilliant work also demonstrated the tuberculosis bacillus in 1882 and the cholera germ the following year.

Even old knowledge, such as James Lind's discovery of the cure of scurvy (1750) and Jenner's introduction of the smallpox vaccination (1796), was little used.

It was as though an intellectual paralysis had seized every aspect of American medical thought in the mid-1800s. In its ignorance, the medical profession split into warring factions, like contending religious cults.

The naturopaths proclaimed the benefits of a drugless therapy, based on air, light, heat, water, and massage. The homeopaths treated patients with drugs that, in healthy persons, would produce the same symptoms as the disease being treated. The drugs were given in extraordinarily thin dilutions. The osteopaths restored the "natural balance" of the body by correcting spinal alignment through manipulation, though they were also open to the concepts of surgery and medication. The hydropaths believed in hot baths, cold baths, and enemas as the roads to health. What we think of as physicians today were then labeled as allopaths.[4]

There was some surgical knowledge, but even "successful" surgery, such as an amputation, was frequently followed by infection, hemorrhage, and death. No surgeon ventured into the chest or the abdomen or the brain. Since surgery is based upon anatomy, and anatomy is learned by dissecting cadavers, it is of interest that in 1861, several states still prohibited dissection by medical students. Many army surgeons learned their anatomy by carving upon the wounded. Some, like W. W. Keen and J. S. Billings, learned well and became the great teachers and clinicians of the next generation.

Instruments that we take for granted, like the thermometer, were a mystery to most Civil War doctors. The Union Army possessed only twenty thermometers, although the device had been invented centuries before. The clinical use of thermometers was taught in every French school of medicine at the time.

Fewer than a dozen Union Army doctors could use an ophthalmo-scope and even fewer could use the laryngoscope. Most surgeons did not use hypodermic syringes for the control of pain; they simply sprinkled morphine powder into the wound.

Without a scientific basis for practice, it is no surprise that doctors in the war and on the frontier were mystified by the most common disease (malaria) and the most common symptom (diarrhea).[5]

Malaria, then called the ague, autumnal fever, chills and fever, or the shakes, was thought to be caused by the "bad air" found near swamps. Its transmission by mosquito and its cause by the protozoan plasmodium were utterly unknown. The use of quinine for malaria was familiar to many doctors at that time, but the drug was often in short supply and most doctors were unfamiliar with its proper dosage.

Diarrhea was usually ascribed to bad water or greasy food, and its clarification into subtypes caused by shigella, salmonella, staphylococcus, camphlobacter, amebas, vibrio, clostridia, and giardia lay far in the future. Even the simple construction of latrines was looked down upon by many line officers and even a few medical officers. The concept that drinking another man's filth might be harmful seemed too complex for some military minds.

The fiscal shortcomings of that era seem astonishing in the light of today's billions for invisible airplanes and computerized tanks. The Senate, in 1863, refused to spend more than 18¢ a day for food for soldiers in the hospital. No matter that those trying to recuperate were dying of starvation; the Senate was adamant. The same year, the House defeated a bill that would have provided trained cooks for the army.[6]

The Battle of Manassas in 1862 demonstrated the incompetence of the Union ambulance services. Wounded men lay on the field for up to a week suffering agonies of pain, thirst, and hunger. Surgeon General William A. Hammond proposed an ambulance corps, but the proposal was vetoed by both Edwin Stanton and Gen. Henry W. Halleck. It was not a good time to be a wounded soldier.

During the war, 230,000 Union soldiers received gunshot wounds, while 225,000 died of diseases, usually typhoid or other dysenteries. In January 1865, the official strength of the Union army was 832,931; of these, 309,395 were absent, either sick, on leave, or AWOL—a loss rate of almost 40 percent.

Relevant to the theme of this book, it is necessary to discuss the venereal, sexually transmitted diseases. Syphilis is caused by a microscopic organism, *Treponema pallidum*. It is difficult to see under the microscope and was not visually identified until 1905. The first blood test came two years later, and an effective (if painful) treatment, Salvarsan, was introduced in 1910. In the primary stage of syphilis, a small, painless ulcer appears, usually on the genitals. Several weeks later, the secondary stage is marked by transient fever and a rash, which clears up spontaneously. The patient may then feel well for years, until the third stage develops. This is the fatal stage, as the infection eats away the brain, the blood vessels, and many other vital organs.

Gonorrhea is caused by a bacteria, *Neisseria gonorrheoea,* and causes a painful urethral discharge in men (formerly known as the clap or the gleet) and infection of the cervix in women. The bacterium was identified by Albert Neisser in 1879. Effective treatment was not available until 1945, with the introduction of penicillin. The third major venereal disease of the 1860s was lymphogranuloma venereum (more on this later).

Dr. Allan M. Brandt described the many hazards in introducing a rational public policy toward venereal disease control. Fear of a disease will lead to irrational preventive measures. In 1900, doctors claimed that syphilis could be spread by touching pens, pencils, toothbrushes, drinking cups, and bedding. In 1917, U.S. Navy doctors removed the doorknobs from its battleships, fearing that the knobs were a source of infection.[7]

Education, too, failed to control infection. Most educational programs were antisex rather than antidisease. Posters and pamphlets showed young men disfigured and consumed by loathsome infections, but as one medical officer noted, "It is difficult to make the sex act unpopular."[8] In response to such classic posters as the 1918 one proclaiming, "A German Bullet Is Cleaner Than A Whore," most soldiers might respond, "But not so interesting."

Compulsory health measures also have been a disappointment. During World War I, 20,000 American women were arrested and held in concentration camps on suspicion of carrying venereal disease. And the disease rates still climbed.[9]

Is treatment effective? In 1943, the incidence of syphilis was 72 cases per 100,000 population. In 1956, it was 4 cases per 100,000, thanks to penicillin. But funding for venereal disease programs was cut, and the rates have more than tripled since 1956. Treatment alone is not the answer.[10]

Even with modern methods, we have difficulty controlling venereal disease. We should be compassionate toward the Civil War doctors, both North and South, who struggled, largely in ignorance, to control these same diseases. What physicians had to offer venereally infected patients in the eighteenth and early nineteenth century merits consideration.

In the eighteenth century, the only remedy for syphilis was salts of mercury, such as mercuric gallate and mercuric salicylate. The author recalls a story that James Boswell, the famous biographer of Samuel Johnson, reported this graffito from the wall of a London men's toilet: "A night with Venus, a lifetime with Mercury." This classic pun accurately reflected the difficult and chronic course of venereal disease treatment in that era.

During the American Revolution, of the 360 patients at Albany Army Hospital on August 20, 1777, there were fourteen cases of "lues venerea," the term used then for syphilis.[11] The manual used by doctors at that time, Van Swieten's *The Diseases Incident to Armies,* reflecting the then-current belief that syphilis and gonorrhea were the same disease, gave this definition: "Small ulcers appearing at the extremity of the penis, or on the prepuce, are called venereal chancres," adding that if "there arises a difficulty and pain in making water, and a running of yellowish matter . . . it is then called a gonorrhea." Many remedies were suggested, including a teaspoon two times a day of "corrosive sublimate 12 grains, rectified malt spirit, two pounds."[12]

During the next great conflict, the War Office, in 1814, ordered that "Women infected by venereal disease shall in no case be allowed to remain with the army, nor to draw rations." (Presumably, women without venereal disease were allowed to draw rations.) Elsewhere, the War Office limited each company to not more than five women.[13]

The Civil War produced more casualties than any other American war. It also produced a medical report too heavy for most librarians to lift: the multivolume *Medical and Surgical History of the War of the Rebellion,* published in sections in the 1880s. The portion dealing with venereal diseases[14] is a historian's gold mine of information about the Union Army.

Venereal disease was more common at the beginning and at the end of the war and less so during its progress. Venereal disease was more common in troops stationed in or near cities, and rarer in combat field troops.

Among white troops, there were reported 73,382 cases of syphilis and 109,397 cases of gonorrhea. The rate of all types of venereal disease was 82 cases per year per 1,000 men. This rate was higher, 87, just before and just after the war. The incidence among "colored" troops was lower: an annual rate of 34 cases of syphilis and 44 cases of gonorrhea per 1,000 men.[15]

At this point, the record becomes confusing because three venereal diseases—syphilis, gonorrhea, and lymphogranuloma venereum—appear to have been mixed together in the record and perhaps occurred simultaneously in the patients. The lymphogranuloma of sexual contact is caused by yet another bacterium: *Chlamydia trachomatis,* and tends to produce plum-sized swellings in the lymph glands of the groin. These swellings are termed "bubos," and when they burst and drain pus were described as suppurating bubos.

In the surgeon general's report, 426 men were sick enough to require hospitalization for venereal disease. Of these, 53 cases were diagnosed as gonorrhea, of which 3 had "complications of suppurating bubo." The remaining 373 cases were diagnosed as syphilis, 41 with "gonorrheal complications" and 77 with "suppurating bubo."[16]

The confusion of diagnosis was equally matched by the confusion of treatment. Many military surgeons reported on their remedies for venereal diseases and on their degree of success. A few of their observations are summarized here.

Surgeon William R. Blakeslee of the 115th Pennsylvania Infantry reported that gonorrhea "was greatly modified and in most cases completely subdued by injecting [presumably urethrally] a solution of chlorate of potash, one drachm in eight ounces every hour for 12 consecutive hours." He then reduced the dosage over the next three days. At Las Lunas, New Mexico, Surgeon Allen F. Peck of the 1st New Mexico Mounted Volunteers found that gonorrhea "readily responded to treatment. With much inflammatory action in the first stage, I generally prescribe a saline cathartic, rest, cooling lotions and low diet. After this stage has passed, I found balsam of copaiba, powdered cubebs and magnesia given as a bolus, four or five times a day to be very effectual. At the same time, I used an injection of chloride of zinc, two to four grains to the ounce of water, once or twice a day."[17]

Surgeon Isaac F. Galloupe of the 17th Massachusetts used hourly injections of a weak solution of sulfate of zinc for gonorrhea, and treated syphilis by cauterization of the chancre, "followed by the continuous application of black wash." Galloupe reported, "Rapid and complete recovery was secured in all cases . . . without secondary disease."

On the California coast, at Fort Bragg, Surgeon P. W. Randall of the 1st Cavalry stated, "For gonorrhea, my treatment, which is successful, consists of a thorough cleansing of the alimentary canal, rest, low diet, the balsam and cubebs internally, with urethral injections of nitrate of silver, sugar of lead or sulfate of zinc." Surgeon J. G. Brandt of the 26th Massachusetts, then stationed at New Orleans, expressed "No faith in the empirical use of balsams and diuretics, so long considered specific in this disease." Brandt preferred to treat gonorrhea with injections of sulfate or chloride of zinc. Later, he reported that in certain cases he used mercury "until the gums were affected, which condition was kept up for ten or twelve days."[18]

At Sacramento, California, the 5th Cavalry surgeon, David Wooster, seems to have used smallpox vaccination as a treatment for syphilis. "I inoculate every case of chancre. If the virus take, I treat locally and hygienically alone; if it fails to produce chancre after the third inoculation, I use protiodide. The cures in both series of cases is generally reasonably prompt, occupying from fifteen to rarely sixty days."[19]

In the mountains of central New Mexico, at Fort Stanton, Surgeon Peck cauterized primary chancres with nitrate of silver, followed by "black wash" until the sore healed.

Surgeon Ezra Read of the 21st Indiana used a steam bath and mercury vapor to achieve "mercurial fumigation, which deposits the mercury upon the surface of the body." With primary syphilitic chancres, Read used cautery followed by the mercury vapor baths as "the best method."

Surgeon Warren Webster, at Fort Larned, Kansas, described the ravages of untreated syphilis upon the Kiowa and Arapaho, "victims of the most desperate forms of constitutional syphilis, evidencing itself in lost noses, vacant palates and the vilest cutaneous affections." Reed, who treated both Native Americans and whites, recorded his "unwavering belief in the efficacy of mercurial treatment."

Surgeon E. A. Tomkins of Fort Yamhill, Oregon, described an unfortunate soldier with syphilis who, over a period of about four months, was treated with potassium iodide in sarsaparilla, corrosive sublimate, lunar caustic, calomel, black draught, emetics, blistering, iron, quinine,

and external chloroform. At the end of the treatment, he was in severe
pain, with one leg badly swollen and cold, barely able to walk.[20]

It is a medical truism that when there are many remedies for the same
disease, it is likely that none of the remedies are much good. Such seems
to have been the case in the then-prevailing treatment of venereal diseases.

One of the weakest points of the Union defense was in the Far West.
Confederate forces from Texas easily overran the New Mexicans early in
the war, although the Union forces from Colorado finally succeeded in
driving the Rebels south. The California volunteers, who arrived later,
had very limited success in their forays against the Ute, Navaho, and
Apache forces. Many reasons have been given by historians for this Federal
ineffectiveness—inexperienced leadership, Southern sympathies, supply
shortages, and low morale—but a factor often overlooked is disease, in
particular, venereal disease.

During the Civil War, the West was divided into several military
departments: the Department of the Northwest (Mississippi River to the
Rockies, north of Kansas), the Department of New Mexico (New Mexico
and Arizona), and the Department of the Pacific (the entire West Coast).
Comparing the venereal disease rates of these departments, as well as
other groups, at various times shows the size and variability of the problem.
The rates shown below reflect cases per 1,000 men per year.

United States Army, 1860	82
Department of the Northwest, 1862	50
Department of the Pacific, 1862	461
Department of New Mexico, 1863	168
Columbus Barracks, Ohio, 1889	462
British Army, 1890	200[21]

The human meaning of these bare numbers may be given substance
by considering an imagined regiment of California volunteers arriving in
Arizona Territory. Reflecting the incidence of venereal disease in the
Department of the Pacific, 461 men out of every 1,000 (almost half!)
have venereal disease. The affected men have a variety of symptoms:
swollen and painful testicles, oozing sores on their genitals (often just
cauterized that day by the surgeon), pain and hesitation with urination,
and fevers that leave them weak. Imagine a man on horseback with these
symptoms, bouncing across the desert, pursuing or being pursued by
hostile Apaches or by the battle-hardened Texas volunteers. This much
pain and disability, even liberally treated with whiskey, does not make for
effective soldiering.

How did this disease problem with the western soldiers grow so serious? There are several answers. Years of military statistics have shown that the soldier most likely to get infected is young, recently recruited, native-born, in a noncombatant role, and stationed near a city.

The majority of the California recruits were young farmers or miners from the Mother Lode country. They were sent to training camps near San Francisco, Sacramento, and Los Angeles, cities already well established as centers of prostitution and wild living. The California camps were notorious for drunkenness and insubordination. Pvt. Robert Kerr was shot by a firing squad for killing an officer. Five recruits were murdered, one committed suicide, and one died while resisting arrest. When the same troops arrived in the Southwest, they continued their rampage of drunkenness, gambling, and wild women. Two sergeants were shot by their own men, and a cook at Fort Wingate was stabbed.[22]

When Carlton's California Column reached the Rio Grande, the troops were accompanied by a considerable number of the West Coast prostitutes with whom they had exchanged diseases 1,000 miles back. This assortment of infected men and women soon brought the epidemics of disease and dissolution to New Mexico.

The New Mexican men themselves had already been busy with the women near the training camps in their home state, at Albuquerque, Santa Fe, and Las Lunas. With this situation of loss of command and control, general demoralization, spreading infection, and ineffective treatment, it is surprising that the Californians and the New Mexicans performed as well as they did.[23]

Horace Cunningham considers the question of venereal disease in the Confederate Army. There seems to have been less infection than in the Union Army, perhaps because with fewer economic resources, the men spent more time in the field and less time near urban centers. Most venereal disease was treated at sick call, and only serious cases were sent to hospital. Emory Hospital in Virginia registered forty-seven venereal disease admissions between January 1, 1864, and April 12, 1865. Because of the growing problem farther south, a separate hospital for unusually serious venereal disease was opened in March 1864 at Kingston, Georgia. The North Carolina 21st Regiment listed a total of fifty-nine venereal infections between April 1862 and April 1864.[24] Most histories of this era conclude that the rate of infection was higher in the Union Army, but the reporting system broke down as the South was invaded and accurate comparisons will never be possible.

Charles Haydon of the 2d Michigan kept a remarkable Civil War diary. In it he mentioned many comrades who had been "injured" while "storming a masked battery" (a term current at the time for contact with female genitals) and wished that his colleagues would pursue the "Rebels as eagerly as they pursue the whores."[25]

Remedies used by the Confederate surgeons included pokeroots, elder, sarsaparilla, sassafras, jessamine, and prickly ash. Stubborn cases of gonorrhea could be cured by a mixture of silkweed root, whiskey, resin, and blue vitriol, according to one surgeon.[26] It seems as though the Confederate doctors were just as much in the dark as their Yankee colleagues.

The continuing havoc of venereal disease was seen in the years after the war. Since none of the treatments of 1865 eradicated the gonococcus or the syphilis spirochete, the boys in blue and gray marched home, still for the most part contagious.

Gonorrhea gave the men urethral strictures, while their wives and sweethearts contracted pelvic inflammatory diseases and the gonococcal arthritis seen in the late phases of the disease, as well as having infertility problems or tubal pregnancies. But the ravages of tertiary syphilis were worse. The destruction of the brain caused "generalized paralysis of the insane," leaving the victim staggering and psychotic (although brain syphilis was less common in the South, where malarial fevers killed the spirochetes). The complication of tabes dorsalis caused crises of intense pain, incoordination, loss of sensation, loss of reflexes, paroxysms of disturbance in the function of the stomach and larynx, inability to retain urine, failing of sexual power, and destruction of the bones and joints. Gummas, erosive syphilitic tumors, ate through various organs; rupea caused rashes of blisters, followed by scabs; ecthyma produced crops of pus-filled pimples on top of plates of hardened skin. With these complications, the disease marched forward to produce a lingering and revolting death.

Waitt estimated that one-third of the men who died in Union and Confederate veterans' homes were killed by the late stages of venereal disease.[27] No one knows how many Union and Confederate wives and widows went to their graves, rotted and ravaged by the pox that their men brought home, or how many veterans' children were blinded by gonorrhea or stunted by syphilis. Like ripples in some Stygian pond, the wounds of war spread long after the shooting died away. The bacteriologist Hans Zinsser, in his classic book *Rats, Lice and History*, makes the case that disease has changed history more than generals, politicians, or religion.[28] Venereal disease in the Civil War may not have changed history much, but it certainly made the discomforts of war considerably worse.

Chapter Eleven

રાજ

Parallel Lives

THE TRADITIONAL VIEW of men and women during the Civil War is familiar: Men put on uniforms and went to war; women stayed at home, worked, sighed, and wrote sentimental letters. The women who did go to war nursed the wounded. When romance bloomed, it was between a man and a woman.

While these traditional role descriptions fit most of the participants in the great conflict, there were some notable exceptions. Several hundred of the combatants in uniforms were women disguised as men, and unknown thousands of the amorous encounters of the war were between men and other men.

Was there homosexual activity during the Civil War? Certainly, no soldier was disciplined for "homosexuality," because the term was not introduced until 1895. Other terms, carrying clearly homosexual connotations, either pejorative or neutral, came even later: "faggot" in 1910, and "gay" around 1950. What about more ancient terms, such as "sodomy," traceable to 1297 A.D., and "buggery," only a century newer?[1] Although these latter terms were well known in the 1800s, no record has come to light of a Civil War soldier having been disciplined for either offense, although there are records of three pairs of U.S. Navy sailors who were court-martialed for such activity.[2]

In 1865, aboard the USS *Shamrock,* John C. Smith and Louis Grant were charged with "improper and indecent intercourse with other." Witness Daniel Nevels testified that he saw Smith do to Grant "that what was indecent, immoral and a violation of nature." Henry Smith, quartermaster, and William Anderson were reported to the same review board for the same offense a few days earlier. In October 1865, Capt. George M. Dansom of the *Muscoota,* based at Key West, referred Henry Williams, seaman, and William Stewart, ordinary seaman, for trial, with charges of "an unnatural crime."[3]

While mention of homosexual behavior in the Civil War era is rare, citations of male prostitution are even rarer. On May 13, 1862, the Richmond *Dispatch* published an article denouncing the Cyprians who "have been disporting themselves extensively on the sidewalks and in hacks, open carriages, &c, in the streets of Richmond, to the amazement of sober-sided citizens compelled to smell the odors which they exude, and witness the imprudence and familiar vulgarity of many of the shame faced of the prostitutes of both sexes."

Perhaps there was almost no homosexual behavior in 1861–65. The incidence of homosexuality today is between 1 and 10 percent (experts differ). Male-male attraction is probably present at birth in future male homosexuals; it would be surprising if our biology has changed much in a mere 130 years. If a conservative 1 percent figure is true, then at least 10,000 of the boys in blue were physically attracted to other boys in blue—and might well have been attracted to boys in gray as well, if a wall of bayonets had not separated them.

If there are few Civil War military records reflecting male-male sexuality, what can be said on the subject during that era? An answer starts with Walt Whitman.

Whitman's poetry and his nursing of the Civil War wounded are known to anyone who has attended a good high school. Whitman's diary, however, reveals other diversions not usually mentioned in high school English classes.

On the night of October 11, 1862, Whitman met David Wilson walking near Middaugh Street in Brooklyn. Whitman wrote that Wilson, who was a blacksmith's apprentice living on Hampden Street, "slept with me." The next afternoon, Whitman and his new friend went for a walk together. Whitman was forty-three; Wilson was nineteen.[4]

On October 22, 1862, Horace Ostrander came to see a friend who was hospitalized and met the now-famous volunteer nurse. Whitman "slept with" Ostrander five weeks later.[5]

On September 3, 1862, Whitman reported, David Spencer, a deserter from the 2d New York Light Artillery, "slept with me." Whitman noted that Spencer was somewhat feminine and had never been in a fight or had a drink of whiskey.[6]

On October 3, 1863, Whitman met Jerry Taylor of the New Jersey District 2d Regiment during a visit to Washington, D.C. Taylor "slept with me last night," Whitman recorded.[7]

Perhaps these youths were merely cold and homeless; perhaps "slept" means only that. Perhaps Whitman was as straight as an arrow. This would have been a surprise to Oscar Wilde, who in 1882 spent the afternoon with Whitman and declared, "There is no one in the great wide world of America whom I love and honor so much."[8] Or to Sidney Lanier, who complained that Whitman's "argument seems to be that because a prairie is wide, therefore debauchery is admirable."[9] Or to Fred Vaughn, who lived for years with Whitman and is honored in Whitman's *Manuscripts:* "I have found him who loves me, as I him, in perfect love."[10] Or to Whitman's lover Peter Doyle, who recalled, "I never knew a case of Walt being bothered up by a woman. . . . his disposition was different. Women in that sense never came into his head."[11] Or to Edward Carpenter, who, when a young man, was the delighted recipient of Whitman's fellatio, which he demonstrated years later to Gavin Arthur. In 1923, Arthur was twenty and Carpenter was eighty. Carpenter, an ordained Anglican priest, writer and gay mystic, asked Arthur to spend the night. They discussed Whitman.

> "How did he make love?" I forced myself to ask.
> "I will show you," he smiled. "Let us go to bed."
> We were both naked and we lay side by side on our backs, holding hands. . . . He snuggled up to me and kissed my ear. . . . I gave myself up to the old man's marvelous petting. I of course had a throbbing erection but he ignored it for a long time. Very gradually, however, he got nearer and nearer. . . . At last his hand was moving between my legs and his tongue was in my bellybutton. And then when he was tickling my fundament . . . and I could not hold it any longer, his mouth closed just over the head of my penis and I felt my young vitality flowing. . . . He did not suck me at all. It was really *Karezza.*[12]

Whitman's *Notebooks* listed dozens of men, such as "Tom Egbert, conductor, Myrtle Avenue, open neck, sailor-looking." "April 17, 1862. The hour or two with Henry W. Moore, evening . . . and in Bleecker Street—the brief 15 minutes. . . ." "Aaron B. Cohn . . . appears to be 19 years old . . . fresh and affectionate." "Dick Smith, blond, driver 14th Street, meet at office every night."[13] Whitman's boys, whom he had nursed in the Washington hospital, often wrote to him after their release, with frequent mention of going into "Ward Master's Room to have some fun."[14] These are a small sampling of the jottings and diary entries with which the poet filled many whole notebooks. The evidence seems overwhelming that Whitman's powerful preference was for men, and in his case, younger working-class men. He found them by the dozens—on streetcars, in the hospital, on the sidewalks.

Such information about homosexual life in the 1860s outside of Whitman's poems, notebooks, daybooks, and unpublished manuscripts is much rarer, but not entirely absent.

The office of the provost guard at Fredericksburg noted on June 11, 1862, "Private Thomas Stewart, Company A, First Pennsylvania Artillery, was dressed in a female dress and very disorderly when arrested."[15]

George McClaughtery, a private in Capt. Bryan's Company of Virginia Artillery, CSA, wrote to his sister in 1865: "The boys . . . rode one of our company on a rail last night for leaving the company and going to sleep with Captain Lowry's black man."[16]

Confederate general James J. Archer, according to Mary Chesnut, had the nickname of "Sally." After Archer was captured at Gettysburg, he was imprisoned at Johnson's Island. The diary of Capt. Robert Bingham (44th North Carolina) notes, "We had a jolly party in our room tonight. Captain Taylor got some whiskey in a box under other things and so not noticed and we had General Archer down and they all got drunk together and got to hugging each other and saying that they had slept together many a time. Taylor called him Archer and hugged him—cursed at every word, much to old [Chaplain] Allen's discomfort." What does this entry really mean? We have only the words themselves.[17]

In 1852, "Grumble" Jones (the future Gen. William E. Jones, CSA) wrote a letter attacking Gen. William W. Loring, with whom he served on the frontier. "I hope you had a good time of it. I have seen no wife. Your stomach may have been satisfied with one of these one-night fellows. I have seen a dark-complected boy said to be yours. . . . if you remember you have a love scrape about this time with one of your captains . . . you and this captain quarreled. You wanted me to take your part . . . and to swear for you. I prefer . . . to tell the truth. I have incurred your everlasting hatred by so doing. You flamed my ruin at Panama . . . after we crossed the Isthmus you again wanted me to take sides against your sweetheart." Do these words mean what they sound like today? The rest of the letter does nothing to clarify the issue, but it is not difficult to see a male-male romance.[18]

In the spring of 1864, Massachusetts soldiers stationed at Brandy Station, Virginia, put on a ball. The local women, secession-minded and few in number, would hardly fill the need for companions. Younger soldiers, in particular the drummer boys, dressed as ladies for the evening. A letter home a few days later noted that "some of the real women went, but the boy girls were so much better looking they left . . . no one could have told wich of the party had fell on a hatchet." A comrade agreed: "We had some little Drummer boys dressed up and I'll bet you could not tell them from girls if you did not know them . . . some of them looked almost good enough to *lay* with and I guess some of them did get laid with." Does this mean what it sounds like? The letter writer adds to his wife, "I know I slept with mine."[19] Is this shameless pederasty, or a description of the communal sleeping arrangements? Or, at a distance of 130 years in time, culture, and language, is it possible to know exactly what happened after the ball was over, after the dance was done?

A major at the same ball was captivated by one young "lady." He finally cornered "her" in the drawing room, at which point "she" lifted up "her" dress and asked the major how he liked what he saw.[20] Today this event might evoke a cloud of words—gender confusion, transvestism, drag queen—but the exact meaning of those events back then continues to remain unclear.

Claims of homosexuality in the recent best-seller *Conduct Unbecoming: Gays & Lesbians in the U.S. Military* have set off a small historical storm. The author asserts that Confederate major general Patrick Cleburne was attracted to men, based upon the memoirs of Cleburne's adjutant, a man much younger than Cleburne, who stated that he shared the general's tent and often his blankets. Historian Dennis Kelly at Kennesaw Mountain National Battlefield Park disagrees: "It is utterly sinful what this author has done. People who don't understand the 19th century are trying to project things into the past," and noted that when he was an infantryman in Korea he shared a sleeping bag—to keep from freezing to death. Randy Shilts, the late best-selling author, believes that just the opposite prevailed: "In the old days when they did biographies of people, biographers felt obliged to make excuses and explanations."[21] Certainly, any assertion about the past needs a strong foundation.

Even if male-male offenses were almost never reported, the law was ready to meet the challenge, as shown in a remarkable book published in 1850 by Joseph Mayo, later the mayor of Richmond: *A Guide to Magistrates: With Practical Forms for the Discharge of Their Duties Out of Court.* In chapter XCVIII, headed "Sodomy and Bestiality," Mayo states, "This violation of the law of nature and the express ordinance of God is sometimes alluded to in the law books as the offence not even to be named among christians. There is but one instance of it to be found on our records, and with that exception, the crime is known only in Virginia through the judicial history of other nations." The author's comment suggests that arrest for same-sex behavior was indeed rare in that era. The rest of the chapter is devoted to fill-in-the-blank forms, to ease the work of puzzled magistrates. An example is the "Form of Certificate of Commitment for Sodomy":

To the Clerk of the County Court of said County: I, J.T., a Justice of the said County, do hereby certify that I have, by my warrant, this day committed C.D. (if free negro or slave, state which) to the jail of this County, that he may be examined (or tried) before the County Court of said County, for a felony by him committed, in this, that he did, on the _____ day of _____, 18_____, in the said County (here state the offense). Given under my hand, this _____ day of _____ in the year 18_____.

The author uses the term "detestable and abominable crime against nature" to describe all forms of carnal connection, whether they be with man, boy, or beast, but does suggest in Form Eight that with beasts the magistrate should name the species.[22]

It is worth further noting that in cases of sodomy between men, the author called for white persons to be committed for examination, but blacks to be committed for trial.

The guide for magistrates has nine different administrative forms for dealing with a crime that, according to the author, had only been prosecuted once in the history of Virginia, perhaps reflecting the hold that same-sex behavior has on the emotions of society. We thus have a crime that was said to have hardly ever occurred, that could not be named or described, that could be punished with five years in prison, and that had the power to disturb "the peace and dignity of the Common-wealth of Virginia." Both the psychology and true incidence of homo-sexuality in the 1860s appear to be mysteries.

Answers to these mysteries may lie in several areas. Homosexuality as a category did not exist and hence was not considered. People may have been more tolerant of others' lives at that time. The selective destruction of records may have been even more complete than those reflecting hetero-sexual life. Discovery of records in the future may clarify these issues. In the meantime, there is also the assertion that Abraham Lincoln himself may not have been entirely heterosexual.

Abraham Lincoln, the man known to every American, is perhaps the most unknown figure of the Civil War, at least in his private and personal life. William Herndon, his law partner for sixteen years, described Lincoln as the most "shut-mouthed" man he ever knew.[23] Leonard Swett, who knew Lincoln eleven years on the legal circuit, declared: "He always told only enough of his plans and purposes to induce the belief that he had communicated all; yet he reserved enough to have communicated nothing.[24] David Davis, a circuit judge who knew Lincoln well, wrote, "I knew the man so well; he was the most reticent, secretive man I ever saw or expect to see."[25]

What was the mystery, the puzzle, the missing link to the secret Lincoln? It may have been a physical attraction to men.

Is this concept merely some flight of fancy, cooked up on today's cauldron of revisionism, muck-raking, and radical political correctness, some apotheosis of "outing," or is it a theory that might have some merit, that might explain a facet of one of America's most complex and remarkable heroes?

Certainly, since the day of his death, Lincoln has been adopted by groups claiming he was "one of us." The thousands of Lincoln books include tomes claiming that Lincoln was a spiritualist, a biosopher, a supporter of high tariffs, an enemy of tobacco, a friend of communism. Is the suggestion that Lincoln might have had some trait of homosexuality merely another cry that "he was one of us"?

Settling any controversy over what Lincoln "really" believed has perplexed writers for more than a century. For every claim, there is a counter-claim. He has been called a born politician and a failure at politics. He has been claimed by Christian fundamentalists, Unitarians, and agnostics. When war threatened, it is claimed both that he tried to keep peace and that he cynically manipulated events to bring war. He has been called a military incompetent and a strategic genius. His policies on clemency have been called too tender-hearted and too ruthless. His Emancipation Proclamation has been called cynical propaganda and the most Christian act in our nation's history. The slaves worshiped "Massa Linkum," yet he urged the deportation of all blacks to Africa.

Arguments can be made, and facts found, to support all of these contradictory views.

What of the sources of our truths about Lincoln as a man? Herndon's two-volume biography is painfully honest, but Herndon accepted as fact vague and contradictory memories, often fifty years old.[26] The ten-volume authorized biography by Nicolay and Hay, Lincoln's secretaries, was censored by Robert Lincoln and shorn of every negative nuance.[27] The more closely the Lincoln sources are examined, the more obscure grows what is certain. With this disclaimer of finding the "real" Lincoln, the arguments regarding possible homosexuality or bisexuality may be presented.

The first consideration is the strength of Lincoln's inherent interest in women. He married at age thirty-one, certainly late for frontier Illinois. What did he do between puberty and age thirty? The first chief event is his romance with Ann Rutledge; there is no particle of proof that they were in love, or were engaged, or that Lincoln was long perturbed by her death. This romance was largely a tale embroidered by Herndon upon the slimmest of facts and a distant cloud of gossip.[28]

After the mythical heartbreak of Rutledge's death in 1835, there is the affair of Mary Owens. Here the evidence is strong: Lincoln's own letters. A close reading of his actual words reveals the most reluctant of lovers; half of his effort was devoted to telling Mary how unhappy she would be if she married him. In letters to his friends, he intimated that he found her distressingly fat and showed his relief and gratitude when she rejected his tepid offers of matrimony.

A later "romance" with Sarah Rickard seems, on closer examination, to have been a leftover of Joshua Speed's interest in Sarah, not Lincoln's. After Speed married another woman, he sent Lincoln to see how Sarah was taking the news.[29]

Thus, the approximately seventeen years of Lincoln's sexual maturity before marriage seem to have contained no serious involvement with any woman, and in actual fact, his one documented "romance," that with Mary Owens, was more of an antiromance, with Lincoln backpedaling and discouraging her until she dropped him.

Perhaps Lincoln had no sexual drive, a deficient libido? Here the historians are in utter confusion. Herndon said, "Lincoln had terribly strong passions for women, could hardly keep his hands off them." Yet, Edgar Lee Masters declared, "Lincoln was an undersexed man,"[30] and Nathanial W. Stephenson stated flatly that Lincoln "lacked the wanton appetites of the average sensual man."[31]

Since the authorities are in total disagreement about the strength of Lincoln's heterosexual impulses, perhaps an inquiry on a different line will shed light on his early adulthood and even on his marriage to Mary Todd.

When at age twenty-eight Lincoln rode into Springfield, Illinois, to set up his law practice, the town, with a population of 1,400 already had eleven lawyers, and Lincoln was broke. He reined in his horse at Joshua Speed's store and inquired about the cost of bedding. Speed figured the bill would be $17, and Lincoln said, sadly, "Cheap as it is, I have not the money to pay. But if you will credit me until Christmas [seven months away] and my experiment here as a lawyer is a success, I will pay you then. If I fail in that, I will probably never pay you at all." Speed wrote afterward, "I thought I never saw so gloomy and melancholy a face in my life."[32]

Speed suggested a plan "by which you can avoid the debt and at the same time attain your end. I have a large room with a double bed upstairs, which you are very welcome to share with me." Lincoln took his saddlebags up the stairs, returned beaming with pleasure and said, "Well, Speed, I am moved.[33]

"Thus it was that Joshua Fry Speed and Abraham Lincoln passed the first hours in their bed together. . . . how much Speed contributed to the development of Lincoln in the four years that they slept together is idle speculation, but their kindred hopes and ambitions fused into a unity and understanding which was never broken."[34]

Later, President Lincoln appointed Speed's brother, James, to the attorney general's office. When some members of the cabinet objected, Lincoln replied that he knew "he could trust the man, since he had slept with his brother for four years."[35] After Walt Whitman was fired from the Department of the Interior by James Harlan, who found *Leaves of Grass* "outrageous," James Speed gave Whitman a job in the attorney general's office.

On January 1, 1841, the day that Speed sold his store and he and Lincoln left the bed they had shared, Lincoln broke his engagement to Mary Todd and became too depressed to attend to his duties in the state legislature.[36] Three months later, Speed went to Kentucky to attend to family business; Lincoln went with him. In February of the following year, when Speed married, Lincoln wrote that it took him ten hours to calm down after reading the news. When Mary Todd Lincoln was pregnant with their first child, her husband wanted to name the child after Joshua Speed, but Mary prevailed and named the boy after her own father. The emotional bonding between Lincoln and Speed suggests the closest of male-male friendships, beginning with four years in the same bed.

Yet, as with any Lincoln story, there is a doubt. A century ago, having a bed to oneself was a luxury. Siblings, indeed whole families, might share one bed. In the rural hotels and taverns, the traveler often shared the bed with a stranger. The soldiers' tents were so crowded that they slept like spoons, all turning over at the same time. During many of the years between 1837 and 1841, while Lincoln and Speed slept together, they also shared the same room with William Herndon (before he married in 1840) and with Charles R. Hurst, another clerk at Speed's store downstairs.[37] Was this a frontier *ménage à quatre* or an economic necessity—or nothing at all?

In his eighteen years of marriage, before going to the White House, Lincoln traveled a wide circuit, both judicial and political. Unlike his colleagues, however, Lincoln seemed to go home as little as possible and preferred to spend his nights with unmarried men.[38] One of these companions, Ward Lamon, later became his bodyguard.

Lincoln was notoriously careless about his personal safety, and accepted an escort or bodyguards only under protest. In the summer of 1862, when he began to spend more time at the isolated cottage of the Soldier's Home, outside the city limits, an infantry guard was posted nearby. At first, regular infantry were assigned to this task, but soon two companies of the 150th Pennsylvania took their place. Lincoln grew to like these Pennsylvanians, especially Company K, with whose captain he became very friendly.

Friendly enough for Lincoln to invite the captain to share his bed on autumn nights when Mrs. Lincoln was away from home.[39]

Lincoln and Mary Todd and their marriage have been the subject of endless speculation. Herndon's entirely fictitious account of the 1841 New Year's Day wedding fiasco, with Mary in her bridal veil and the marriage supper hot in the kitchen, stood up by an errant Lincoln, sets the tone for the Lincoln-Todd literature. Where factual material is absent, the gap has been filled with spurious remembrance, idle speculation, and psychobabble.

Certainly, the Lincolns had their share of troubles—more than their share. Lincoln was not an easy husband, Washington gossip was vicious, and several of their children died. These well-known events certainly took their toll on Mary's precarious mental balance. It is highly likely that sexual inter-course stopped after the birth of Tad, in 1853, as Mary Todd Lincoln had serious gynecological problems.[40]

But perhaps Mary sensed that something was missing, some funda-mental attraction that can be the glue and reassurance in a good marriage. Such an intuitive, yet unprovable, factor could unhinge a more stable woman than Mary Todd.

Most Lincoln scholars believe that he was closer to Joshua Speed than to any other person, male or female, in his life. Perhaps a parallel might be drawn with the relationship of Emily Dickinson and her sister-in-law, Susan Gilbert. Speed and Lincoln seem never to have quarreled, but otherwise Paglia's characterization seems relevant: "By every standard except the genital, the stormy thirty-five year relationship between the two women must be called a love affair."[41]

Following the principle of Ockham's Razor, a Lincoln attraction to men, perhaps only manifest as relative ease in male company, is the least complex key to the distance that Lincoln put between himself and the women in his life. It is the most parsimonious explanation of the plaintive and tender letters exchanged between Lincoln and Joshua Speed when each took the momentous step of marriage. And it lies utterly beyond either proof or disproof.

Women served in many capacities in the Civil War. Most such women, even when they served in nontraditional roles, still assumed a female public persona. Women worked as clerks in the Treasury Depart-ment, as munitions workers, as vivandières, as nurses, and volunteered as daughters of regiments, but in all such roles they retained their identities as women.

A small group, however, probably between 500 and 1,000 women, served in combat units disguised as men. Many were killed or wounded.

A recent wave of interest in warrior women, both Union and Confederate, has produced two books,[42] three review articles,[43] a novel,[44] and even a coloring book.[45] The stories of a few of these women will illustrate this phenomenon.

At the opening of the war, one of the volunteers in Company F of the 2d Michigan Infantry was Pvt. Franklin Thompson. In 1861, Thompson's unit was building fortifications and learning soldier life on the outskirts of Washington, D.C. Thompson worked as a male nurse in the brigade hospital and later as a mail carrier. Unknown to comrades, Thompson actually was Sarah Emma Edmonds.

After an initial baptism of fire at the First Battle of Bull Run, Edmonds was appointed as a spy. Disguised as a male slave and given the name "Ned," she penetrated the Rebel defenses at Yorktown and was immediately pressed into service building fortifications. The next day, she arranged to be a water carrier, in which role she could hear all the Confederate gossip about troop dispositions. That night, "Ned" escaped back through the lines with her information.

Over the succeeding months, Edmonds saw much combat as a soldier, an ambulance worker, and an orderly to Gen. Philip Kearny. Even more astonishing than her adventures as Ned were her forays through the Confederate lines in a new disguise: Bridget, an illiterate thick-brogued Irishwoman peddling homemade pies. (Edmond's mother was an Irish immigrant, providing a role model for the accent.)

The Second Battle of Bull Run found Edmonds, now disguised as a black woman, cooking at Confederate headquarters, listening for useful information. After service at Fredericksburg and in Kentucky, Edmonds was hospitalized with malaria. She feared having her gender revealed during a bout of fevered confusion, and on April 17, 1863, the regimental records noted that "The beardless boy, a universal favorite," had deserted.

In civilian life, after recovering her health and now Emma again, she wrote a fictionalized version of her spy career, *Nurse and Spy,* which sold 175,000 copies. She donated most of the proceeds to charity. In 1867, she married Linus Seelye and assumed the name Sarah Seelye. In this new role, she bore three children and adopted two more. She and her husband labored with the Freedman's Bureau and performed other acts of Christian charity, but the Southern climate reactivated her malaria and the Seelyes moved north.

In 1883, as part of her application for a medical pension, she told her story to a reporter for a Detroit newspaper. After a sudden wave of publicity, old comrades rallied to support her case, and the next year Congress granted her a medical pension for malaria and several combat equestrian injuries received on spying missions. When the money finally arrived, five years later, it totaled $100.

In 1897, she was accepted into the Grand Army of the Republic Post at Houston, Texas, the only woman to receive such an honor. A year later she was dead, the victim of a final attack of malaria. Her gravestone is inscribed "Emma E. Seelye—Army Nurse."[46]

A woman of much different temperament, but of equal daring, served as Lt. Harry T. Buford in the Confederate Army. Lieutenant Buford began life as Loreta Janeta Velasquez, born to a wealthy Cuban family. Velasquez was a dreamer, who fancied herself a new Joan of Arc and had the money to equip herself with disguise, uniform, horse, and servant, and travel as an "independent" self-commissioned officer. Her initial combat experience was (like Edmond's) First Bull Run. Velasquez, in her own opinion, had so distinguished herself on the field of battle that she applied directly to "Stonewall" Jackson for a promotion. He offered her a recruiting commission, which she rejected.

Her next combat experience was at Ball's Bluff, where the fleeing Federal troops were slaughtered. There her blood lust curdled and she sickened of the sight of dying men. Her next assignment was as a railroad detective, checking the papers of suspicious persons. This new career was brief and she was soon at Fort Donelson, just before its capture. She escaped to New Orleans, was arrested as a spy, released, and then jailed again for cross-dressing, in episodes worthy of Molière.

She next appeared at Shiloh, taking the second lieutenant's place when he fell in battle, but the eventual Confederate defeat in that two-day struggle again cooled her ardor for combat, and her enthusiasm was further chilled by a dislocated shoulder.

Upon her recovery, she worked for the South again, smuggling medical supplies from Cuba disguised as a British widow, but her restless nature soon brought her to Tennessee, where she crossed and recrossed the lines in a variety of guises, gathering information on Federal forces.

Compounding the confusion in her own life was a passionate yearning for one Captain DeCaulp, with whom she had served as Lieutenant Buford; meanwhile, DeCaulp expressed his love for Loreta Velasquez, who he had met in another setting. Lieutenant Buford finally revealed her true identity to DeCaulp, who, after recovering from his shock and confusion, married her. Unlike in an opera with a happy ending, DeCaulp died a few weeks later. The heartbroken widow sought solace in a return to duty, and in the fall of 1863, she returned to spy work. Soon she was in the North, being interviewed by Lafayette Baker, head of the Federal investigations, who soon retained her services, little suspecting that she was a double agent. Trips to the South and Canada in a variety of guises and under a variety of names led to an assignment from Baker—to catch herself!

Through Byzantine maneuvering, she became a courier for a ring of crooked Federal officers who were counterfeiting Confederate bonds and selling them in England. As the South collapsed, Loreta headed for Europe with $100,000 in cash, to escape Federal retribution. By the late 1860s, she was in New Mexico and California, with a new husband. A decade later, she was in Brazil, at which point she fades from history.

Is her story true? Are her memoirs, *The Woman in Battle*,[47] to be believed? Researchers who have devoted years to this question say yes—but.[48] Some of her adventures seem to be true and can be verified, while others, of more doubtful validity, stand as wonderful examples of imagination.

Less dramatic, and probably more typical, was the career of Pvt. Albert Cashier, who served three years with the 95th Illinois. Every part of his military career is on file at the National Archives. Albert enlisted on August 6, 1862, in Boone County, Illinois, at the age of nineteen. He was 5 foot, 3 inches tall with blue eyes, auburn hair, and a light complexion. He was accounted for at every muster until his release at Camp Butler in August 1865, where he received his bounty and his tobacco allowance. He had lived through forty battles without a scratch.

For the next four decades, Cashier worked as a farmhand and handyman and served as caretaker to his church. He never married. In 1911, he was hit by an automobile (not common then) and suffered a fractured femur. The doctor soon learned that Albert was really a woman, Jennie Hodgers, but true to the doctor's oath of confidentiality, he preserved her secret while arranging admission to the Soldiers' and Sailors' Home at Quincy, Illinois.

Two years later, after some erratic behavior, Albert was committed to a public mental hospital and the news was out. National headlines told the secret. Old comrades rallied to her support, testifying to Albert's bravery in combat and public good works in later life. Albert/Jennie died at Watertown State Hospital in 1915, at age seventy-one. The local post of the Grand Army of the Republic arranged for the burial. Her headstone reads: "Albert D. J. Cashier, Company G, 95th Illinois Infantry."[49]

Many other women served as men, although less detail is known about their lives. John Evans served eighteen months in the Pennsylvania Volunteers; after he was wounded, he was discovered to be Mary Owens. Satronia Smith Hunt enlisted in an Iowa regiment, along with her husband. He was killed in battle, but she survived the war. Mary Stevens Jenkins enlisted in a Pennsylvania regiment, was wounded during her two years of service, and was mustered out without her sex being discovered. Elizabeth

Niles and her husband, Martin, were on their honeymoon when war broke out. She cut her hair, and they both enlisted in the 4th New Jersey Infantry and served together through many engagements.[50]

Nellie K. enlisted with her brother in the 102d New York and fought at Antietam, Chancellorsville, Gettysburg, and Lookout Mountain. Mrs. L. M. Blalock joined the 26th North Carolina with her husband, stating that she was his younger brother. She fought in three major engagements before leaving the service. Mrs. Amy Clarke also joined with her husband. While serving with Gen. Braxton Bragg in Kentucky, she was wounded and captured. In Gen. Philip Sheridan's memoirs, he mentions a teamster and a private who got drunk together and fell into a river. When rescued and revived, they both proved to be women.[51]

Amy Clarke of Iuka, Mississippi, was thirty years old when she joined her husband's cavalry regiment. Later, she enlisted in the 11th Tennessee. Her true sex was not discovered until she was wounded and captured. Lizzie Compton was not easily discouraged. She enlisted in eight different Union regiments, but each time her gender was discovered and she was discharged. She was, however, on active service long enough to be seriously wounded at Fredericksburg.[52]

What is one to make of these soldier women? The army's official answer was that they never existed. Gen. F. C. Ainsworth of the Records and Pension Office stated in 1909 that there was no record of any woman ever enlisted in the army during the Civil War.[53]

Since the record suggests that Ainsworth was wrong, a more productive question might be that of motivation. Some otherwise excellent historians gave these women very little credit. Bell Wiley considered them somewhat bizarre.[54] Mary Elizabeth Massey assumed that most were prostitutes.[55] Speculation using today's terminology might include lesbianism, transsexualism, and transvestism. A fairer opinion, based on more recent evidence, might be that such women typically joined to be with a beloved husband or simply believed passionately in their cause, whether it be Union or Confederate.

As in other wars and other times, devotion to an ideal seems far more important than whether the soldier is male or female, or favors the same or a different gender in choosing a lover.

Chapter Twelve

ta

Against Her Will

RAPE HAS LONG BEEN RECOGNIZED as a crime of violence, not of sexuality. The hatred, aggression, and lust for dominance found in rape accounts for its manifestation in men who already have willing or available partners. The very compliance of these partners may lessen the ardor of the potential rapist for the available. He desires, most of all, the terror and humiliation of his victim.

Still, rape can be classified not only as a crime of violence but also as a sexual crime because of the body parts involved and the possibilities of pregnancy and venereal disease.

Since historians have usually focused on other aspects of the Civil War, it may seem strange to think of rapists in blue and gray, but the record speaks for itself. Confederate rapists are somewhat harder to locate than Union ones, since unknown persons set fire to the Confederate Army court-martial records about the time of Lee's surrender, but a survey of less than 5 percent of the Federal court-martial records, preserved in the National Archives, have yielded more than thirty trials for rape.

Not surprisingly, scrutiny of these records reveals the usual stories of force and violence. In spite of the likely fate of hanging or shooting if arrested, rapists still worked their will. A few of their stories will illustrate this point.

At dusk on February 27, 1865, in a cabin on the north side of the Catawba River in South Carolina, Pvt. Robert Opdyke of the 38th Ohio Volunteers was awakened by the screams of "a woman of African descent." She was being held down by Daniel Kunkle of Company C and by three other unidentified men, while Pvt. Thomas Killgore, of the same unit, raped her. Opdyke testified at the trial that Killgore "laid in between her legs, bobbing, then Kunkle tried to rape her but did not succeed. [Killgore] said he wanted to see what she had for a thing; he then put his foot on her leg, pulled up her dress and threw a [flaming] torch between her legs." Killgore received ten years at hard labor, Kunkle four years.[1]

At Lynchburg, Pennsylvania, in the summer of 1865, Sgt. Maj. Alfred Waxey of the 8th Pennsylvania cavalry went with Lt. D. W. Davis of the same regiment to the house of William Johnson, a "colored citizen." Johnson testified that "he commenced hugging and kissing my wife. Then the light went off. . . . I then told him that if this woman [Fannie, his wife] had given him any cause to come here to take her, but not to impose on me. He then struck me twice. . . . I left the room in which they were, went into another, got on my pants and shoes and jumped out the window . . . because I was afraid the gentlemen were going to kill me. I went to the Provost Marshal. No one came that night." Sergeant Major Waxey was reduced to the ranks with loss of pay.[2]

Pvt. Adolph Bork, Company H, 183d Ohio, was tried for the rape of "Susan, a woman of color," who testified that "he took out his revolver and said, 'God damn you, I will force you to do it.' He said he would blow me to pieces if I didn't let him do it. I was sitting with a child on my lap belonging to another woman, and I got up to go out. He told me not to go out. . . . He came then and put a hand on my breast and pushed me on the bed. He tried to do what he undertook, but didn't do it. He said, 'If you don't do what's right, I'll bust you open.' [She was nine months' pregnant.] I told him to let me alone, that he hurt me. He said he didn't give a damn if he did. He got on top of me. He entered my person with his private member as well as he could. He completed the act. He used force." Susan finished her testimony by adding that she had a husband; they had been married by a "colored exhorter."

That same day, in addition to the rape, Bork "did willingly and maliciously assault and shoot with a pistol ball one Private Ludwig Sweitzer." Bork was sentenced to be "shot with musketry."[3]

Some attempts at rape involved money. Pvt. William Van Buren of Company B, 212th Illinois, who was stationed at Camp Denison, had a few drinks in town and accosted Mrs. Ellie Farnan and her daughter. He offered them money for "some skin." They saw this as "insult and abuse," beat up Van Buren, and then called the guard. Capt. F. L. Rupill arrested Van Buren and returned him to the Farnan house to face his accusers. Mrs. Farnan's statement was recorded as follows: "You god damned old son of a bitch, you had the impudence to offer a decent woman like myself a dollar and my girl, that I'm raising, three [dollars]." The hapless Van Buren got a month in the guardhouse.[4]

Patrick Manning, while stationed at Natchez, proved equally as maladroit at fiscal negotiation as Van Buren but was more violent. Manning was a private in Company B, 8th New Hampshire, and tried to assault Miss Clara Grier. At the trial, she testified, "He took hold of me and attempted to throw me down and I hollered and he kicked me. He asked me if I wanted five dollars. I said no. He asked if he could stay with me. I said no. I am a quadroon. He was drunk." He was found not guilty of attempted rape, but for other crimes he got three years at hard labor with a ball and chain.[5]

Pvt. Frederick D. Wells of Company D, 90th Battalion, New York Veteran Volunteers, while absent without leave, "did enter the house of one Mary Harvey of Winchester, Virginia, and did then and there attempt to commit a rape upon . . . the said Mary Harvey, striking her on the face and head for resisting his violence and attempting to defend herself." Wells received three years at hard labor with a 24-pound iron ball attached to his left ankle by a 6-foot chain.[6]

The trial record of Corp. George Hakes of Company F, 6th Michigan Cavalry, notes that he "did ravish the wife of one Cornelius Robinson, a loyal colored citizen of Frederick County, Virginia. This near Winchester, on or about the 19th day of November, 1864." The sentence was dishonorable discharge and two years at hard labor.[7]

Sergeants Danbridge Brooks and William Jackson, both of Company G, and Corp. John Sheppard, Company I, all of the 38th Regiment of U.S. Colored Troops, entered the Richmond, Virginia, home of Washington Crawford and stole a pair of white kid gloves, a silver thimble, a white shirt, a satin vest, a dark blue overcoat, and 8 pounds of butter. In addition to these thefts, Sergeant Jackson raped Mrs. Crawford, Sergeant Brooks raped a Miss Eliza Woodson, and Corporal Sheppard raped both Mrs. Crawford and Miss Woodson. All three men were hanged.[8]

Pvt. John Forrest, of Company M, 3d Massachusetts Heavy Artillery, "did seize and attempt to throw Mrs. Francis Parker, with avowed intent of committing outrage upon her person, saying at the same time, 'Let me fuck you,' or words to that effect. This near Fort Saratoga, District of Columbia, on or about the fourth day of February, 1865." Forrest was dishonorably discharged and sentenced to six years at hard labor.[9]

Mrs. Frances West was a widow, living near Morrisville, Virginia. On the night of September 9, 1863, Pvt. Thomas Dawson entered her home and "did forcibly and violently and against her will have sexual intercourse with [her] . . . thus committing the crime of rape." Dawson, of Company A, 19th Massachusetts Volunteers, was hanged with the approval of Abraham Lincoln.[10]

On July 29, 1863, near Lebanon, Kentucky, Pvt. Stephen Stillwell visited the home of Joseph Blair. Stillwell, upon learning that Blair was away, told Mrs. Blair that some stolen government horses were being held at a house a mile or so away and compelled her to go there and make inquiries on his behalf. She departed, leaving Stillwell alone in the house with her sister, Mrs. Sallie McKune. This was apparently what Stillwell had in mind, because, "by force and against her will and consent did then and there have carnal knowledge of, and connection with, her body . . . [there being] no one within hearing of her voice or call." Stillwell, a member of the 37th Kentucky Volunteers, received fifteen years at hard labor in the state penitentiary.[11]

Death by firing squad. That was the fate of three privates from Company H, 2d New Jersey Cavalry. On March 12, 1864, Thomas Johnson, John Callahan, and Jacob Snover, all armed, broke into the home of Miss Margaret J. Brooks, a resident of Shelby County, Tennessee. After a violent struggle, Johnson and Snover held her down, while Callahan raped her. Then the other two men took their turns raping her. When the three men departed, they took $250 in cash. They did not have long to spend it.[12]

On the first day of August 1863, in Blount County, Tennessee, "Abe [a man of color], the property of one Samuel H. Henry, did commit a rape upon the body of Mrs. Creger, a citizen and respectable white lady." Abe was sentenced to hang and Lincoln approved the verdict.[13]

Another Missouri soldier with troubles was Pvt. William T. Cox of Company I, 8th Missouri Cavalry. On the night of October 18, 1862, in Green County, Missouri, he entered the home of one Richard Rose and found there Nancy Rose, Richard's wife. Cox then "did forcibly and with violence and threats commit a rape . . . without the consent of said Nancy Rose and contrary her will." The Court found him guilty and sentenced him to be "shot to death with musketry."[14]

The court record for Pvt. George Nelson of Company F, 13th Regiment of U.S. Colored Troops, was brief and to the point: "[He] did commit rape on the person of Indiana Rose, in Dixon County, Tennessee." Nelson was hanged.[15]

Wild gunfire marked the crimes of John Carroll, a Wisconsin Volunteer. Under the cover of darkness, Carroll, who was already absent without leave, entered the home of Elisha Gidon, forced Mr. Gidon out of the house at gunpoint, and then, holding his pistol at Mrs. Gidon's head, forced her to have intercourse with him. Mr. Gidon used this time to summon help and returned with Mr. and Mrs. Reyes Flores. Carroll fired at the rescue party, wounding Mrs. Flores. Company D of the 20th Wisconsin Regiment lost a member when Carroll stood before a firing squad a few days later.[16]

McMinnville, in Warren County, Tennessee, was the scene of the crimes of Jacob Leonhart, a saddler with the 26th Independent Pennsylvania Battery. He entered the home of Mrs. Jane L. Young, knocked her down with his fist, and "did then and there, feloniously and against her will, attempt to commit a rape upon the person of 'Sally,' a negro woman in the employ of said Jane L. Young." Leonhart was sentenced to a penitentiary for the duration of the war, with a 12-pound iron ball chained to his left leg.[17]

Pvt. James Robinson of Company G, 6th Cavalry, Missouri State Militia, together with Pvt. Samuel B. Stewart, left camp at night without permission, went 6 miles to the Vernon home, where they stole a blanket, a coat, two pairs of ladies' hose, and a silk mantilla. They then "did lay violent hands upon and did throw to the floor the said Letta L. Vernon, with remarks that 'You have to submit to our wishes,' and then attempted to violate her person." Stewart received five years in prison, Robinson three.[18]

An unusually inventive and cruel rape was perpetrated by Pvt. Charles C. Hunter of Company I, 7th Kentucky Cavalry. The trial transcript notes that on the morning of May 18, 1864, he "did enter the residence of Mrs. Mary Melissa Kirkesey and, after having bound her firmly with a leather strap, running the same through her mouth, thereby suppressing her cries, did then and there brutally ravish her person." The Court gave Hunter eighteen years in the penitentiary at Nashville.[19]

Employees of the army came under military law, as seen in the case of Mr. Robert H. Hughes, "colored teamster in the employ of the U.S. Quartermaster's Department." Hughes "did make a violent assault on the person of Lucy B. Batkins, a white woman, resident of New Kent County, Virginia, and did attempt by force and threats to commit a rape on her person." Lincoln approved the sentence of death by hanging.[20]

Justice was swift and final for two soldiers of Company E, 72d New York Volunteers. Privates Ranson S. Gordon and Daniel Geary went "to the house of Mrs. Mary E. Stiles, a resident of Prince George County, Virginia, and did by threats and violence . . . commit a rape on the person of said Mary E. Stiles." Both soldiers were hanged.[21]

Pvt. William Jones of the 3d Wisconsin Cavalry had a wild time the night of February 25, 1864. He was absent without leave near Drywood, Kansas, and began his evening by burglarizing the home of Steven Howard, taking $107 in cash. He then entered the William Martin home, robbed the husband, and raped the wife. Jones was stood in front of a firing squad.[22]

A Vermont private escaped with his life after a brutal rampage in which he went absent without leave and, near Warrentown, Virginia, encountered one Pricey McCoy, whom he beat, bruised, raped, and "evilly treated." The criminal, Charles R. Rogers of Company E, 3d Vermont Volunteers, had his head shaved in front of his company, was drummed out of the service, and was sentenced to five years at hard labor.[23]

Sentries are supposed to be alert, sober, and well behaved. On June 18, 1864, Sgt. Charles Sperry of Company E, 13th New York Cavalry, was none of these things. He deserted his post (near Langley, Virginia), got drunk, and "did beat, strike and bruise one Annie L. Nelson, a maiden of about 15 years, then and there, feloniously, with attempt to ravish her by force and against her will." The Court sent Sperry to the firing squad.[24]

Pvt. John Cornish was a recipient of President Lincoln's clemency. Cornish, of Company G, 30th U.S. Colored Troops, "did seize Sarah Potter by the arm and attempt to force her from the house for the purpose of committing a rape upon her person." He was sentenced to hang. Lincoln reviewed the case and commuted the sentence to life imprisonment.[25]

A story of Chaucerian low farce, mixed with brutality, was heard by a military commission at Salisbury, North Carolina, as they took up the case of "Alfred Locke, colored, a free man." Roseann Hendrick testified that about two hours after dark, she was at Mary Sloan's house. A man banged on the door and said, "God damn you, open the door or I will set fire to the house." The women asked who was out there. The voice replied, "A Yankee, God damn you. . . . I want to fuck you." Then their visitor broke down the door, jerked Mrs. Sloan out of bed, and choked, kicked, and beat her. Mrs. Hendrick, who was hiding under the bed, testified, "He got her choked down and just went to ravishing her." Locke did not detect the second woman, who escaped Mrs. Sloan's fate.

Another witness, John Franklin, a "colored free man," explained Locke's hope for amorous success at the Sloan home: "[Locke] told me that there was two black men . . . had gone to Mrs. Sloan's in the night and had passed themselves for Yankees and gone in and screwed them." It remained unexplained why any of the parties concerned would mistake Locke's regional accent for a Yankee twang.

The Court had other concerns. They sentenced Locke to hang. Lincoln approved the sentence, but Locke escaped on his execution day and the file concludes with telegrams to and from the War Department, debating the next move.[26]

The rape charges against Pvt. William H. Cole resulted in an unusual flux of petitions and penalty revisions. Cole served with the 109th New York Volunteers and from January 1863 was stationed at the village of Laurel, in Prince George County, Maryland. In late 1863, he was charged with the rape of a fifty-year-old woman, Mrs. Alvisa Brown, wife of one Nicholas Brown. She stated that the rape occurred in May 1863. Cole denied the accusation, claiming that he was drunk and did not remember anything about the matter. Cole was convicted and sent to Albany State Penitentiary in New York with a ten-year sentence.

In March 1864, three of Cole's comrades, Ezra Bills, Ixes Brink, and Silas Tripp, submitted a two-page sworn statement that they had often visited the Brown household (consisting of Alvisa and Nicholas Brown and their daughter, Ellen Elizabeth England), and that it was no ordinary home. The three soldiers said that many members of their company spent time with the Browns, who procured whiskey for the soldiers, and that Alvisa and Ellen drank with the troops and that the women were drunk several times. "We each of us further depose that we are satisfied that the said Alvisa and the said Ellen are lewd women and that the said Nicholas Brown is cognizant of the fact and that they keep a bawdy house." Ezra Bills further stated that once Ellen was in bed with a man and that her mother was present and knew of it. Ezra and Ixes signed the statement with an "X" and Silas in a fine hand. Samuel Brown, J.P., attested to the signatures.

A petition from Cole's hometown friends stated that Cole "from his childhood . . . has been a peaceable and quiet citizen and that we have never heard any charge or complaint against him . . . except that occasionally he was a little wild." Cole's father, Jacob, was said to be eighty years old, "aged and infirm," and his mother, Rhoda, was age seventy. The petitions were forwarded to the president on July 9, 1864, by Mr. Hotchkiss, with a request for pardon. That same day, Lincoln wrote, "Pardon, according to above request," and Cole was free.[27]

On November 7, 1862, Pvt. William Eliott of Company G, 8th U.S. Infantry, attempted "to commit the crime of rape upon the body of a colored woman named Kate Brooke, this on the premises of her master, R. M. Johnson, of Rectortown, Virginia." Eliott was given life in prison.[28]

John Bell had the distinction of being the first man to be legally executed in Kansas. Bell, a private in Company I, 2d Kansas Cavalry, was sentenced to hang for a rape committed near Iola, Kansas, on the Fourth of July. He was to be executed five days later (no lengthy appeals in 1862!) but the hanging was delayed until dawn the next day, because a great crowd of men, women, and children had gathered on the appointed afternoon, annoying the local commander, who objected to the carnival atmosphere.[29]

In a 1912 letter, a former Confederate soldier reminisced, "I killed a member of the 18th New York who was trying to rape a lady near White Chimneys in New Kent County and many other such acts."[30]

In Vicksburg, "a couple of the disbanded Marines were out on a spree and had taken it into their heads to make a descent upon the house of a Mr. McDaniels. . . . they attacked the portion of the house occupied by colored people and, breaking in the door, entered to the great terror and fright of the inmates who at once commenced a series of screams and squawks and . . . a severe drubbing by the loudest of the frail feminines." This attempt at rape was driven off by the guard.[31]

At Waterloo Landing, Alabama, a court-martial was held for Pvt. Edward Hays, Company L, 4th Kentucky Cavalry, in February 1865. He was accused of taking twelve-year-old Nancy Short into the woods, lying on top of her to "see a little fun," covering her mouth, and attempting to rape her. Hays was age fifty. He was given two years at hard labor.[32]

In a letter dated October 1, 1863, Arabella Speairs of Fluvanna County, Virginia, wrote, "Virginia Shields . . . gives the most awful account you ever hard, of the treatment of our people by the Yankees. . . . she is a woman that can be relied upon, for I have known her from her birth, and she says she saw from her window a lady of the highest respectability taken in the broad daylight and stripped naked in the street and then her person violated by ten drunken Yankees, all because she was a true Southerner and her husband in the army. Shoot them, dear husband, every chance you get. [Virginia] says she saw a little boy about 12 years old, caught by one of those [Yankee] demons and castrated and tied to a lamp post until he died, because he gloried in being a rebel."[33]

While Yankee soldiers raped some Southern white women, their major victims were black women. The psychology seemed a mixture of forbearance toward whites plus a wish to prove to both blacks and whites that the white masters (and mistresses) could not protect their property. Such a crime against black women was most potent in the presence of Southern white witnesses. The forces of emancipation raping the beneficiaries of this charity—the irony is hard to miss.

Returning Confederate veterans and, later, Ku Klux Klan members raped black women, probably to vent feelings of revenge and to establish dominance. Indeed, the fate of black women at that time seems to have been victimization by every side.[34] A startling example was described by a Yankee prisoner who was being marched to Shreveport, watched by three heavily armed "ragged, wretched and wild ruffians." At a lunch stop, the three Rebels encountered a slave woman, "a bit buxom, but not unattractive." They ordered her to come near. "Each one of the trio in turn raped the helpless negress and after they finished their lustful desires they turned to me, one of them saying, 'Now, Yank, it's your turn.'" The Yankee refused their invitation and the woman retired in tears. The diarist, Pvt. Louis Kakuske, was particularly horrified by the white women who watched the rape, clapped their hands, and "laughed as if they were applauding actors at a theater."[35]

In general, rape was treated as a very serious offense, but sentencing

was capricious and black soldiers seemed much more likely than whites to receive the death penalty.

There is evidence that there was less rape during the Civil War than in comparable conflicts;[36] indeed, only twenty-two men were executed for rape.[37] British journalist Edward Dicey commented on how well-behaved Federal troops were compared with European soldiers, "due, probably, to the fact of the privates being mostly married, and all men of some kind of education. . . . In truth, the almost morbid sentiment of Americans with regard to women, while it renders them ridiculously susceptible to female influence, protects women in that country from the natural consequences of their own misconduct."[38]

While all observers note that rape was relatively rare, this was not a comfort to those who were the unlucky exceptions.

Chapter Thirteen

ૐ

An Officer and
a Gentleman

RANK HATH ITS PRIVILEGES, but also its responsibilities. Noblesse oblige. To earn command means to earn respect. In some eras, that respect came from fear, or from social caste, or from wealth. In the Civil War, with most commissioned officers chosen by local election or by political patronage, rather than through long professional training, their moral obligations tended to reflect the communities that sponsored them.

The majority of officers did their duty, but the seductions of power, the distance from hometown restraints, and the wartime breakdown of moral standards blended with the immemorial contrariness of human nature to lead some officers very far from being gentlemen.

Jerome Potter, second lieutenant of Company K, 102d Ohio Volunteers, had in his unit one Pvt. Calvin C. Rice. Potter, who was about to go home on leave, announced to his brother officers that Rice's wife, Julia, was in his opinion attractive and sexually available, and that while he was home on leave he intended to take her to bed.

When Potter returned from leave a month later, the 102d Ohio was camped at Clarksville, Tennessee, where Potter soon began to regale officers and enlisted men alike about his amorous successes back in Ohio. In the elegant and formal words of the trial records, Lieutenant Potter:

> Falsely and maliciously did publish and speak of and concerning the said Julia Rice, the following false and slanderous words, or words to the same effect, to wit: "I screwed (meaning he had carnal intercourse with) Rice's wife (meaning said Julia Rice) when at home in Ohio. I had a good time with Mistress

Rice (meaning said Julia) and got all I wanted (meaning thereby that he had carnal intercourse with said Julia Rice). I had sexual intercourse with Rice's wife," and then and there he, the said Jerome Potter, exhibited to said officers and soldiers a pair of stockings and garters and declared and said that he had taken them from Mistress Rice's legs with his own hands, which statements were untrue. Potter further said: "I screwed Rice's wife and had a good time with her. I wonder what Rice would say if he knew it."

It would seem that the trial board was less amused than Potter. They ordered him to be dismissed from the service, and the order was approved by Maj. Gen. William S. Rosecrans.[1]

Capt. Augustus Steuernagel, acting assistant adjutant general with the 68th New York Volunteers, was stationed at Atlanta in the autumn of 1865. The court records note that the captain had been drunk most of the month of August, but their major concern was with his household arrangements. The first witness at his trial was Nancy Peirce, a native of New Orleans and apparently Steuernagel's mistress. She had returned from an errand to find the captain in her room, on top of a sixteen-year-old mulatto girl named Fanny Edwards. The curtains were up, exposing the room to the street. When Peirce asked him what he thought he was doing, Steuernagel replied, "You damned Irish bitch, if you don't get out . . . I will bust a chair over you." The judge advocate, apparently taking a lively interest in this encounter, asked, "In what position did you find the accused and Fanny Edwards, the colored girl, in your room?" Miss Peirce, a keen observer, replied, "He was on top of her and she was lying there naked and did not have any clothes on at all, with her feet crossed on top of his back. He was in his shirttail and he had his pants about half off of him."

The judge advocate apparently was slow to comprehend the import of this scenario and inquired further: "What did the accused do to this mulatto women when he was lying on top of her?" Miss Peirce, retaining her grasp of the essentials, replied, "He was screwing her. . . . I looked five or ten minutes and have seen the whole thing."

Not to be deflected in the search for truth, the Court then asked, "Did the accused have sexual intercourse with . . . Fanny Edwards?" Miss Peirce, maintaining her composure, answered, "Yes, I did see it."

Further testimony showed that the captain tried to hit Nancy with a chair, that she threatened him with his own saber, and that when the guard was summoned, she was on the front porch shouting, "Lieutenant, kill the son of a bitch. He has got the clap. I will not stay with him any more and now I seen him on top of a negro woman." Captain Steuernagel was dismissed from the service.[2]

Capt. Adolph Lamburg of Battery F, 2d U.S. Colored Artillery, lived sixteen months with a colored woman named Mollie Gray and openly acknowledged her to be his wife, "to the great prejudice and scandal of the service." He was found not guilty. The reviewing officer disagreed with the verdict, stating that the Court had ignored the evidence before it. "The Court, having been dissolved, however, the case could not be remanded."[3]

Second Lt. Charles Walsh of the 1st New York Dragoons, while stationed at Port Tobacco, Maryland, got so drunk that he "was reeling on his horse," according to witness Corp. Hiram Miller. Walsh and another intoxicated man dismounted from time to time to smash windows, including those of Miss Eliza Quinn. When this method of gaining her favors failed, Walsh then offered her $5 "for the alleged purpose of violating her person." After being arrested, Walsh failed to cooperate in his confinement. He was dismissed from the service.[4]

A warm autumn evening near Montgomery, Mississippi, was the undoing of 1st Lt. Thomas C. Baldwin of the 7th Iowa. He was later charged with conduct unbecoming an officer and a gentleman, in that "on the night of the second day of September, 1862, he did take a Negro wench into his tent, took her to bed with him and lay with her until nearly midnight, with his tent doors open." Perhaps a gentleman would have closed the tent doors. Baldwin was dismissed from the service.[5]

Capt. John Smart's dereliction is unmistakable in the trial summary: "He . . . did become drunk and while in that condition did conduct himself in a very disgraceful manner, by entering a tent where the sutler of the 25th Regiment had spread a table for visiting officers from another regiment. He, Captain John Smart, did then and there piss upon the food and dishes there spread out. All this at the camp of the 25th Regiment, Illinois Volunteers, near Murfreesboro, Tennessee, on or about May 10th, 1863." This action earned him a dismissal from the service.[6]

There are many wartime legal cases in which those on guard duty have failed as adequate sentinels. One of the more remarkable examples occurred with 2d Lt. George W. Parrott of the 16th Illinois. While on guard duty near Edgefield, Tennessee, in December 1862, he "did become drunk and have sexual intercourse with a Negro or colored woman, in the presence of his guard and did remain on said . . . colored woman, 30 minutes or more, until Corporal Ellis made him get off." The other sentinels were described in the court proceedings as so drunk as to be "unfit for duty." Lieutenant Parrott forfeited six months' pay.[7]

Personal initiative and the holding of a second job are not necessarily evil, but they proved the undoing of 2d Lt. John Miller of the 14th Illinois Volunteer Cavalry. In the spring of 1863, he was stationed at St. Louis, Missouri, where he was found tending bar "in a house of prostitution and ill fame, and this in the uniform and while wearing the emblems of his rank and position as an officer." The Court found this to be inappropriate behavior, and he was dismissed from the service.[8]

In May 1863, at the 2d Division Hospital, 3d Army Corps, near Potomac Creek, Mrs. Mercy M. Whippey of Camden, New Jersey, came to visit her wounded son. First Lt. George W. O'Malley of Company E, 115th Pennsylvania, volunteered to act as "as safeguard and protection . . . to her during her stay at camp." Just before midnight, according to the court record, O'Malley did "commit an assault with intent to commit a rape upon the person of Mercy M. Whipey (she being on her bed) and did attempt to ravish her." This apparently was quite unwelcome, and when she protested, he held her down "with great force and violence and kissing her against her will and consent and manifesting by other actions his intent . . . of having carnal connection with her person." This failure to be a safeguard and protection earned O'Malley six years at hard labor, a sentence approved by Lincoln.[9]

On September 24, 1865, on the night train between Tennessee and Alabama, 2d Lt. Henry Mente of 42d U.S. Colored Troops "did allow himself to be treated with undue familiarity by one Lucy Nobles, a white woman cook for Headquarters Mess." Miss Nobles's apparently willing amours occurred "in the presence of several enlisted men and colored women, servants of the regiments." It was the public nature of these midnight revels that the Court saw as "forfeiting the respect of the men of the regiment and bringing disgrace upon his uniform as an officer." Lieutenant Mente joined the ranks of other cashiered (dishonorably discharged) officers.[10]

Second Lt. John W. Stiles of the 34th Massachusetts learned the hard way about the rules of military etiquette. In early April 1863, near Fort Lyon, Virginia, "while on fatigue duty [he] did, with two noncommissioned officers, of said company, visit and drink whiskey at a low hovel, kept by Irish and Negro women." While the court record saw this as "degrading himself in the opinion of his men," it does not specify which aspect of the activity was considered especially degrading.[11]

Col. William S. Fish, 1st Connecticut Cavalry, got himself into deep trouble. He was convicted of fraudulent claims regarding the sale of horses, as well as one instance of misappropriating almost $4,000 in gold bullion. He was also accused of attending "a ball at a public house of prostitution, kept by one Annette Travers, wearing his uniform as an officer," but the Court specified that there was "no criminality in the act, it appearing that it was done by the accused in the discharge of his official duties." Whatever his official duties at a hooker's ball, Colonel Fish's sentence of a year in the penitentiary and a $5,000 fine was approved by Abraham Lincoln.[12]

At a court-martial convened at Atlanta a few weeks before Christmas in 1865, Capt. Dan W. Lyon of Company I, 138th U.S. Colored Troops, was accused of a variety of offenses. On October 21, he had been AWOL all day and around midnight appeared at the office of the provost marshal "in a state of intoxication and in company with a lewd woman." Why Lyon thought the provost marshal would welcome such a visit is unclear, but, with an apparent talent for making the worst of a bad situation, he then struck his newfound female companion twice and, in the presence of the provost marshal, called her a "Goddamned lying bitch."

Two weeks later, while off duty, Captain Lyon approached the police guard of his regiment, cursed them in a drunken frenzy, and tried to seize their weapons. When they declined to give up their muskets, he ordered them arrested and then, distracted by a new thought, wandered off to a camp of "colored refugees," where he encountered Pvt. James Fitzpatrick of A Company, who was in bed with Mrs. Fitzpatrick. Lyon ordered the soldier out of bed and climbed in to take his place, "keeping the woman in bed with him." A few nights later, Lyon took "a colored woman into his tent and had sexual intercourse with her." He was dismissed from the service.[13]

Military life could also be perilous to medical officers. Surgeon William Woodward of the 58th Illinois was approached by Pvt. Charles Franklin of Company D, who was suffering from "a private disease." The regimental pharmacy lacked the proper supplies, so Woodward collected $5 from Franklin and purchased the required medication. The surgeon was accused of "accepting payments for services rendered," since medical care was a free benefit for Federal troops. At the court-martial, Woodward was found not guilty after testifying that he had refunded the money.[14]

On a warm summer afternoon, on the public road near Tullahoma, Tennessee, Lt. Harvey John of the 49th Ohio Volunteers encountered Mrs. Catherine Farmer. What he wanted, she did not. According to the trial transcript, Lieutenant John assaulted her, beat her, and did "forcibly and unlawfully ravish and carnally know Mrs. Farmer, against the will of said Catherine Farmer." The lieutenant was cashiered and sentenced to two years in the penitentiary.[15]

The trial of Lt. Col. William A. Carrie of the 8th Pennsylvania Cavalry produced some contradictory testimony. The principle charge was that in full uniform, he was present "for at least two full hours at a fandango [at] the disreputable dance house of a negro woman and there engaged in drinking and dancing among some of his own soldiers and with negro women." The owner of the house was said to be one Martha Jane Botts. In her testimony, Botts stated that she lived on Twelfth Street in Lynchburg, alone, and was the cook for five gentlemen who took their meals there. Sgt. James McNichols of Company H contradicted her. He saw the colonel "dancing with a yellow woman." Mrs. Botts testified that the colonel was at her home for only a few minutes and not the two hours claimed by others. The Court was not convinced. Colonel Carrie was sentenced to be dismissed from the service.[16]

Hilton Head, South Carolina, is today an elegant destination resort. It felt the same way to Capt. James A. Book of Company A, 72d Pennsylvania Volunteers, during the Civil War. He overstayed his leave by eight days and upon his return told his commanding officer, "Oh, I have been having a gay time. You can put me under arrest. I have been under arrest before and it don't hurt me."

Book's high spirits (or uncontrolled alcoholism) led him deeper into trouble. Several weeks later, about two in the morning, accompanied by his orderly, he rode over to the building housing negro women and their children and demanded entrance. When refused, he fired his revolver through the wall. The terrified inhabitants unbarred the portal, and Book and his orderly led their horses through the dormitory. The general commotion and gunfire created an alarm, and the guard was called out.

At his trial, Captain Book served as his own counsel, created a spirited defense, and managed to lend confusion to almost every issue. (Regarding the dormitory gunfire, Book claimed that there had been "scrabbling noises" in the dormitory and that he was duty-bound to investigate.) He was found guilty on five of the six charges.[17]

The trial of Capt. William H. Newman, Company D, 1st Arkansas Volunteers, was much briefer. He was charged with "publicly cohabitating" with a mulatto girl. Testimony showed that she was his cook, and he was found not guilty.[18]

In the days before penicillin (and precise diagnosis), Mother Nature was less forgiving. Capt. Joseph Bushfield of the 2d Virginia Volunteer Infantry "did at Irontown, Ohio, on the tenth of October, 1862, and at diverse other times during October, have unlawful carnal intercourse with a lewd woman." He was most unlucky in his choice of partner, as he "became diseased with syphilis, or clapp, in consequence of which [he] has been unfit for duty . . . this known to officers and men." The captain was dismissed from the service but probably carried his illness into civilian life.[19]

For many months during the winter of 1862–63, Capt. Levi Bryte of the 3d Virginia Volunteers "frequently and in a public manner visited a house of ill fame outside the picket lines and remained overnight." Although he did this without his commander's permission and in a manner that caused him to neglect his official duties, it was only after several dozen nights away that judicial notice was taken of his nocturnal habits. Whether Lieutenant Bryte was smitten by one young woman in this house near Sutton, Virginia, or by a stable of Old Dominion beauties is unknown. It is recorded that he was dismissed from the service.[20]

The Federal steamboat *Izetta* was the stage for some operatic scenes in the autumn of 1862. Whether the opera was grand or soap can be debated, but the adventures of Lt. Col. Timothy C. Moore of the 34th New Jersey Volunteers are a matter of public record. As the *Izetta* plied her way down the Ohio River, Moore's eye was caught by Elizabeth Klein, the wife of one Cpl. George Klein of the same regiment. The corporal's opinions are not recorded, but his wife seems to have been cooperative in the colonel's efforts to "lie with and have sexual connection with one Elizabeth Klein."

This wild mènage continued for three days, while the paddle wheels churned the river waters. Then Col. William H. Lawrence, commanding the regiment, ordered Mrs. Klein put off the boat. While Lawrence's back was turned, Mrs. Klein departed, but to the stateroom of Lt. John Schwartz, rather than to the banks of the river. The moonstruck Colonel Moore continued to visit Mrs. Klein and created such a rumpus in his new bower that he, Lieutenant Schwartz, and Mrs. Klein were all brought to judicial attention. The colonel was dismissed from the service, but Lincoln, weighing his value to the war effort, restored him to duty.[21]

Felix de Fontaine, a Confederate newspaper correspondent, was pleased to report the wide variety of transgressions noted among Yankee officers. "The commission of atrocious crimes and all sorts of disgraceful offenses by officers, high and low, from colonel to lieutenant, is of daily occurrence." While de Fontaine listed half a dozen different crimes, he took greatest offense at the tendency for Federal officers to "keep company with negresses."[22]

De Fontaine might have been surprised to find that Rebel soldiers and officers could also be flawed. Many Virginia homes opened their doors to Confederate wounded. Capt. Boling Williams received several gifts from his sweethearts/nurses, including some unexpected ones: In the back of his diary are three prescriptions for gonorrhea. Some men from Louisiana married in Virginia, when they already had wives back home. One Louisiana officer was exposed when he wrote to both wives and accidentally switched envelopes.[23]

Henry Harrison Walker, the future Confederate brigadier general, was stationed at Jefferson Barracks in 1856 and wrote about John H. Forney, the future Confederate major general:

> Old Forney was down from Fort Snelling . . . he expressed a wish to shag something. I told him I thought I could gratify him. I had been to see the widow several times and knew exactly how to get in. I told Forney how to act and how to imitate my voice. He goes over, finds a window open, jumps in and undressed himself before the widow woke up. He stayed with her all night, saying as little as possible, while she, told him every secret I had. In the morning she woke up and discovered her mistake. She immediately kicked him out and covered herself up head and ears until he had dressed and gone. This has brought her wrath down on me and she reviles me for all the rascals in the world.[24]

Confederate general Rufus C. Barringer had an illegitimate son by a black slave, Roxana Coleman. This son, Warren C. Coleman, was at one time the wealthiest black man in North Carolina. Beginning as a rag collector, barber, and candy store owner, by 1869, when he was only twenty years old, Mr. Coleman was wealthy enough to pay $600 for a half acre of business land. The general's legitimate son, Paul Barringer, does not mention Warren Coleman in the Barringer family history.[25]

Capt. Henry Snow of the 28th Colored Troops seems to have been dazzled by the trappings of power. In his 1865 court-martial at Cairo, Illinois, it was charged that he did "allow three of said recruits . . . to accompany him to a hat store and purchase and present to him a hat, and immediately afterward, upon their solicitation, did permit them, in charge of a corporal and guard, to visit a house of ill fame." Captain Snow was dismissed from the service.[26]

Brig. Gen. Eleazer A. Paine of the United States Volunteers had a somewhat checkered career. In October 1865, he was brought to trial on twenty-seven different charges, including calling his superior, Maj. Gen. H. W. Halleck, a "God damned coward and a damned rascal." Paine was sentenced to be reprimanded, but the sentence was remitted.[27]

It would not be amiss to include one noncommissioned officer in this catalog of malfeasance. Sgt. James Wheeler of Company J, 2d Battalion, 14th United States Infantry, stationed at Camp Chimborazo, was ordered to turn out his detachment. Wheeler refused. Maj. James Miller ordered the Sergeant placed under "close arrest." At the court-martial, the major was asked what happened next. "I went into my office and found the sergeant sitting on my bunk with his Penis in his hand in the act of committing a nuisance. I ordered him to stop. . . . he refused and I put him out." Pvt. Alias Mondon, another witness, was asked, "did you see the prisoner commit a nuisance?" Mondon replied, "I did. He pissed in the Quarters. . . . he was half-drunk but not staggeringly drunk." Wheeler was reduced to the ranks and fined $10 a month for the duration of his service.[28]

Medical officers also were not immune to misbehavior. Dr. J. W. Jamison, acting assistant surgeon, U.S. Navy, entered the house of Mrs. J. M. Carrow and her niece, Miss Margaret Harrell, and "made proposals to them for sexual intercourse." When they refused, Dr. Jamison "seized hold of Miss Margaret Harrell and attempted by force to carry her into another room to ravish her person." All of this occurred in the jurisdiction of the Sounds of North Carolina in the spring of 1863. A few days later, Capt. Charles Lyon, provost marshal, held a hearing, to which Dr. Jamison was escorted by "Mr. Cushing, Paymaster of the U.S. Steamer *Hunchback*." During the hearing, Dr. Jamison called Captain Lyon a "damned fool" and a "son of a bitch," which did not help his case. The incident was referred to higher authority for discipline.[29]

Another opera buffa is seen in the career of one young officer, whose commission was a gift from Lincoln himself. The officer disgraced himself in a hotel, was the butt of some gentle Lincoln humor, and finally redeemed himself on the battlefield.

In 1861, Lincoln wrote, "Because of his relationship to the late Senator [Stephen] Douglas, I wish James Madison Cutts, Jr., to be a Captain in some part of this new Corps."[30]

Cutts next surfaces in the public record two years later, while serving as acting judge advocate general for the Department of the Ohio. On October 10, 1862, while occupying Room 79 at the Burnet House in Cincinnati, Cutts was struck by the singular beauty of the woman in Room 80. That afternoon he was caught peeping through the keyhole at her and her husband. His embarrassment was not sufficient to prevent a second attempt at voyeurism.

That night, around half past eleven, Cutts noted that the object of his fascination had retired to her room and that her husband was in the corridor below. Taking a suitcase from his room, Cutts moved quietly into the hallway, set his improvised stepladder against the door of Room 80, and climbed gingerly up. As his eyes rose to the height of the transom window, he found his quarry "partly undressed, previous to retiring." His eyes met hers. Her husband appeared in the hallway. "This to the great outrage of the feelings of the lady and her husband and to the great scandal and injury of the service."[31]

At that time, the Swedish minister to the United States was one Count

Piper. On reading a report of the Cutts's trial, Lincoln remarked to John Hay that Cutts "should be elevated to the peerage . . . with the title of Count Peeper," a remarkable double pun.

Cutts had been in trouble at the same time for quarreling with Burnside's aide-de-camp. Lincoln wrote a confidential memo to Cutts:

> Although what I am to say is to be, in form, a reprimand, it is not intended to add a pang to what you have already suffered upon the subject to which it relates. You have too much of life yet before you, and have shown too much of promise as an officer, for your future to be lightly surrendered. You are convicted of two offenses. One of them, not of great enormity, and yet greatly to be avoided, I feel you are in no danger of repeating. The other, you are not so well assured against.

Lincoln concluded with a homily against quarreling, and returned Cutts to duty because of his gallantry in battle.[32]

The case of Capt. Edward McD. Reynolds, U.S. Marine Corps, illustrates 1864 views on morality. A reviewing board had found him "mentally, morally, professionally and physically fit for the performance of all the duties of his office," but there were questions on the morality issue. On return from blockading duty in the South Atlantic, he was admitted to a naval hospital for "dyspepsia caused by excessive use of tobacco and urethritis caused by sexual intercourse." Further testimony showed that while on Pacific duty in 1857, his "moral character was so bad" that his commanding officer declined to introduce him to ladies visiting the ship. Further, while stationed in Mexico, "he was in the habit of going to balls which were not reputable and dancing all night with improper women in his uniform." The investigators further noted that in 1860 his wife had divorced him for adultery. A higher review board, consisting of a rear admiral, a commodore, and a colonel of the marines, found Captain Reynolds morally unfit for service, and Secretary of the Navy Gideon Wells was so annoyed at the opinion of the lower board that he placed all of its members on furlough for three months.[33]

One general seemed intent on saving himself from sexual temptation by marinating his brain in whiskey: "General Meagher is lying in the tent of the chaplain of the 20th, as drunk as a Beast, and has been so since Monday [four days], sending out his servant for liquor and keeping his bed wet and filthy. I have directed Colonel Gates to ship him tomorrow if he does not clear out."[34]

Officers in the Civil War were usually well known to their men and to their community. Millions of soldiers wrote letters home, commenting, among other things, upon their homegrown superiors. An officer's family, preacher, and friends knew much about his behavior. But even with this scrutiny and with all the printed regulations governing good behavior, many strayed far from the path of duty.

Chapter Fourteen

🕊

Generals Nuisance

IN EVERY LIFE, there is opportunity for mischief. In the military world, one of the differences between officers and enlisted men is that the former have greater scope and latitude for their misdeeds and are held, at least by implication, to a higher standard of behavior; thus their transgressions seem more worthy of note. This holds true for general officers, even more than for the lower grades of commissioned officers.

Half a dozen Civil War generals acquired reputations unusual enough to merit examination in the context of this book. They include H. Judson Kilpatrick, Joseph Hooker, Daniel E. Sickles, Benjamin F. Butler, and Edward Johnson.

Kilpatrick graduated from West Point on May 6, 1861, and three days later was appointed captain, 5th New York Volunteers (Duryee's Zouaves). A month later, he was severely wounded at Big Bethel; upon his recovery he was appointed lieutenant colonel, 2d New York Cavalry. In the years that followed, he fought in many battles, was wounded again, and was breveted major general for his services associated with Sherman in Georgia and North Carolina. After the war, he was twice U.S. minister to Chile (1865–68 and 1881). In 1868, he left the Republican party and joined the Democrats in supporting Horace Greeley. His political enemies raised the question of improper conduct during his military years, and the testimony from that investigation, still on record at the National Archives, reads like today's tabloids.

Dr. R. Blacknall of Durham Station, North Carolina, stated under oath: "He came here early in April 1865 and made my house his headquarters. I occupied the west end of the house with my family and General Kilpatrick occupied the east end with a woman who on their first arrival I was informed was Mrs. Kilpatrick. General Estes occupied a room in the center of the house with another woman and I was at first led to believe that these women were respectable but they soon made their appearance in male attire and the one under General Kilpatrick's charge was known as 'Charley' and the one with General Estes was known as 'Frank' and I soon discovered them to be women of dissolute character.

"They were vulgar, rude and indecent, but fitting companions for a man of General Kilpatrick's character and they forced themselves upon my family in a low vulgar manner. The privacy of my family was not respected by them, neither was the wardrobe of my two daughters, they appropriating their dresses and underclothing." Dr. Blacknall was further enraged by Charley and Frank riding about the town dressed "in their indecency."

James H. Miller of Raleigh testified: "I was an officer of the 5th Ohio Cavalry, commanding Company 'L' in General Kilpatrick's command and was well acquainted with the General and his staff. . . . it was generally understood in his command that General Kilpatrick had a woman with him all through the campaign . . . dressed in men's half uniform clothes." Miller went on to say that this woman was with him at the Durham Station headquarters. Later in the campaign, Kilpatrick was accompanied by a woman named Alice, who rode in a closed carriage in Kilpatrick's head-quarters train. The general introduced Alice as a Yankee schoolteacher who had been stranded in the South at the outbreak of hostilities and said that he was conducting her north to safety. Miller noted, "It was the general belief of the command that he carried her with him for purposes less honorable than those alleged by him."

There is a marvelous battle story in Miller's narrative. In North Carolina, at Monroe's Cross Roads, Wade Hampton's sudden dawn attack on Kilpatrick's headquarters (a two-room log cabin) found Alice at home and the General escaping "with nothing on but his pants." Miller himself held the headquarters flag during the two-hour battle and then returned it to the color bearer. In Kilpatrick's official report, the general gives credit to Alice to saving the flag from capture "by concealing it under her garments." Miller concluded by noting that Gen. L. G. Estes would endorse the non-Alice version of that flag rescue and that Alice accompanied Kilpatrick when he departed for Chile in his new role as ambassador.

Five other citizens came forward to make statements about Kilpatrick's sojourn in North Carolina. Mrs. Robert Morris testified that Generals Kilpatrick and Estes were accompanied by women dressed as men, "women of disreputable character and lewd habits; on one occasion they entered her dooryard and in a rude and insulting manner tore from the ground her choice flowers." Mrs. Eugene Eckels confirmed the story of Charley and Frank and the two generals, and described a fifth person in the mènage: "a yellow woman named Molly who was in the family way. . . . she said that General Kilpatrick was the father of her child." Mrs. Eckels noted that when Charley first arrived at Kilpatrick's new headquarters, the general "kissed Charley affectionately . . . and this excited suspicion as their sex."

The next witness, recorded as "Mrs. James Dick (colored)," described Charley: "She had black eyes and black hair and dark complexion," while General Estes's companion Frank had fair skin and light blue eyes. "I have often seen General Kilpatrick in bed with Charley hugged up close. I know that Charley was a woman for I have seen her naked and I have seen her making water and she always sat down to do it." Mrs. Dick also observed the unfortunate Molly doing the washing. "It was ladies under linen and it was in one instance stained. Molly was in the family way and she told me that General Kilpatrick 'done her so' and now was trying to go back on her but she should stick to him and make him take care of the baby, for it was his."

Edmund Hill, a servant of Alexander Eckels, confirmed Mrs. Dick's observations, adding, "I know the white women were women for I have seen them making water and they always let down their pantaloons and squatted down and I also saw the shape of their breasts." Mrs. Leddy Garrett, who served with Edmund Hill, was in close agreement: "I . . . often saw General Kilpatrick in bed with Charley. I know she was a woman for I have seen her naked and no man was ever made like her . . . General Kilpatrick was very fond of Charley and used to lie pretty close to her in bed."

Whatever the purpose of this long-ago testimony, Kilpatrick seems to have survived it, and continued his political career.[1]

Joe Hooker graduated from West Point in 1837, in the same class as Braxton Bragg and Jubal Early, and distinguished himself in the Mexican War: He was breveted captain at the siege of Monterrey, breveted major for his gallantry at the National Bridge, and breveted lieutenant colonel for his actions at Chapultepec. In the Civil War, he further enhanced his military reputation at Yorktown, Williamsburg, Fair Oaks, and Malvern Hill. He was wounded at the Dunker Church, but returned to command the Army of the Potomac, where he threw away his reputation at Chancellorsville. He redeemed himself at the "Battle Above the Clouds" near Chattanooga and finished the war as a major general.

During the American occupation in Mexico City, he was a great favorite with the Spanish ladies, who called him *el capitan hermoso* ("the handsome captain") and *el buen mozo* ("the good boy"). Hooker was a man of strong opinions and never hesitated to inform his Southern colleagues of the wrongness of their views on slavery and states' rights. He lost few opportunities to make a new enemy or irritate an old friend, and during his life many unfortunate words escaped the fence of his teeth. (In 1848, Hooker testified against Winfield Scott, his commander. Thirteen years later, Scott, who had forgotten nothing, blocked Hooker's initial request for a Civil War command. More on that later.)

In 1849, Hooker was assigned to the army post at Sonoma, California. Bored with peacetime military duties, he resigned his commission in 1853. He was well known at the Blue Wing Tavern, just off the Sonoma Plaza, and his patronage is still noted by a bronze plaque. Hooker, unsuccessful as a farmer, went into the firewood business; he obtained an army contract to supply wood at $15 a cord, hired one Peter Albertson to transport the wood to Benicia and to the Presidio, and relaxed at the Blue Wing. In 1854, Albertson sued Hooker for $1,200 in unpaid wages and attached the war hero's fourteen yoke of oxen as security. The judge who heard the case ordered Hooker to pay $802.

Later, James Hallock, the woodcutter, sued Hooker for $295 in unpaid wages. The case was settled out of court. Even with the lawsuits, Hooker did well, as the army paid him $8,775 for the wood delivered.

Shortly after resigning his commission, Hooker signed an IOU for a $485 gambling debt he owed to Joseph Neville, who had, in turn, used the IOU to satisfy a debt that he owed to Thomas Nugent. Nugent sued Hooker, who won his case by pointing out that gambling debts were illegal and therefore uncollectible. This received wide publicity, and it is likely that Hooker's future poker partners played for cash only.

Henry Halleck (Lincoln's future military advisor) and William T. Sherman (future leader of the march through Georgia) were in business in San Francisco in the 1850s. Hooker owed them money, had gathered the amount of his debt, but seems to have gambled it away the day before the payment was due.

When the Civil War came, Hooker wished to go to Washington to plead for a command, but he had not the money for a ticket. A San Francisco friend of his, Billy Chapman, a saloon keeper and faro dealer, gave Hooker $1,000 in cash and enough cigars and whiskey to make his sea voyage pleasant.

In Washington, Winfield Scott delayed Hooker's appointment, and the future "Fighting Joe" was a civilian spectator at the First Battle of Bull Run. A few days later, he arranged an audience with Abraham Lincoln and told the President, "I am a damned sight better General than you, Sir, had on that field." Lincoln, looking for military success rather than modesty, arranged for Hooker's appointment as a brigadier general of United States Volunteers. In the autumn and winter of 1861, he commanded troops in the suburbs of Washington, D.C., and gave his name, unwittingly, to Hooker's Division.[2]

This seems the place to consider Hooker and hookers, i.e., as a term for prostitutes. Twelve authorities illustrate the range of opinions as to whether the general gave his name to the ancient profession. The authoritative 1933 *Oxford English Dictionary* lists thieves, fishing vessels, and Amish as various types of "hookers" but makes no mention of prostitutes. The 1976 *Supplement* to the *OED* lists the word as American slang for prostitute, giving its earliest use as 1845.

William Craigie's 1942 *Dictionary of American English* cites the Corlear's Hook area of New York City, where houses of ill fame were concentrated, catering to the sailors of the busy harbor. Craigie found "hooker" as a term for prostitute in use in 1859.[3] H. L. Mencken was in full agreement with the Corlear's Hook derivation; in the Gen. Joe Hooker origin, he said, "there is no truth whatever."[4]

A University of North Carolina professor has found an 1845 letter written by a student to a classmate, using "hooker" in the sense of prostitute: "If he comes by way of Norfolk, he will find any number of pretty hookers in the Brick Row, not far from French's Hotel."[5]

The 1968 Dictionary of the Underworld, published in London, gives the same derivation as Craigie, and cites the source as Bartlett's Americanisms, published in 1859.

Robert Wilson, editor of *Playboy's Dictionary of Forbidden Words,* derives "hooker" from Old English *hok,* an implement used by thieves to hook and steal items through open windows. Wilson concludes that prostitutes were called hookers because they were also thieves.[6] William and Mary Morris, for their *Dictionary of Word and Phrase Origins* (1971), wrote to the eminent Civil War historian Bruce Catton, who acknowledged that the term had been used even before the Civil War but stated that the district near Constitution Avenue in Washington "became known as Hooker's Division in tribute to the proclivities of General Hooker."[7]

Two other sources are even bolder, if less accurate, in their derivations. Allen Work, in his *Everyday Words from Names of People and Places* (1980), claims that hookers were named for Civil War General "Fighting Joe" Hooker, who arranged such distractions "to bolster the morale of his men."[8] The May 1969 issue of *Avant Garde* magazine attaches its origin to "General Joe Hooker, a handsome figure of a man who, during Civil War days, spent so much time in the red light district of New Orleans that the area became known as 'Hooker's Divisions.'"

The 1979 *Webster's Dictionary of the English Language, Unabridged* gives no prostitute meaning to "hooker." The 1976 *American Heritage Dictionary*—

New College Edition lists prostitute as one of the six meanings of "hooker," but gives no derivation.

Following the adage "where experts differ, the ignorant may choose," I choose to believe that the term "hooker" was well known in everyday male circles as one of many prewar terms for the ancient trade but leapt to prominence with the fortuitous arrival of Joe Hooker himself, his order concentrating the whores in Washington's Murder Bay, and his personal weakness for female charms.

But back to the man himself. After Burnside's disastrous 1862 defeat at Fredericksburg, Hooker set about proposing himself as the new commander of the Army of the Potomac. Postmaster General Montgomery Blair opposed the appointment, citing Hooker's well-known and excessive love of "John Barleycorn."

Lincoln had few illusions about Hooker and, six days after placing him at the head of the Army of the Potomac, wrote him a classic letter of caution: "I believe you to be a brave and skillful soldier . . . you have confidence in yourself . . . you are ambitious, which, within limits, does good rather than harm." Then Lincoln admonished Hooker for his habit of denouncing his colleagues and for his opinion that the country needed a dictator: "Of course, it was not for this but in spite of this that I have given you the command. Only those generals who gain successes can set up Dictators. What I now ask of you is success, and I will risk the Dictatorship."[9]

The Richmond *Dispatch* was less kind than Lincoln and greeted Hooker's appointment with a review of his California days: "he failed in farming and applied himself most industriously to borrowing money . . . and drinking whiskey whenever and wherever he could obtain it."[10]

Another commentary was made by Charles Francis Adams, grandson of John Quincy Adams, proper Bostonian, railroad expert, lawyer, historian, and an officer with the Massachusetts Cavalry, who remarked in his autobiography, "when Hooker was in command . . . the headquarters of the Army of the Potomac was a place no self-respecting man liked to go, and no decent woman could go. It was a combination barroom and brothel."[11]

In September 1864, after Rosecrans's defeat at Chickamauga, Hooker was given command of the newly formed 20th Corps and rushed to Nashville, where he distinguished himself. Others were less impressed; when Gen. Henry W. Slocum was informed that Hooker was to be his new superior, he submitted his resignation, asserting, "My opinion of General Hooker, both as an officer and a gentleman, is too well known to make it necessary for me to refer to it in this communication."[12]

When the commander of the Union Army of Tennessee was killed, Sherman passed over Hooker, who was senior, and selected O. O. Howard in his place. Hooker asked to be relieved of his post; Sherman obliged him and wrote home to his wife, "Howard . . . is a man of mind an intellect. . . . he was a junior Major General to Hooker, who took offense and has gone away. I don't regret it; he is envious, imperious and [a] braggart. Self prevailed with him and knowing him intimately I honestly preferred Howard."[13]

Hooker rarely missed a chance to insult even his most active benefactors. Hooker attended a Union League meeting in September 1864 in Brooklyn. Always popular with the public, he was greeted with a frenzied standing ovation. Lincoln's bid for reelection was only four weeks away, and he very much needed support. The best that Hooker could say on this occasion for the president, who had helped him in every way, was, "and on the whole [Lincoln] has done tolerably well."[14]

In a letter still preserved in the Library of Congress, Henry Halleck wrote to Sherman, "He [Hooker] is most unmeasured in his abuse of me. . . . the funny part of the business is that I had nothing whatever to do with his being relieved [of command] on either occasion . . . and he knows that perfectly well. His animosity arises from another source. He is aware that I know some things about his character and conduct in California and, fearing that I may use that information about him, he seeks to ward off its effect by making it appear that I am his personal enemy."[15]

Gen. George Stoneman, who knew Hooker well in California, tried to analyze his character: "He could play the best game of poker I ever saw until it came to the point when he should go 1,000 better, and then he would flunk." Hooker said that at Chancellorsville, it was neither concussion nor whiskey that had paralyzed him, but loss of confidence in himself, when he alone was responsible.[16]

Hooker was a maze of internal contradictions. His virtues were numerous: He brought spirit, discipline, and sanitation to demoralized divisions, he had personal courage, he even predicted two weeks in advance that Gettysburg would be the site of a great battle.[17]

But on the other hand, his acid tongue, his arrogance and high-handedness, manifested in part by drinking, gambling, and womanizing, diminished his potential for greatness.

Daniel Edgar Sickles, unlike Hooker, was no professional military man but was instead the quintessential political general, a type unknown in the twentieth century. Sickles could exhaust a thesaurus, but brass, cheek, impertinence, gall, chutzpah, flair, presumption, and self-service might be a good start.

He was admitted to the New York Bar at age twenty-one (after studying under Benjamin Franklin Butler, of whom more quite soon), and at age twenty-two was elected to the New York State Legislature. In those days of Tammany Hall, bone-deep corruption, and machine politics, it is certain that Sickles was precocious in the unscrupulous ways of mid-century urban government and that his election was neither a fluke nor a result of any campaign for cleaner politics.[18]

When he was twenty-eight, he married Theresa Bagioli, the seven-teen-year-old daughter of an Italian music teacher. The same year, through political connections, he was appointed secretary of the United States Legation in London, where he served two years before returning to New York and, at age thirty, being elected to the state senate. At Albany, he was entangled in four years of shady deals, bad debts, and marital infidelity. This term of shameless corruption and immorality pre-pared him for his next step: election to Congress.

About two years after settling in Washington, D.C., he discovered that his lovely Theresa (perhaps disenchanted with her husband's numerous affairs) had become the lover of Philip Barton Key, the son of the author of the "Star Spangled Banner." Sickles browbeat Theresa into writing and signing a confession of guilt, armed himself, and in cold blood found and shot Key to death.

At the murder trial, Sickles escaped the gallows by the first American usage of a plea of temporary insanity. Freed by this act of legal acrobatics, in which he introduced his wife's forced confession of adultery into evidence (from whence it was reprinted in every newspaper), Sickles returned home and ostentatiously told his wife he had forgiven her. To his surprise, she did not forgive him; Theresa soon died, most likely of shame and chagrin at her public disgrace.[19] (After all, this was 1858, not 1993.)

Sickles was next in the public eye in 1861, when Lincoln authorized him to raise troops. The Excelsior Brigade, with Sickles as its colonel, went to war. Sickles, doing well for a total amateur, led his troops at Seven Days and Chancellorsville and emerged as a major general.

Gettysburg was different. Although ordered by Meade to occupy the Round Tops, Sickles moved forward into the infamous Peach Orchard, where, in a few hours, half his corps was dead or wounded and Sickles lost his own right leg.[20]

His adventures were not just on the battlefield. Ever the irresponsible bon vivant and raconteur, Sickles told the following story on himself. Lincoln was visiting Sickles's headquarters. Noting the president's melan-choly, Sickles suggested that all the women present should line up and kiss old Abe. They agreed, but none would go first. Sickles addressed Princess Salm-Salm (the wife of one officer) and told her that as she was the youngest and most courageous woman present, she should start the parade. The princess objected that she was too short to kiss so tall a man, but Sickles told her that if she would reach up, Lincoln would surely meet her halfway—and so he did.

That evening, when Abe told his wife, Mary Todd Lincoln, she was not amused, and at a later dinner she snubbed Sickles in spite of the president's attempt to make peace. Lincoln turned to Sickles and remarked, "I am told, General, that you are an extremely religious man." Sickles avowed that he deserved no such credit. Lincoln continued, "I believe that you are not only a great Psalmist, but a Salm-Salmist."[21]

In 1866, now a civilian with a wooden leg, Sickles was appointed military governor of the Carolinas, where he proved to be such a tyrant and vengeful despot that he was removed by Andrew Johnson in 1867. Two years later, utterly unchastened, he arranged his own appointment as ambassador to Spain. After four years of insolent incompetence, in which American-European diplomacy reached a new low, Sickles resigned—to devote himself full-time to a torrid love affair with Isabella II, queen of Spain!

Apparently, being a queen did not involve much day-to-day work; Isabella and Sickles lived openly together in Paris, where he schemed to put her son, Alfonso (only one of many claimants), on the throne. When Isabella returned to Spain, Sickles remained behind in Paris and occupied himself with a fresh project: hatching a Tammany Hall–style plot to end the French Republic and place his friend, Louis Philippe Albert, on the throne vacated by Napoleon III. Failing in this, and in a later Spanish marriage, Sickles returned to New York, where he was appointed chairman of the New York State Monuments Commission. He headed the commission for twenty-six years, until he was removed for graft, theft, and corruption. This dark picture of arrogance, meddling, dalliance, thievery, and conspiracy is relieved by two bright spots: Sickles secured the land for New York's Central Park and that for Gettysburg National Monument.[22] Before the final bar of justice, where men's hearts are weighed, these two accomplishments may help counterbalance his manic proclivities for sexual and political intrigue.

Benjamin Franklin Butler, military governor of New Orleans in 1862, is remembered by Southerners as "Beast Butler." How did he gain such a title?

Butler was admitted to the Massachusetts Bar in 1840. His skills as an attorney and as an investor brought him sufficient wealth so that he maintained three homes and owned the cup-winning yacht *America*.

He was intensely involved in politics most of his life and served in both houses of the Massachusetts Legislature, as well as in the Congress, where he played a leading role in the attempt to impeach Andrew Johnson. He was defeated in three bids for the governorship of Massachusetts but was elected on his fourth try. He was always outspoken and aroused endless animosity.[23]

Although frequently accused of graft and corruption, Butler was never proved to be guilty of anything, although it is unclear whether this was from cleverness or innocence. On May 1, 1862, the city of New Orleans surrendered to Union forces, and Butler entered the city on horseback as its new chief executive. In his six-month tenure, he improved sanitation (yellow fever was a major problem) and preserved the peace, but his hanging of William Mumford (for pulling down the United States flag) and his seizure of $800,000 in gold bullion, left with the French consul, brought international denunciation. He is remembered best, however, for his Order No. 28.

Butler confronted a problem. The men of New Orleans, even though they far outnumbered the Yankees, offered no resistance to the occupation— but the women were a different matter.

Butler usually rode out with no guard, only an orderly. A few days after his arrival, as he passed a balcony, the five women above pirouetted, raising the hems of their skirts, and presenting their nether parts to his gaze. He remarked loudly, "Those women evidently know which end of them looks the best." When Flag Officer David Farragut (remembered for his quote, "Damn the torpedoes, full speed ahead") visited the city as Butler's guest, a chamber pot full of urine was emptied, from an upper floor, onto the admiral's head by one of the secessionist ladies of New Orleans. The following day, a third Union officer, on his way to church, received a face full of spit, delivered by yet another well-dressed secessionist female.

Butler knew that arresting or physically punishing the women would result in a riot or insurrection, which he had not the troops to suppress. He wanted to protect himself and his men from insult, without giving the ill-mannered women an opportunity for martyrdom. Any order for maintaining the peace would need to be self-executing. On May 15, 1862, he had published the following order:

> As the officers and soldiers of the United States have been sub-
> ject to repeated insults from the women (calling themselves
> ladies) of New Orleans, in return for the most scrupulous non-
> interference and courtesy on our part, it is ordered that hereafter,
> when any female shall, by word, gesture or movement, insult or
> show contempt for any officer or soldier of the United States, she
> shall be regarded and held liable to be treated as a woman of the
> town, plying her avocation.

Butler's staff was concerned that the order would stir up violence and further resistance, but the old politician's instincts were true; there were no further incidents. Butler noted in his autobiography that the ladies behaved themselves because they did not want to be considered whores and the whores behaved themselves because they wished to be considered ladies.

Without a single shot fired or arrest made, Butler restored the peace. The reader may judge for himself or herself whether Butler's order was the work of a beast or of a practical and humane wartime administrator.[24]

Another controversial general was Edward Johnson, who graduated from West Point in 1838. He distinguished himself so well in the Mexican War that his home state of Virginia presented him with an engraved sword. After secession, he resigned from the U.S. Army and accepted appointment as colonel of the 12th Georgia Volunteers.

He was wounded in the leg at McDowell, Virginia, in 1862 and spent a year in Richmond recuperating. Since the unmarried Johnson had both money and friends in the Confederate capital, he had ample means for a busy social life.

He seems to have commanded attention by his strong personality and loud voice, rather than by physical good looks: He aided his crippled gait by use of a long staff (which later led his men to dub him "Old Club"), he winked without ceasing because of a disorder of one eye, and to literally top it all off, his skull was cone-shaped in layers, described by Mary Chesnut as resembling an antique beehive, or the Pope's tiara. Between his three-tiered skull and his gimpy leg was a bulky, bearlike body that projected a powerful roar, a voice that penetrated every corner of a room.

His locomotive energy propelled him to hundreds of social events in his convalescent year, and at each one he shouted sweet nothings into the ears of many women, proposing marriage to one in a voice that could be heard across the room, and a few days later booming his impassioned interest to another girl, in this case his young cousin.

"Old Club" charmed some women by sheer, unrelenting force of personality, by his enormous presence; his stentorian speech made it seem that he filled not only his ample uniform but whatever space surrounded him.

Whether his many proposals of marriage were rejected or never seriously meant is unknown, but when "Stonewall" Jackson called Johnson to command a division of the Army of Northern Virginia, "Old Club," the leviathan lover, was still unmarried. When he died at age fifty-seven, nine years after the war, his body lay in state in the state capitol, with flags at half mast. There was no widow to mourn him; the man of 10,000 bellowed sweet nothings and 1,000 proposals had never had a bride.[25]

The Lord's Prayer asks not only that we be delivered from evil, but that we should not be led into temptation. One of the most remarkable apostles of temptation in the Civil War was Miss Anna E. Jones, a young woman who had an impact on the lives of half a dozen generals.

Annie was born in Cambridge, Massachusetts, in 1844. When her parents died, a conservative minister and his wife became her guardians. In 1861, when she was seventeen, she left home against her guardians' wishes and went to Washington, D.C., to be a nurse. Not surprisingly, she was refused because of her age. In her sworn statement, made in March 1864, she said:

> I then procured a pass from General [John E.] Wool to visit the different camps in and around Baltimore. I had no particular object or business in the Army, but went out of curiosity. I spent some months in this way. In the various camps, I was furnished by the commanding officer with a tent and sometimes occupied quarters with the officers.

She claimed that in the autumn of 1862, she spent time as a guest of Gen. Franz Sigel at his headquarters near Fairfax Court House. Her next host was General Stahl, from whence she "joined General Kilpatrick's command and went to the front as a friend and companion of General Custer." Annie claimed that Kilpatrick became jealous of Custer's attention to her and charged her with being a Rebel spy.

Lt. Charles Shepard was assigned to investigate the espionage charge and prepared a voluminous report, dated February 2, 1863. Shepard ascertained that Annie had come to Virginia with the 135th Regiment of New York Volunteers as a Daughter of the Regiment. Several of the officers had given her the countersign, which enabled her to pass freely through the guardposts. The report concluded that the spy charge was baseless and had originated in a letter penned by a jealous female rival. In a post-script, Shepard described his investigation as "very amusing."

Annie's penchant for daring living continued, however, and September 1863 found her locked in Old Capitol Prison, where she soon "became intimately acquainted with Captain Mix, Mr. John S. Lockwood, the Superintendent Clerk and others. . . . . in consequence of Mr. Lockwood's intimacy with me . . . Mr. Ward discharged him."

Annie was released from prison after giving her word that she would stay away from Virginia and the District of Columbia, but within three weeks she was back, wangled a pass from a Major Wybert of the Treasury Department, and was being stopped by sentries who recognized her from previous escapades. Her new home in Washington was Mrs. McCormick's boarding house, a hotbed of secession sympathizers. After a brief stay, Annie swindled the landlady out of her board and departed for Boston with Mrs. McCormick's bonnet.

Annie filed an accusation against Mr. William Wood, of the prison, implying that he had given her money in exchange for sexual favors. He replied that she had arrived at prison in rags, having been "camping with a regiment," and out of his compassion, "she received $50 . . . for the purpose of obtaining a new and clean outfit."

Annie's ability to instigate investigations is seen in Gen. George Custer's rebuttal to her accusation, written in March 1864, two years after he met her: "She remained at my headquarters until she could ascertain whether her services were required at any of the hospitals. . . . a general order was issued . . . prohibiting all females from accompanying the army." At this time Custer sent her away, but three weeks later, she reappeared, "under an escort furnished by Major General Warren." Annie asked to visit the front-line fortifications, but Custer sent her away again. His report concluded that "Her whole object and purpose in being with the army seemed to be to distinguish herself by some deed of daring; in this respect alone she seemed to be insane. Her claim of intimacy with me and General Kilpatrick is simply untrue."

In June 1864, she wrote to Abraham Lincoln, claiming "I have never violated my parole," and stating, "I am an orphan and an unprotected girl . . . the victim of the fiendish malice of . . . the Superintendent of Capitol Prison and of Colonel [Lafayette] Baker."

In April 1865, the judge advocate general of Massachusetts wrote to Secretary of War Edwin Stanton that Annie must be kept out of the hands of Fernando Wood: "We were unwilling that she should be used as a political tool . . . in last fall's campaign and left to commence [law]suits under the direction of her new advisers."

Here is a woman, in actual fact still a girl, who managed to involve herself with six generals, not to mention the lesser ranks and various civilian functionaries, many of whom were hard put to defend themselves or had their careers ruined. What was this phenomenon?

What contemporary terms best describe this Annie? Liberated woman? Pathological liar? Feminist patriot? Borderline personality? Clever double agent? Sexual Munchausen's syndrome? Whatever the reality of Annie's inner life, she left a four-year trail of officers who seemed to be no gentlemen.[26]

Gen. "Stonewall" Jackson had a well-deserved reputation for piety and moral conservatism, but even he may have had weaknesses of the flesh, as shown in this note attributed to Gen. Ezra A. Carman:

Stonewall Jackson was not a youthful saint; he was fond of horse races and has his full share of the hot blood and indiscretions of youth. It is known and not denied by those conversant with the facts that he was the father of an illegitimate child. Major [Jedediah] Hotchkiss (May 14, 1895) informed me that this was known to Jackson's military family among whom the matter was frequently discussed. When a cadet at West Point and on a visit to his home he seduced a young girl at or near Beverly and the result was a child, which Jackson acknowledged and to which he frequently made presents and sent money. The late Asher [Waterman] Harman also confirmed this and had knowledge of the fact before the war. Dr. [Robert Lewis] Dabney when hunting material for his life of Jackson was horrified to learn this fact and utterly refused to believe it.[27]

Col. Henry W. Brown of the 3d New Jersey Volunteers never did receive the brigadier general's star he long desired, but he seems worth including here in this brief roster of picaresque officers.

Henry's military career began with a five-year hitch as an enlisted man (1839–44), with the 4th U.S. Artillery. In the following eight years, he moved three times, twice opening a candle factory, and in 1852, he went to California, where he went broke digging for gold.

His fortunes seemed rescued by the coming of war, and in late 1861, he was already a lieutenant colonel of the Volunteers. By the next year, he was a full colonel. When his brigade chief, Brig. Gen. George Taylor, was killed at Manassas, Brown was wounded in the pelvis. When he recovered, he was even more severely wounded at Spotsylvania and returned home on a stretcher, bitter and irritable.

In the domestic world of Henry Brown, he started life as Henry Barnes, but changed his name when he abandoned his first wife, Susan, and enlisted in the U.S. Artillery. Around 1843, he began to live with Rebecca Pierson, a widow with three children. In spite of Henry's frequent brutality, destructive rages, and economic instability, Rebecca and Henry stayed together for twenty-six years. After the breakup in 1869, Henry disappeared and went to his first wife, still the "Widow" Barnes. She wouldn't let him in the door; after all, he had been gone for thirty years.

In 1873, passing himself off as twelve years younger than his real age (quite a feat for a man with a bullet hole through his pelvis and a second bullet hole through one thigh), he married twenty-five-year-old Marion J. Smith, who soon presented him with three children. When Henry filed for a pension, Susan obliged him by dying, but Rebecca and Marion both made claims upon his pension, not only while he lived, but also after his death and well into the next century, a source of endless confusion for the Federal pension authorities.[28]

Also worth examining here is Clara A., whose diary was described by Robert W. Waitt. She was born in Richmond in 1848 and entered the profession of prostitution at age fourteen. During the war, her one-woman establishment was in Locust Alley, near the Ballard and Exchange Hotels. She always operated alone, having no pimp, partner, or employee, and catered only to the carriage trade, a tribute to her unique talents. At age forty, she married well and helped found one of the South's leading department stores. The entries in her journal might shed light on some of the military figures of the day, if her cryptic character descriptions could be connected with known historical persons.

> General Limpy, the food fop—he must do the undressing. Shoes, too.
>
> Big brass, big belly. Since my rule, he brings only Yankee money. Wonder where he gets it. Wonder what old sourface would say if he knew one of his plate-lickers had so much Yankee money.
>
> The Maryland Governor? Do it bending over, bark sometimes.
>
> Bubblehead says the war will soon be over. Says Grant knows what they talk about before their own generals. Says there are spies everywhere. I'll bet big belly is one. Says one more push at Williamsburg Road or Petersburg and I will be servicing Grant or Meade. I wonder what a Yankee will feel like?
>
> Rednose Mayo had some of his bully police break in 7 houses around the corner last night. I sent $50 in metal this morning. Let them come *here*!
>
> Four big generals last night came together. Red beard really has red hair all over. They brought two more barrels of wine and twenty blankets. Must sell some of the blankets. Have too many.
>
> Redbeard brought the hero. I wondered why he came here, when he could get all he wanted free. All he can do is play.
>
> Christ! The praying general was brought in today by Preacher H. He is rough and brutal. After I serviced him, he dropped to his knees and asked God to forgive me for my sins![29]

Clara's diary entries for November 16, 18, 21, and 22, 1863, mention sexual services to a wounded hero general. The November 17, 1863 Richmond *Examiner* reported that Lt. Gen. John B. Hood (wounded September 20, 1863, at Chickamauga) was in Richmond "enjoying all the hospitalities that the social circle of his entertainers can bestow.[30]

A further intriguing footnote to the sexual history of the war is the recent discovery that the buildings on Locust Alley, the street favored by the top courtesans, were owned by Miss Elizabeth Van Lew, the leading agent in the Union espionage ring organized by Thomas McNiven.[31]

Clara's remarkable, if fragmentary, journal hints at the vast subterranean life, now lost to history, that seems to have existed during the War Between the States and was extirpated by three generations of censors, leaving only a two-dimensional picture of that era, a pale, shadowy, diaphanous ghost of the robust reality that was shared by some men of all ranks, from the newest recruit to the most exalted general.

Chapter Fifteen

૨ે

Clerical Error

SINS OF THE FLESH are common enough among the laity, and excite little public comment, but when such sins are committed by the guardians of public morality, by those persons whose profession it is to regulate and denounce carnality, then whole new vistas open up.

In the recent past, television evangelists have been especially in the public eye for trysting with prostitutes and fiddling with church secretaries. The television news cameras and the resourceful photographers of the tabloids have brought us, in living color, men of the cloth scuttling out of seedy motels, struggling with their zippers, and wronged women naming names, flanked by their attorneys and press agents. In this sordid business, the only thing that is truly new is the availability of mass communication.

The urges, lusts, and infatuations are as old as history. Each era has had its fallen angels; in the time of the Civil War the champion of indiscretion may well have been the Very Reverend James Cook Richmond, priest of the Protestant Episcopal Church and chaplain to the 2d Wisconsin Regiment of Infantry Volunteers.

Richmond's beginnings were conventional enough. He was born in Providence, Rhode Island, in 1808 and graduated from Harvard in 1828. Like many middle-class sons, he went to Europe for further study, in this case to Gottingen and Halle, in what is now Germany. In 1833 he was ordained priest; over the next twenty-eight years, he was a missionary in Maine and Illinois, held pastorates in several churches, and traveled extensively in Europe. The Muses called him frequently, and he penned at least three works, "A Visit to Iona in 1846," "A Midsummer Day Dream," and the first canto of an epic poem entitled "Meta-Comet." As we will see, his urge to write caused him to be remembered in the War Between the States, but probably not in the way he had intended.

When the great conflict opened, Richmond was age fifty-three;
with the 2d Wisconsin he marched off to war. Two years later, for reasons
as yet unclear, Chaplain Richmond was not with his regiment but was
living in Washington, D.C., where he had become infatuated with Miss
Rosa Bielaski, a young copyist (typewriters were not yet invented) who
worked in the Treasury Building. In April and May 1863, his increasingly
disturbed and apparently unwelcome letters to Miss Bielaski form a
remarkable record of a mind obsessed.

> April 4, 1863—*For two eyes and one heart only.*
> My own dearest darling Rosa,
>   You have made me perfectly happy by your affectionate
> acceptance of my devoted love and by the modest and tender
> manner in which you receive the offering of a heart which has
> been yours from the moment when my eyes, with astonishment
> and rapture, fell upon your qualities and I feasted my soul on
> your charms and physical perfection.
>   I thought your eyes the brightest and most tender, resembling
> both lightning and fire, your carriage most majestic and graceful
> . . . your countenance beaming with intelligence and modest
> love . . . your bosoms and your lovely body . . . perfectly pro-
> portioned . . . great round mountains of delight . . . rising out
> of the odoriferous Valley of Cashmere.
>   I am satisfied that your pouting lips, your twin hillocks
> with their rosy blossoms, your majestic snowy mountains
> [here the chaplain's fascination with her buttocks first appears]
> with their Assantic Dell and the sweet hairy valley between
> your perfect legs . . . shall I one day possess them? The Prince
> of Love, of which I spoke yesterday, alluding to the "ramrod
> and ballocks," even now larger, stiff and rising at the thought.
>   1. This is his small state in quiet rest [a drawing of a limp
> phallus appears]. 2. This is his state in your presence, I may say
> his Roseate state [there is a drawing of a tumescent phallus
> labeled "9 inches long"]. 3. This is the state he longs for—the
> delight of Rose and her lover is here too intense for expression
> [drawing of coitus]. Prick now nearly out of sight.

Three weeks later, Richmond's conviction that Rosa loved him seems
to have grown. He was sleeping less and less and on April 29 spent most
of the night in furious composition, his prose speckled with bits of verse.

> Midnight. In bed. Oh, my sweetest, infinitely, ineffably beloved
> darling Rose, am I not made the happiest man this night from

the most wretched? O Rose, am I not in thy tender love in ten thousand times ten thousand Paradises? Rosa loves me! (O thanks to God!) Rosa said the breach had made her sick. O the delightful and delicious darling. This morning I had no Rose and the world was empty. Tonight, I know that Rosa positively loves me. You need to hide it, my dear, sweet, snowy sweet—you love me, even me. And this my joy that such a maiden—the sweetest damsel that ever offered me her love—that she should love me! But I dare trust myself no further now for I am undressed and in bed, and my body begins to grow unruly and furious that I cannot here, now, tonight, feast upon your glowing charms.

One in the morning. It is useless, dear Rose. I put my light out and attempted to sleep—but in vain. The image of your charms has prevailed and I have once more lighted my light to write, as well as think of thee, sweet Mon-Rose in this very bed, with me alone. What a bliss to think of! And now I wish to correct some expression in the poem I gave you and carry it further. You remember I had described the coral-tipped hillocks in front and the great snowy mountains in the rear of your array of charms.

The expressive word which describes fully the *gushing* of love, is that very word. And now I think of it there another word most expressive . . . I do not like to omit one of those epithets which much pleased you in that part of the poem which I read to you on the walk, when I told you that this talk of Ramrod and "bullocks" . . . what the men call "bollocks," i.e. the two balls at the foot of—you remember I mentioned this at the time I read you the descriptions of your *Mighty Mountains* of which I confess I am a little proud, both of the mountains as mine, and the poetic description: Rich, large, round, white divinely fair.

My Rosa's mountains grandly are. Now I want to make the whole stanza read as below, and I think I will set it to music and dedicate it to you and it certainly will be popular. Thus: New Music: Some thoughts on the charms of Miss Bielaski— dedicated humbly and piously by her humble admirer to Miss Rosa Bielaski . . . it almost makes a man's mouth water to read it.

Dearest Rosa, it makes my mouth water, I hope my head will soon be between thy mountains, moving in adoration, that my lips there between your marble but warm columns be allowed to meet your middle bearded lips . . . in infinite kisses where the doors are more fragrant and divine than the per-fumes of Damascus. I would give more for one smack there, even for one prolonged smell of the Odors of Rose than for all the proud Attar of Roses.

> There, far below, great mountains rise,
> More white than driven snow.
> Twice blest who here may feast his eyes,
> Or on those mountains go.
> Rich, gushing, round, O maddening fair,
> My Rosa's juicy mountains are.

I think the "gushing" is fine and expressive. I have seen fatter girls with fatter cheeks, and therefore with fatter mountains than yours. Though I have often observed the great size of yours, without the keep of crinoline and I think there is not a finer proportioned a pair of Joy Hills in the whole city. Blest experience will soon convince me of the truth of my thoughts . . . I see in my mind's eye, rather my heart's eye, the two hills, the dear back above them, long, fair, dimpled (women have a dimple in the center, just where the two hills taper into the waist) and gently and gracefully growing less.

If you descend, they grow greater until they fairly bulge with delight—a man madly eyes everything, and rushing to the sweet encounter of love, insanely and furiously thrusts his hand and his head and his nose and his lips and his hi-diddle-dee—what am I saying? Well yes, his ++++ into Rosa's ++++ . . . Well, Rosa, dear, I must stop or I might go too far into ++++ *difficulty*: though I suppose it goes easy enough by this time . . . for my part I don't like tight fits or hard work or new undertakings, what the poets would call Virgin Enterprises.

"Fragments of verses on the charms of Miss Rosa Bielaski—On Rosa's Twin Forts:

> Fair, soft, chaste hillocks rise,
> And heave with rapture's sighs,
> Beneath the hazel eyes.
> On the tops are coral fires,
> The beacons of all sweet desires.

Note—written while undressed in bed and sheet thrown off. I have touched the verse with the head of the Prince of Love, a lovely dwarf only nine inches in height!

Thursday morning, six o'clock, in bed. I wake from dreams of my Rose, again to think of Rose . . . I met thy infinite sweetness yesterday. My hours and minutes have been nothing but *roses*. There is one word to express thy charms . . . that part in which I should love to dwell longest, I ever *mount* so high and ascend the mountain not yet descended—for you know, dear Rose, the Jungfrau (i.e., virgin) Mountain in Switzerland, is so

called because no one has ascended her. So I poetically fancy
that the two greater mountains in thy rear (not to say the twin
hillocks with coral tips in the front) of my Rose are untrod by
man. I really care nothing for the footsteps of those who have
gone before, or even several men have been on thy great mountains of joy [Richmond seems unaware of the potential for insult
here] provided absolutely and strictly that hereafter, my private
property Rose no man but me shall touch them again.

Following this last letter, things seem to go downhill. His ensuing letters
are shorter, and the handwriting is ever more frantic and scratchlike. On
May 1 he asks to see her "on matters of importance" and to give her
more poetry. He begs her to meet him at four in the afternoon "at the
open gate south of Treasury." Six days later, he writes on a smaller sheet
of paper that he must meet her, but the details are lost in a desperate and
indecipherable scrawl.

Then follows an undated message on a very small piece of paper, in
which a note of threat appears: "Miss Bielaski, if you wish, I will send a
copy of this letter to your mother. If you prefer any other course . . . I am
waiting at the entrance to the grounds south of the Treasury."

On May 10, 1863, an official of the Office of Internal Revenue,
Treasury Department, sent a memo to the Secretary of War: "A certain
Mr. Richmond, a chaplain in the Army, has annoyed one of the ladies
engaged as a copyist in this office. His behavior has been very scandalous: a
part of the proof of which I send herewith. I have no doubt that he is insane."

On May 16, a Mr. J. Hereford submitted his investigation of the
matter. Hereford observed Richmond passing notes to the Treasury mes-
sengers and arranged for Superintendent William B. Webb of the Metropolitan Police to arrest Richmond. At the station, Richmond was found
to have several letters in his possession and admitted writing them, "but in
extenuation stated that he was partially insane or that God in His infinite
wisdom had deprived him of reason at the time that he wrote them."

The Reverend Mr. Jackson at the Army Hospital told Hereford that
he knew Richmond to be "a really wicked, lewd man and probably
insane" and recommended dismissal from the Army and placement in
"an Insane Asylum."

If Richmond had gone to a psychiatric hospital today he would
probably have been diagnosed as bipolar, manic type or as having neuro-
syphilis or, less likely, a temporal lobe disorder. But no such facilities or
knowledge existed then. As it was, he agreed to leave Washington, D.C.,
and soon did.[1]

In a truly remarkable example of self-deception and two-mindedness (perhaps even hypocrisy), the very week he was packing his belongings to leave Washington in disgrace, the Reverend Richmond made one final political appearance: as the chaplain of the "One-legged Brigade," convalescent veterans at St. Elizabeth's Hospital. When this group visited the White House to meet with the president on May 22, 1863, Richmond was their spokesman. He alluded to his work in "driving the devil out of Washington." Lincoln replied that he looked forward to the Evil One being brought to the White House on his stumps, incapable of further rebellion.[2]

Three years after his departure from Washington, D.C., the Reverend Richmond was in the public eye one final time, the victim of murder on July 20, 1866. Richmond then owned a farm near Poughkeepsie, New York, and had a sharecropper named Richard Lewis. The Lewis family, according to the *Poughkeepsie Daily Eagle,* "bore a bad character," and there had been a lawsuit between Richmond and Lewis. Some of the difficulty may be reflected in Richmond's continuing eccentricity:

> He was one of the best educated and most talented . . . men we ever met with, although his peculiar religious views and his eccentricities caused him to be looked upon as insane by many persons, and he was actually an inmate of an asylum once or twice. . . . his religious views caused him considerable trouble at several places where he preached and for some time before his death he only occupied the pulpit occasionally, preaching also at times in public halls and in the open air.

The nature of the final problem was revealed in testimony. Mr. Lewis was heard to remark, "Now I am going up to ask Mr. Richmond what he meant by calling my mother and sister all the black strumpets and whores he could turn his tongue to." He then struck the former chaplain a terrific blow on the left side of the face, which ended his life. One witness testified that James Lewis, Richard's father, said, "Give it to him this time for you will have to pay for it; give it to him for he hasn't got half enough."[3]

Looking back over Richmond's life, his mental problems took the form often seen in religious professionals: extreme ambivalence, an unhealthy fascination mixed with fanatic opposition. His sexual obsession with the Treasury secretary and his denunciation of Mrs. Lewis's morals seem to be two sides of the same coin.

South of the Mason-Dixon line, another man of the cloth had stepped over the line of propriety. This miscreant had been a guest at one of the great plantation houses in Georgia, Montevideo. The pillared, white-painted mansion was the family seat of the Reverend Doctor Charles Colcock Jones, whose rich plantation at Maybank gave him, his ancestors, and his heirs the leisure to write the 1,200 pages of letters now preserved at Tulane University. The Joneses were community leaders in Liberty County, dedicated Christians, educated and literate gentry—and absolutely convinced of the correctness of slavery. The Reverend Doctor also had little use for Yankees, whom he described as "violators of public and private peace and happiness, despisers of law, justice, integrity, and truth, and scoffers at the great law of the Living God."

The alleged offender in this story was the Reverend William Slates Lee, who was a house guest at Montevideo from July through September 1860; the purpose of his stay was to make a copy of a church history previously prepared by Dr. Jones. Reverend Lee appeared to have impeccable credentials: He was the son of a highly esteemed minister of South Carolina, he was married (his wife was in the North for health reasons), he was a prominent member of the Presbyterian church in Columbus, Georgia, and he was the superintendent of the Sunday school, president of the Young Men's Christian Association, and principal of a high school for young ladies.

On Monday, August 26, 1861, eleven months after Reverend Lee's departure from Montevideo, Dr. Jones wrote to him. After a flowery first paragraph in which he cited Lee's credentials and virtues, Dr. Jones came to the heart of the matter.

> You were right under my roof but a short time before you debauched a young Negro girl—a seamstress, and one of our chambermaids. And you continued your base connections with this Negro woman week after week until your took your final leave! Of the hundred of men of all classes and conditions and professions—men of the church and men of the world, married and unmarried—who have been guests in my house for days, weeks, months, and some for years, you, sir, are the only man who has ever dared to offer to me personally and to my family and to my neighbors so vile and so infamous an insult. You are the only man who has ever dared to debauch my family servants—it being the only instance that has occurred— and to defile my dwelling with your adulterous and obscene pollutions. Had you been detected, I should have driven you instantly out of the house and off the premises, with all the accompanying disgrace which you merited; and I regret that the law affords me no redress under so serious an indignity and injury.

The proof of your criminality is of so clear a character as to remove all doubts. There is the free, unconstrained confession of the Negro woman herself in full detail; there is the correspondence between the time of your connection with her and the birth of the child—a mulatto, now some time born; and there is the resemblance to you beyond mistake. In this last proof I do not rely upon my own convictions. I have submitted the child to the inspection of three gentlemen in the county who know you well personally and are familiarly acquainted with your countenance and physiognomy, and they without hesitation declare its resemblance to you to be as striking as possible. And all who have seen it are of the same opinion. The evidence is amply sufficient to warrant the submission of the case to the session of the Columbus church for action.

And now, sir, what are your former Christian friends to think of you? You have sinned under the most forbidding and aggravating circumstances, and it is difficult to conceive of a more degrading and hypocritical course of wickedness and folly, or one which argues a greater destitution of principle or more callousness of conscience! I never have been more deceived in a man in all my life. How have you wounded the Saviour, and brought disgrace upon religion, and given occasion for the ungodly to triumph! What an injury you have done to the soul of the poor Negro! What disgrace and ruin of character have you brought on yourself! I pity you, and try to pray for your redemption. You know well what your duty is toward God and man, and I hope you may find grace to perform it.

I voluntarily offered you my name on your school circular. I request you take it off. You have betrayed my confidence and injured me grievously, and I cannot look upon you as I once did nor hold any further intercourse with you.

On the twenty-fourth of the following month, Dr. Jones received a reply from two of the elders of the Presbyterian church in Columbus, John Johnson and A. G. Redd. Reverend Lee had shown them Dr. Jones's letter. Johnson and Redd questioned the evidence cited in Jones's letter. They accepted that a mulatto child had been conceived at the time of Lee's Montevideo sojourn, but they raised question about the reliability of any mother's claim of paternity, and even more question about the reliability of facial features of a newborn. They noted that the slave woman was doubtless instructed in morals and religion—but so was the accused. They note their legal advisors' opinion that in bastardy cases the woman usually conceals the true father. Johnson and Redd noted that the woman gave no alarm and could not have been offered a promise of marriage both because she was a slave and because Lee was already married. The letter concludes with a plea for additional evidence.

Dr. Jones replied October 16, noting their arguments and finding them empty or irrelevant. Of course there could have been no promise of marriage, "no contracts of marriage obtain between whites and blacks." The issue of marriage was a nonissue. As to character, the parties were both of "good character," so one's word was as good as the other's. The resemblance of children to their parents was *a law of nature* and not to be denied. Jones suggested that age and social station gave Lee an advantage over the slave girl, which overcame her moral training.

A more telling rebuttal in Dr. Jones's letter came with the story of a second black girl, this one in the village where Mr. Lee taught school. She charged Lee with fathering the child she carried. He denied the charge and urged that she be punished, which she was. (The nature of the punishment was not mentioned.) When the child was born it was mulatto. Jones noted that even "under punishment" the girl insisted on Lee's paternity. Lee was acquitted by the trustees of the school.

Jones concluded with the remark that if his servant had been white, any court of justice would have convicted Lee. He urged the elders to "preserve the purity and character of Christ's Church, which He has bought with His own Blood."

John Johnson, session clerk, replied on November 18, enclosing a sworn statement of innocence, signed by Lee, and asked Jones if he would act as prosecutor or whether, in Jones's opinion, the church session should take action.

In the final letter of this exchange, Jones replied on Christmas Day, 1861. With barely concealed impatience, he pointed out that a sworn statement of innocence is no more conclusive than any other claim of innocence, and that evidence is more reliable than any assertion of the accused. Since he was not a member of their church, he thought it quite improper for him to respond to their request that he advise them what to do; he did suggest that the first six chapters of the Presbyterian book of discipline could give them all the guidance that they needed.[4]

There the matter rested, at least as reflected in the papers of the Jones family. Whether Reverend Lee was convicted of this crime or others, in this world or in the next, is unknown.

Chapter Sixteen

⁊

Love

IN THE PRECEDING CHAPTERS, the operant word has been "lust," and rape, adultery, passion, seduction, and prostitution have been the dominant themes. But another four-letter word is "love," and it would unfair, it would be unbalanced to make no mention of it.

The best minds of our literary heritage have tried to capture love, to name it, to identify it, and it would be futile to make any attempt to rival them. But it would not be futile to note that in war, perhaps even more than in peacetime, the emotions that include compassion, tenderness, affection, warm regard, and sympathy are much in evidence, and it would be remiss not to touch upon them now.

The nation's authority on Civil War love letters may be Dr. Susan Cooper of the National Archives. During eleven years of research on other subjects, she has unearthed over 100 letters by men and women who, long ago, poured out their hearts in words meant only for each other. Time and chance have let us share their sentiments.

Four of these letters come from the dead letter file of the prisoner of war camp at Point Lookout, Maryland. This first excerpt is from a letter intended for Stephen Daniel: "May 16th, 1885. My dear husband, You may imagine how great has been my anxiety and what a dreadful state of suspense I have been in for the past six weeks, not having heard from you. . . . we are all well and getting on as well as could be expected, in the absence of one whose presence is so essential to my happiness. . . . how long seems each day as it brings no tidings from my beloved."

On June 19, 1865, Sallie (whose last name is unrecorded) wrote to John: "I looked for you home yesterday but was sadly disappointed. Boatload after boatload but no John. Oh, my dear husband, how can I bear it much longer, my patience is nearly worn out. . . . I feel like something will happen that we will never meet on earth again, oh, John, how I long to see you and hear your voice once more. I feel like my heart is almost broken. . . . time drags so heavily—farewell. May God protect you is my daily prayer."

Another lost letter was written in 1863 by a soldier to his "Dear Little Wife . . . I never get tired of being loved or being told of it. . . . if I had a choice between a Major General's Commission and your presence here for an hour, you could come as fast as the [railroad] cars would bring you. . . . I love you, little wife, and you must not allow your imagination to worry you into the belief that absence . . . will affect my love for you."

On September 10, 1863, Elisha Allen wrote to May Hobbs Allen and marked the envelope "private." This young soldier confided: "I have pleasant memories of your warm passionate love. Do you remember the first kiss I gave you? I should love to drive down the road again on a fine autumn day and as before kiss your sweet lips and press you to my bosom, to hear you say, 'I will marry you.' It flooded my heart with rapture."[1]

There is no shortage of love in these anguished outpourings.

The author's great-grandfather, Emanuel Lowry, wrote to his financée, Phoebe Colborn, on May 30, 1861: "Today, there is nothing to keep back the free heart that goes out on wings of fancy, wearing garlands of sweetest flowers to crown your brow. O, to feel your heart beating against mine once more again and your kiss of purest affection trembling on my lips . . . the heart struggles with mighty waves of tenderness—its every chamber overflowing with exquisite harmonies." While this serious young man also devoted many pages of the same letter to the internal policies of the Disciples of Christ and to his analysis of the coming war, he saved his warmest words for Phoebe, to whom he would be married for forty-five years.

Other authors have collected some outpourings of the heart. An Iowa woman wrote her soldier husband, "Do you ever wish you had me for a bedfellow? I have wished you were here more than once when I would get ready for bed. But I feel in hope that we can have that privilege before long, don't you?"

Samuel Cormany, back on duty after a short home leave, wrote in his diary that he and his wife "didn't sleep much last night" as the "reunion so buoyed up our affections that we had a great deal of loving to do."

In the antebellum years, Joseph Lyman wrote to his wife, "I antici-pate unspeakable delight in your embrace" and "look forward to your voluptuous touch." His Laura replied, "How I long to see you. . . . I'll drain your coffers dry next Saturday, I assure you."[2]

Mary Chesnut, the famed Southern diarist, wrote of the brief meteor of love that flashed through the life of Decca Singleton. "Decca was the worst in love girl I ever saw." The young lady in questions and her fiancé,

Alex, were to be married, but military duties delayed his arrival and "she wept like a water nymph." At last they were joined. A year later, as Alex lay wounded, Decca died of the complications of childbirth and was buried in her wedding frock. Mrs. Chesnut wrote, "Is she to be pitied? She said she had had months of perfect happiness. How many people can say that? So many of us live long dreary lives and happiness never comes at all."[3] Who can doubt the truth of Mary Chesnut's observation?

Rita Mae Brown, novelist and explorer of the Southern psyche, spent four months reading Civil War letters. She was struck by the tenderness and respect that the male writers showed to their wives, sweethearts, and mothers. Even in the letters of men to other men, there is rarely a negative comment about women. The contemporary battle of the sexes, aggravated by the writers of television situation comedies and inflamed by the litigation that surrounds harassment, whether real or contrived, has no sympathetic chord in Civil War correspondence. Brown speculates on why men and women seemed to be more respectful of one another in that era. Some factors might be that men and women needed each other in different ways than they do now and that their expectations of marriage were more realistic. They hoped for teamwork and cooperation, and if they got love or beauty or happiness in the bargain, well, that was even more than they had hoped for. Sex roles were clearer then, too. Men who did not support their wives and children were clearly labeled as bad men; women who weren't "into" child care or cooking would have been regarded as very peculiar.[4]

Family ties and the wish for family approval seem to have been strengthening factors in 1860 and were rarely perceived as burdensome. Love back then seemed to have its rapture built on a more solid foundation of practical reality.

Lest we conclude with the notion that love in the Civil War was only sober and level-headed, let us consider this final letter, written by Maj. Gen. Godfrey Weitzel, who in his cadet days at West Point had been judged "the most promising cadet."

Many years after his student days, the now-mature General Weitzel wrote to his lady friend, Miss Louisa Bogen: "Metropolitan Hotel, New York, March 4, 1864. My darling Louisa, I have pinched your picture and it does not holler. I have bitten it and it does not holler. I have kissed it and it does not return my kisses. I have hugged it and it does not return my hug. So just consider yourself pinched, bitten, hugged and kissed. I have been dreaming about you all last night. I was back at home and had only 12 hours to stay. You and I sneaked away from the rest of the folks and went upstairs to that little front room in your house and we had such a pleasant time. But alas! It was only a dream."[5]

There was no shortage of tenderness, longing, fidelity, and affection during the Civil War. Quite the contrary—along with all the Cyprians, gambling, tanglefoot whiskey, cursing, and adultery, there was also an ocean of loyalty, consideration, and love.

Chapter Seventeen

છે

Aftermath

THE CIVIL WAR was a watershed in our history. No war before or since changed us so much. The transformations wrought lie in at least four areas.

First, the war settled forever the dominion of Federal over state control. The right of the state to secede was canceled out in the ink of human blood.

Second, the world's largest slave-based economy was brought to an end, which raised us in the esteem of civilized nations but produced a dramatic change in the economy of the South.

Third, the war established forever that a large industrial nation, engaged in modern warfare, will triumph over a smaller, nonindustrial nation.

Fourth, the relationships of the sexes and of the races, both in public and in private, were radically altered, as reflected in this present study.

For white women, the war brought life without men. For some, this was firsthand, as the wife of an absent soldier or as a widow. For others, the change was secondhand: a daughter or a friend whose man was at war. Wives, both rural and urban, learned new skills in management, direct labor, or both. On the farm, women were involved in decisions about purchasing newly available planting and harvesting equipment. In cities and towns, they were the backbone of fund-raising, nursing care, and the work of Sanitary Fairs and the Sanitary Commission.

There was increased publicity about prostitution, out-of-wedlock births, and moral scandals. The sordid world of physical reality was harder to ignore. Women who entered the workplace came to know the man's world firsthand, with its possibilities of sexual harassment, as well as the pleasures and disappointments of a paycheck.

White males by the millions were separated from their homes and families and subjected to epidemics of contagious and often fatal diseases, as well as the possibility of maiming or death in combat. They also were exposed to the flocks of prostitutes that followed the troops. In some units, close to half the troops had venereal disease. After the war, many men had what in other wars was called shell shock, combat neurosis, or post-traumatic stress disorder. Some such men simply brought their problems home (as seen in the novel *Oldest Living Confederate Widow Tells All*),[1] while others chose to take their lessons in violence and male bonding West and became frontier soldiers, gunslingers, or cowboys.

Those who did come home entered a more subtle zone of combat: retaking the role of dominant spouse from a wife who had managed home and children in the years of the husband's absence.

For blacks in general, there was an enormous cultural shift—from being property to being citizens—an abrupt change for which neither blacks nor whites were fully prepared. Generations of separation from their ancestral cultures and from the inner core of white culture, combined with almost total illiteracy, left most blacks floundering in the new freedom. And what was freedom without land, home, capital, or marketable job skills?

For black women, who had been sexually subject to their masters, regarded as livestock by slave traders, and likely to have their children torn from them at the auction block, there was certainly a new set of circumstances to master. There had been a long tradition of passive resistance, secret hopes, and underground railways, but little had prepared them for sudden and universal freedom, an explosive decompression, and a world of choices yet few resources with which to implement such choices.

For black men, the defining of manhood was a major issue. As slaves, they had had neither the chance to protect their women nor a choice in their own occupation or place of dwelling. The concept of a family unit had been virtually meaningless, because an owner could sell or separate slaves at will.

For some black men, change had come earlier, in the form of service as colored troops, but with pay inferior to white troops and always with white officers. Equality and manhood—but not quite.

The relationship of black men and black women after the war was complicated by all the factors just mentioned, plus that of defining themselves as heads of households or as coequals in a marriage. And formal, legal marriage also was a new thing. Property cannot marry, but people can.

In *The Brothers Karamazov*, the Grand Inquisitor asserts that humans are not ready for choice and that for most, choice is not a blessing but a burden.[2]

The abolitionists were too sanguine about the transition from slavery to freedom, and the supporters of slavery were too eager to suppress this evolution, by means of the Ku Klux Klan and Jim Crow laws.

The enormous task of redefinition, for both black and white men and women, even today remains unfinished.

After the dust of the war had settled, the sexual reverberations of the great conflict continued. One arena was that of pensions. A not-atypical contested application for benefits was filed by the widow of Capt. George B. Carse, Company C, 40th New York Volunteers. A 100-page investigation revealed that the Carses had married in 1863, that she had thrown him out in 1876 because of his drunkenness, and that he had died in 1883.

In 1862, he had been AWOL for two months and was dismissed from the service but reinstated. He was wounded in the face and leg in 1863 at Chancellorsville and had 3 inches removed from one fibula.

A dozen of the late captain's friends were interviewed. One said that Carse drank only when in pain; another said that Carse was always in pain. Another swore that Carse never had more than a whiskey before dinner and a bottle or two of wine after the meal. A fourth witness described Carse's self-medication regimen: chloroform, chloral hydrate, absinthe, and whiskey.

Other witnesses stated that on the evening of his death, Carse had been in a drunken altercation with a cab driver and then had gone to "Mrs. Maitin's" bordello, where he died of "a drunken debauch." The examiner concluded that the wound caused the pain, the pain caused the drinking, and the drinking caused his death, therefore death was service connected. The grieving widow received $25 a month until 1919.[3]

Some of the men still on active duty after the war continued the tradition of wild living. In 1870, Lt. William H. Bower, at Camp Stambaugh, Wyoming Territory, "did send by his servant, King Brown, colored, to Mrs. Thomas D. Goodman, laundress of Company E, an obscene and bawdy picture and a page of obscene printed matter upon one of which was written a message of a lewd and filthy character in the handwriting of Lieutenant Bower." Since she did not reply, he sent a second unwelcome message that afternoon. The month before, he had been in difficulty for chasing "Mary Elliott, colored," down the hill behind the officers' quarters.[4]

For the benefit of those frontier soldiers who did not have laundresses to chase, nearly every fort had an annex of low saloons and cribs, where booze and women were always available. Those "hog ranches" were found outside Fort Laramie, Fort Randall, Fort Davis, Fort Fauntleroy, Fort Selden, Fort Kearney, Fort Russell, and Fort Lincoln, among others.

In 1850, at Fort Union, the huge supply depot in northern New Mexico, two prostitutes received as "gifts" from the soldiers 9,400 pounds of bacon, 3,400 pounds of flour, 4,300 pounds of coffee, and 6,000 pounds of sugar. Anticipating an increase in trade in 1861, the owner of Loma Parda, Fort Union's "hog ranch," installed a gambling hall. The year after the Civil War ended, the commander of Fort Union sent seven soldiers to investigate a knifing in Loma Parda. The local alcalde jailed all seven soldiers. Clearly, the war had moved west.[5]

Many men no longer in uniform continued their wartime behavior. Frank Harris, who later wrote a widely suppressed sexual autobiography, spent his early twenties as a cowboy. He noted, "The worst toughs were the ex-soldiers."

In 1866, the Union Pacific Railroad extended its tracks west to Abilene, and the next summer, the first great cattle drive north was on. In September 1867, a thousand cowboys, many of them war veterans, descended on Abilene, and in a month, most of their pay was in the strongboxes of the newly built saloons and whorehouses. Six years later, the railroad moved to Ellison and Abilene died. As the tracks moved steadily west, Wichita and Dodge City rose and fell. The former boys in blue and gray, who had seen the girls of Washington, Richmond, and Nashville, had no reluctance in patronizing the Cyprians of the frontier.[6]

Back at home, the war changed life for women, as they entered the formerly all-male world of the office. The harassment of a Treasury Department copyist by Reverend Richmond has been described earlier. In the Confederate quartermaster general's office, a parallel drama unfolded. A dozen of the male "young bloods" amused themselves by preparing a weekly "Adjutant's Report," in which they each give the details of the preceding seven days' sexual activities. They distributed this report through interoffice mail. Of course, a copy was intercepted. The first female to read it could not comprehend the content; the second woman blushed; the third woman laughed. The recorder of these events described the writing as "fiendishly obscene." None of the men involved lost his job.[7]

The continuation of war-time habits into peace-time life is well illustrated by the *Souvenir Sporting Guide* published by Wentworth Publishers for the 1895 national Encampment of the Grand Army of the Republic, at Chicago. The guide lists four theaters and 28 houses of prostitution. A typical listing is that of Elsie Livingston, who stated, "While out seeing the sights, boys, do not fail to drop in upon Miss Elsie at 828 Grayson Street, and you will be royally entertained. Everything and everybody connected with her establishment is first-class. She has the following ladies to entertain you: Misses Freddie, Annie, Edna, Alice, Blanche, Marie and Grace. Miss Elsie herself is an Ohio girl and will be pleased to see all visitors from home." Since most GAR attendees were over age fifty-five, their interest in this information could hardly be attributed to the indiscretions of youth.[8]

Although the power of native Protestant conservatism, combined with imported Victorian ideals, pushed powerfully toward the *status quo ante bellum,* there was no returning the genie to the bottle. Too many men and women had seen too much, experienced too much, felt too much to ever be the same.

The Civil War uprooted institutions, transformed our politics, influenced the social relationships of half a continent, and wrought changes that still echo down the generations.

Now, two lifetimes after the last shots were fired, these national transformations are still in ferment, politically, racially, economically, and sexually. The unending dialogue regarding what is, sexually, and what ought to be, is just as intense now as it was in 1865. Pre-marital sex, adultery, birth control, sex education, abortion, prostitution, and venereal disease—any one of these can still provoke a lively debate, or painful silence, a century and a half after they became public issues in the great turmoil of the war.

The age of Victorian censorship blotted out most consideration of the sexual aspects of life in the Civil War until recently. Now, with the accumulation of new information and the resurgence of old sources, the vicissitudes of Eros in the lives of our great-grandparents may be seen, and that valid dimension can be added to the history of the blue and the gray.

The manifold dimensions of love and lust in the Civil War stand revealed for those who care to see them.

Notes

ॐ

INTRODUCTION

1. Harold Holzer et al., *The Lincoln Image* (New York: Charles Scribner's Sons, 1984), 21, 98.

2. P. M. Zall, *Abe Lincoln Laughing* (Berkeley: University of California, 1982), 42, 61, 97, 101.

3. Dawn L. Simmons, *A Rose for Mrs. Lincoln* (Boston: Beacon Press, 1970), 91, 96, 131.

4. Gene Smith, *Lee and Grant: A Dual Biography* (Secaucus, NJ: Blue & Gray Press, 1988), 4.

5. Douglas Southall Freeman, *Lee's Lieutenants: A Study in Command,* vol. II (New York: Scribners, 1943), 46-47.

6. Kate Cummings, *Kate: The Journal of a Confederate Nurse,* ed. R. A. Harwell, (Baton Rouge: Louisiana State University, 1959), 46, 136.

7. Carlton McCarthy, *Detailed Minutiae of Soldier Life* (1882; reprint, New York: Time-Life, 1982), 92, 209.

8. Frederick D. Williams, ed., *The Wild Life of the Army* (East Lansing: Michigan State University, 1964), 42.

9. Alfred C. Kinsey et al., *Sexual Behavior in the Human Male* (Philadelphia, W. B. Saunders, 1948), 221.

10. Everett B. Long, *Civil War Day by Day* (New York: Doubleday, 1971), 707.

11. Claudia Pierpont, "A Study in Scarlet," *The New Yorker,* August 31, 1992, 90.

CHAPTER 1: OUR FOUNDING FATHERS

1. Walter H. Blumenthal, *Women Camp Followers in the American Revolution* (New York: Ayer, 1974), 57–93.

2. Edward Park, "Could Canada Have Been Our Fourteenth Colony?" *Smithsonian* (December 1987): 43.

3. Blumenthal, *Woman Camp Followers,* 57–93.

4. Hiram Bingham, "Missionaries versus Man-of-Warsmen," in *A Hawaiian Reader,* ed. A. Grove Day and Carl Stroven (Honolulu: Mutual Publishing, 1959), 47; James A. Michener and A. Grove Day, *Rascals in Paradise* (New York: Random House, 1957), 39.

5. Ibid.

CHAPTER 2: THE BIRDS AND THE BEES

1. David Pivar, *Purity Crusade—Sexual Morality and Social Control* (Westport, CT: Greenwood, 1973), 18-28.

2. Maren Lockwood Carden, *Oneida: Utopian Community to Modern Corporation* (Baltimore: Johns Hopkins, 1969), 5–58.

3. Jamie Sokolow, *Eros and Modernization—Sylvester Graham, Health Reform and the Origins of Victorian Sexuality* (Rutherford, NJ: Fairleigh Dickinson University, 1983), 26.

4. F. C. Fowler, *Life—How to Enjoy and How to Prolong It* (Moodus, CT: 1896), 111–13.

5. Sokolow, *Eros and Modernization,* 26.

6. Mark Twain, "Some Thoughts on the Science of Onanism." See Jacob Blanck, *Bibliography of American Literature,* vol. II, item #3580 (1957), 233.

7. National Archives Record Group 153, NN856.

8. Arthur N. Gilbert, "Doctor, Patient and Onanist Diseases in the Nineteenth Century," *Journal of the History of Medicine* 30 (1975): 217.

9. Vern Bullopugh and Martha Voght, "Women, Menstruation and Nineteenth Century Medicine," *Bulletin of the History of Medicine* 47 (1973): 66.

10. Nancy Sahli, *Women and Sexuality in America—A Bibliography* (Boston: G. K. Hall, 1984), 61, 101, 109, 110, 146.

11. Daniel S. Smith, "The American Sexual Revolution—Evidence and Interpretation," in *The American Family in Social-Historical Perspective,* ed. Michael Gordon (New York: St. Martins, 1978), 426.

12. James Mattood and Kristine Wenburg, eds., *The Mosher Survey of Sexual Attitudes in 45 Victorian Women* (New York: Arno, 1980), 1–24.

13. Carl Degler, "Women's Sexuality in the Nineteenth Century," in *The American Family in Social-Historical Perspective,* ed. Michael Gordon, 403; Carol Z. Stearns, "Victorian Sexuality—Can Historians Do It Better?" *Journal of Social History* 18 (1985): 625.

CHAPTER 3: I TAKE PEN IN HAND . . .

1. Manuscript Collection, Illinois State Historical Library.

2. Robert W. Waitt, Jr., "A Kinsey Report on the Civil War," (Kentucky Civil War Roundtable, Fall 1963, manuscript in vertical file, Kinsey Institute, Bloomington, IN). Waitt writes (1993), "Little did I think when I gave this speech thirty years ago that I would need my notes again. They are gone with the wind. Some of those who shared their files with me were Bell Wiley, Bruce Catton, Ralph Newman, Dave Mearns, Otto Eisenschmil, Burke Davis, Harnett Kane, Cliff Dowdey, Dr. Douglas

Freeman, Dr. Allen Nevins (my old teacher), and the late Mrs. Sarah Jackson, then of the National Archives." Mary Elizabeth Massey cited the Waitt talk in her *Bonnet Brigades* (New York: Alfred A. Knopf, 1966), 262.

3. Bell I. Wiley, *The Life of Johnny Reb* (Baton Rouge: Louisiana State University Press, 1971), 51, 53–58.

4. Ibid.

5. Bell I. Wiley, *The Life of Billy Yank* (New York: Bobbs-Merrill, 1951), 257–62.

6. Bell I. Wiley, *Embattled Confederates* (New York: Harper & Row, 1964), 197–99.

7. James I. Robertson, Jr., *Soldiers Blue and Gray* (Columbia, SC: University of South Carolina Press, 1988), 121–77.

8. Collection of Dr. James Milgra, Northbrook, Illinois. Courtesy of H. M. Madaus.

9. Ibid.

10. Collection at Fredericksburg National Military Park. Courtesy of R. K. Krick.

11. Manuscript at Chicago Historical Society.

12. Manuscript at Pennsylvania State Archives.

13. National Archives Manuscript RG 107, M404, roll #1. Courtesy of R. K. Krick.

14. Collection of Michael Hammerson, Highgate, London, England.

15. Bound Volume #513, Fredericksburg National Military Park. Original from Historical Society of Pennsylvania.

16. Miscellaneous Collection, U.S. Army Military History Institute, Carlisle Barracks, Pennsylvania.

17. John McLean Harrington Papers, Special Collections Library, Duke University, Durham, NC.

18. Civil War Collection, Confederate and Federal, 1861–1865, Federal Collection, box F-22, Letters, folder 14, Tennessee State Library and Archives, Nashville.

19. Stephen W. Sears, ed., *For Country, Cause and Leader: The Civil War Journal of Charles B. Haydon* (New York: Ticknor & Fields, 1993), 4, 13, 34, 71, 75, 86, 104, 152.

20. Courtesy of James C. Frasca of Croton, Ohio, 1993.

21. Original in Milwaukee Public Museum. Copy courtesy of R. K. Krick and H. M. Madaus.

CHAPTER 4: BLUE WITH OATHS

1. John D. Billings, *Hardtack and Coffee* (1888; reprint, Williamstown, MA: Corner House, 1980), 286.

2. National Archives RG 153, General Court-Martial Order (GCMO) #128, May 30, 1864.

3. National Archives RG 153, Records of the Judge Advocate General's Office (Army), entry 15, Court-Martial Case File, file MM2417, cited as RG 153, MM2417.

4. RG 153, GCMO #300, June 14, 1865.

5. RG 153, GCMO #319, June 19, 1865.

6. RG 153, GCMO #327, June 21, 1865.

7. RG 153, GCMO #225, July 22, 1863.

8. RG 153, GCMO #364, December 4, 1864.

9. RG 153, GCMO #62, March 16, 1853.

10. RG 153, GCMO #65, March 16, 1863.

11. RG 153, GCMO #104, April 28, 1863.

12. RG 153, GCMO #624, November 16, 1865.

13. RG 153, GCMO #667, December 22, 1865.

14. RG 153, GCMO #427, August 16, 1865.

15. RG 153, GCMO #513, September 11, 1865.

16. RG 153, NN757.

17. RG 153, NN757.

18. RG 153, NN757.

19. RG 153, NN808.

20. RG 153, MM3059.

21. RG 153, MM2456.

22. RG 153, MM2392.

23. RG 153, MM238.

24. RG 153, MM2410.

25. RG 153, MM2437.

26. RG 153, MM2412.

27. RG 153, MM2413.

28. RG 153, GCMO #179, April 7, 1865.

29. RG 153, GCMO #127, March 8, 1865.

30. RG 153, GCMO #80, February 15, 1865.

31. RG 153, GCMO #115, February 25, 1865.

32. RG 153, GCMO #5, January 4, 1865.

33. RG 153, citation not available.

34. RG 153, GCMO #364, July 13, 1865.

35. RG 153, GCMO #372, July 19, 1865.

36. RG 153, GCMO #412, August 10, 1865.

37. RG 153, GCMO #412, August 10, 1865; RG 153, GCMO #422, August 15, 1865.

38. RG 153, GCMO #84, February 15, 1865.

39. RG 153, GCMO #93, February 18, 1865.

40. RG 393, part 2, entry 1167, vol. 61, GO #20, May 8, 1864.

41. RG 153, GCMO #85, February 16, 1865.

42. RG 153, MM2504.

43. RG 153, GCMO #204, July 2, 1863.

44. RG 153, NN820.

CHAPTER 5: AND THE FLESH WAS MADE WORD

1. G. Legman, "Unprintable Folklore," *The Journal of American Folklore* 103 (July–September 1990): 259–300.

2. Vance Randolph, *Pissing in the Snow* (Urbana, IL: Illini Books, 1986), 24, 84.

3. Vance Randolph, *Roll Me in Your Arms* (Fayetteville, AR: University of Arkansas, 1992), 10–31.

4. Guy Logsdon, *The Whorehouse Bells Were Ringing, and Other Songs Cowboys Sing* (Urbana: University of Illinois, 1989), 1–19.

5. Paul Glass and Louis C. Singer, *Singing Soldiers* (New York: Grossett & Dunlap, 1968), 66, 236, 267, 286.

6. Rip van Winkel [pseud.], *Jeff Davis' Dream,* November 23, 1863, Ohio Historical Society, Patrick Keran Collection, MSS 5, box 1, item 30.

7. John Harrington Cox, *Folk Songs of the South* (Hatboro, PA: Folklore Associates, 1963), 396.

8. Robert W. Waitt, Jr., "A Kinsey Report on the Civil War," address to the Kentucky Civil War Roundtable, autumn, 1963, copy in Kinsey Institute vertical file. Mr. Waitt recalls in a personal communication (1993) that he had seen in the 1960s about ten verses of "The Yellow Rose of Texas," which described in considerable detail the sexual proclivities of the girls in a Galveston whorehouse.

9. E. L. Rudolph, *Confederate Broadside Verse* (New Braunfels, TX: Book Farm, 1950), 15.

10. Sylvia Dannett, *A Treasury of Civil War Humor* (New York: Yoseloff, 1963), 112–14.

11. Randolph, *Pissing in the Snow.*

12. Ibid.

13. David S. Sparks, ed., *Inside Lincoln's Army* (New York: Yoseloff, 1964), 255, 257.

14. Walter Hebert, *Fighting Joe Hooker* (1944; reprint, Gaithersburg, MD: Olde Soldier Books, 1987), 180.

15. Michael Musick, "Spirited and Spicy Scenes," *Civil War Times Illustrated* 12 (January 1973): 26.

16. James C. Frasca, private collection, Croton, IL. Material used with the kind permission of Mr. Frasca.

17. John D'Emilio and Estelle Freedman, *Intimate Matters* (New York: Harper & Row, 1988), 131.

18. Anon. *The Libertine Enchantress, or the Adventures of Lucinda Hartley* (New Orleans: 1863), 1–25.

19. Calvin Blanchard, *The Secret History of a Votary of Pleasure—His Own Confession* (New York: 1866), 1–31.

20. Philocomus [pseud.], *The Love Feast, or a Bride's Experience—A Poem in Six Nights* (Associated Female Press, Blind Alley, Coney Hatch, Maidenhead, 1865), 1–22.

21. James C. Frasca, op cit.

22. Beaumont Newhall, *The History of Photography* (New York: Museum of Modern Art, 1964), 5–19; William C. Darrah, *Cartes de Visite* (Gettysburg, PA: Darrah Press, 1981), 1–14.

23. Morton N. Cohen, *Lewis Carroll's Photographs of Nude Children* (Philadelphia: Rosenbach Foundation, 1978), 6–23.

24. Constance Sullivan, *Nude Photographs—1850–1980* (New York: Harper & Row, 1980).

CHAPTER 6: PROSTITUTION: EAST

1. Ruth Rosen, *The Lost Sisterhood—Prostitution in America* (Baltimore: Johns Hopkins, 1982), 1–10.

2. William W. Sanger, *The History of Prostitution* (1858; Eugenics Publishing, 1939; New York: AMS Press, 1974), 420–550.

3. John M. Murtagh and Sara Harris, *Cast the First Stone* (New York: McGraw-Hill, 1957), 210.

4. Donald Press, "South of the Avenue: From Murder Bay to Federal Triangle," *Records of the Columbia Historical Society of Washington, D.C.* 51 (1984): 51.

5. Franc B. Wilkie, *Pen and Powder* (Boston: Tichnor & Co., 1888), 181–83.

6. Margaret Leech, *Reveille in Washington: 1860–1865* (New York: Harper, 1941), 260–67.

7. John W. Stepp and I. William Hill, eds., *Mirror of War: The Evening Star Reports the Civil War* (Englewood Cliffs, NJ: Prentice-Hall, 1961), 31, 224, 257, 263.

8. Constance McLaughlin Green, *Washington: Village and Capital 1800–1878* (Princeton, NJ: Princeton University Press, 1962), 250–52.

9. Press, "South of the Avenue," 57.

10. Leech, *Reveille in Washington,* 262.

11. Ibid., 264.

12. Ibid., 266.

13. *Official Records,* series II, volume 5, page 628.

14. Leech, *Reveille in Washington,* 261.

15. Ibid., 260.

16. National Archives RG 393, vol. 298, Provost Marshal of Washington, D.C.

17. David H. Donald, ed., *Gone for a Soldier: The Civil War Memoirs of Private Alfred Bellard* (Boston: Little, Brown, 1975), 226, 254–58.

18. "Within Sight of the White House," unidentified newspaper clipping. Geography and map division, Library of Congress #G3851 .E625, 198-, .W5.

19. Donna J. Seifert, "Within Sight of the White House," *Historical Archaeology* 25, no. 4 (1991): 82; Donna J. Seifert, "Mrs. Starr's Profession" (Paper presented at the 1992 Society for Historical Archaeology Conference, Kingston, Jamaica, January 8–12, 1992).

20. Charles Stuart, New York *Citizen,* June 1, 1867.

21. Clifford Dowdey, *Experiment in Rebellion* (Garden City, NY: Doubleday, 1946), 93, 114.

22. Elizabeth Gushee (Virginia Historical Society), personal communication, 1992.

23. Dowdy, *Experiment in Rebellion,* 257.

24. Rita Mae Brown, "Oh, Southern Men; Oh, Southern Women!" *Civil War Times Illustrated* 26 (June 1987): 49.

25. Dowdy, *Experiment in Rebellion,* 114.

26. Richmond *Daily Dispatch,* May 18, 1862.

27. Robert Waitt, Jr., "A Kinsey Report on the Civil War," address to the Kentucky Civil War Roundtable, autumn, 1963, copy in vertical file, Kinsey Institute.

28. Richmond *Daily Whig,* August 17, 1861; September 14, 1861; February 7, 1862; February 12, 1862; February 22, 1862; March 7, 1862; November 17, 1862; November 19, 1862; November 20, 1862; December 5, 1862; December 12, 1862; April 20, 1862. Courtesy Robert E. L. Krick.

29. Waitt, "Kinsey Report."

30. Ibid.

31. National Archives RG 109, entry 448.

32. National Archives RG 153, MM2388.

CHAPTER 7: PROSTITUTION: WEST

1. David Kaser, "Nashville's Women of Pleasure in 1860," *Tennessee Historical Quarterly* 23, no. 4 (December 1964): 379.

2. Charles Smart, ed., *The Medical and Surgical History of the War of the Rebellion,* part III, vol. I, 3rd Medical Volume (Washington, DC: Government Printing Office, 1888), 891–96.

3. James Boyd Jones, "A Tale of Two Cities: The Hidden Battle Against Venereal Disease in Civil War Nashville & Memphis," *Civil War History* 31, no. 3 (1985): 270.

4. Ephraim A. Wilson, *Memoirs of the War* (Cleveland: Bayne Publishing, 1893), 151–53.

5. Smart, *Medical and Surgical History,* 893.

6. Jones, "A Tale of Two Cities," 272.

7. Ibid.

8. Smart, *Medical and Surgical History,* 892.

9. Ibid., 894.

10. Ibid.

11. William M. Chambers, *Sanitary Report of the Condition of the Prostitutes of Nashville, Tennessee,* prepared January 31, 1865, handwritten manuscript, the Western Reserve Historical Society, Cleveland, Ohio.

12. National Archives RG 94, Records of the Adjutant General's Office 1780s–1917, A File MSS #388 (entry 621). Courtesy of Michael T. Meier.

13. Leroy P. Graf and Ralph W. Haskins, *The Papers of Andrew Johnson,* vol. 6, (Knoxville, TN: University of Tennessee Press, 1983), 717–18.

14. Chambers, *Sanitary Report.*

15. Ibid.

16. R. Wallace, "United States Hospitals at Nashville," *The Cincinnati Lancet & Observer,* n.s. 7 (1864): 587.

17. James A. Hoobler, *Cities under the Gun—Images of Occupied Nashville and Chattanooga* (Nashville: Rutledge Press, 1986), 108.

18. Smart, *Medical and Surgical History,* 894.

19. Jones, "A Tale of Two Cities," 273.

20. Chambers, *Sanitary Report.*

21. Jones, "A Tale of Two Cities," 276.

22. Chambers, *Sanitary Report.*

23. Jesse C. Burt, *Nashville—Its Life and Times* (Nashville: Tennessee Book Co., 1959), 60.

24. Stanley F. Horn, ed., *Tennessee's War, 1861–1865, Described by Participants.* (Nashville: Tennessee Civil War Centennial Commission, 1965), 108.

25. Jones, "A Tale of Two Cities," 275.

26. Stanley J. Folmsbee, Robert E. Corlew, and Enoch L. Mitchell, *History of Tennessee,* vol. II (New York: Lewis Historical Publishing Co., 1960), 89.

27. Patricia M. LaPointe, "The Disrupted Years: Memphis City Hospitals 1860–1867," *West Tennessee Historical Society Papers* (1984): 9, 16.

28. Smart, *Medical and Surgical History,* 894.

29. Ibid., 895.

30. Ibid., 896.

31. Ibid.

32. National Archives RG 153, NN790.

CHAPTER 8: BRED UPON THE WATERS

1. Harry Drago, *Notorious Ladies of the Frontier* (New York: Dodd, Mead, 1969), 93-95. On the subject of Sherman's Memphis deportation, Drago (p. 94) claims that it was the steamer *Washington.* There are no citations, and Drago has passed away.

2. National Archives material reprinted in *American Heritage* 33, no. 4 (June–July 1982): 98.

3. Jones, "A Tale of Two Cities," 272.

4. Ibid., 272.

5. Bert Fenn, manuscript in Special Collections of the Public Library of Cincinnati, 1987.

6. Ibid.

7. Ibid.

8. National Archives material, 98.

9. Fenn manuscript.

10. National Archives material, 98.

11. Ibid., 99.

12. Frederick Way, *Way's Packet Directory 1843–1983* (Athens, OH: Ohio University, 1984), 221.

CHAPTER 9: FRENCH LETTERS AND AMERICAN MORALS

1. Norman E. Himes, *Medical History of Contraception* (Baltimore: Williams & Wilkins, 1936), 209.

2. Ibid., 218.

3. Ibid., 230.

4. L. L. Langley, ed., *Contraception* (Stroudsburg, PA: Dowder, Hutchinson & Ross, 1973), 77.

5. Ibid., 84.

6. Ibid., 88.

7. Ibid., 91.

8. James C. Mohr, *Abortion in America: The Origins and Evolutions of National Policy, 1800–1900* (New York: Oxford University Press, 1978), 48.

9. Ibid., 50.

10. Edward Shorter, *A History of Women's Bodies.* (New York: Basic Books, 1982), 194.

11. Mohr, *Abortion,* 52.

12. Ibid., 59.

13. Ibid., 63.

14. Ibid., 68.

15. Ibid., 72.

16. Ibid., 77.

17. Ibid., 80.

CHAPTER 10: THE AILMENTS OF VENUS

1. Francis Randall Packard, *A History of Medical Science in the United States* (New York: Hoeber, 1931), 140.

2. Ibid., 151.

3. Ibid., 178.

4. Ibid., 213.

5. Gert H. Brieger, "Health and Disease on the Western Frontier," *Western Journal of Medicine* 125 (July 1976): 28.

6. George W. Adams, *Doctors in Blue* (New York: Henry Schuman, 1952), 36.

7. Allan M. Brandt, "AIDS in Historical Perspective," *American Journal of Public Health* 78 (April 1988), 367.

8. Ibid., 368.

9. Ibid., 370.

10. Ibid.

11. Rudolph Kampmeier, "Venereal Disease in the United States Army: 1775–1900," *Sexually Transmitted Diseases* 9 (April 1982): 100.

12. B. Van Swieten, *The Diseases Incident to Armies with the Method of Cure,* translated from German (Philadelphia: R. Bell Printers, 1776).

13. Kampmeier, "Venereal Disease," 102.

14. Charles Smart, ed., *The Medical and Surgical History of the War of the Rebellion,* part III, vol. II, 3d Medical Volume (Washington, DC: Government Printing Office, 1888), 891.

15. Ibid., 891.

16. Ibid.

17. Ibid., 892.

18. Ibid.

19. Ibid.

20. Ibid., 893.

21. Lawrence R. Murphy, "The Enemy Among Us: Venereal Disease Among Union Soldiers in the Far West, 1861–1865," *Civil War History* 31, no. 3 (1985): 257.

22. Ibid., 260.

23. Ibid., 263.

24. Horace H. Cunningham, *Doctors in Gray* (Baton Rouge: Louisiana State University Press, 1958), 210.

25. Stephen W. Sears, ed., *For Country, Cause and Leader* (New York: Ticknor & Fields, 1993), 71-75.

26. Cunningham, *Doctors in Gray,* 211.

27. Robert Waitt, Jr., "A Kinsey Report on the Civil War," speech to Kentucky Civil War Roundtable, autumn 1963, copy in Kinsey Institute vertical file.

28. Hans Zinsser, *Rats, Lice, and History* (Boston: Printed for the *Atlantic Monthly* by Little, Brown, 1935).

CHAPTER 11: PARALLEL LIVES

1. *Oxford English Dictionary,* "sodomy," "homosexuality," and "buggery"; S.V. *Random House Dictionary of the English Language—Unabridged,* "faggot" and "gay." S.V.

2. National Archives RG 45, Naval Records, subject file NJ, folder "1860–1870, 1 of 2, Minor Delinquencies and Cases Where There Is No Record That a Court-Martial Was Held," box 284.

3. Ibid.

4. Jonathan Katz, *Gay American History* (New York: Discus Books, 1976), 752.

5. Ibid., 753.

6. Ibid.

7. Ibid., 754.

8. Charley Shively, *Calamus Lovers: Walt Whitman's Working Class Camerados* (San Francisco: Gay Sunshine Press, 1987), 10.

9. Ibid., 13.

10. Ibid., 42.

11. Ibid., 51.

12. Winston Leyland, ed., *Gay Sunshine Interviews,* vol. I (San Francisco: Gay Sunshine Press, 1984), 126.

13. Shivley, *Calamus Lovers,* 55.

14. Ibid., 69.

15. Fredericksburg *Christian Banner,* June 11, 1862.

16. Letter in files of Manassas National Park.

17. Unpublished diary, courtesy of Roger Long, Port Clinton, OH, 1988.

18. Letter courtesy of Gary Hendershot, Little Rock, AR, 1993.

19. Reid Mitchell, *The Vacant Chair: The Northern Soldier Leaves Home* (New York: Oxford University Press, 1993), 119.

20. Ibid., 120.

21. Hollace Weiner, "The 'Outing' of Historical Leaders," San Francisco *Sunday Chronicle—Sunday Punch,* August 15, 1993, p. 6.

22. Joseph Mayo, *A Guide to Magistrates* (Richmond, VA: Colin, Baptist and Nowlan, 1850), 622.

23. Richard Current, *The Lincoln Nobody Knows,* (New York: Hill and Wang, 1958), 12.

24. Ibid.

25. Ibid.

26. William Herndon, *Herndon's Lincoln,* (New York: D. Appleton & Co., 1892).

27. John G. Nicolay and John Hay, *Abraham Lincoln: A History* (New York: The Century Co., 1890).

28. David Donald, *Lincoln's Herndon* (New York: Alfred A. Knopf, 1948), 358.

29. Current, *The Lincoln Nobody Knows,* 41.

30. Ibid., 32.

31. Ibid.

32. Carl Sandburg, *Abraham Lincoln,* one-volume edition (New York: Harcourt, Brace, 1954), 56.

33. Joshua F. Speed, *Reminiscences of Abraham Lincoln* (Louisville, KY: Morton & Co., 1884), 22.

34. Robert L. Kincaid, *Joshua Fry Speed: Lincoln's Most Intimate Friend* (Harrogate, TN: Lincoln Memorial University, 1943), 13.

35. Charley Shiveley, *Drum Beats: Walt Whitman's Civil War Boy Lovers* (San Francisco: Gay Sunshine Press, 1989), 84.

36. Ibid., 78.

37. Donald, *Lincoln's Herndon,* 14.

38. Charles B. Strozier, *Lincoln's Quest for Union* (New York: Basic Books, 1982), 118.

39. Margaret Leech, *Reveille in Washington* (New York: Harper, 1941), 303.

40. Strozier, *Lincoln's Quest for Union,* 88. See also Lincoln's poem about homosexual marriage, 44.

41. Camille Paglia, *Sexual Personae* (New York: Vintage, 1991), 670.

42. Lee Middleton, *Hearts on Fire* (Coolville, OH: Alberta Taylor Civil War Books, 1993); Richard Hall, *Patriots in Disguise* (New York: Paragon House, 1993).

43. DeAnne Blanton, "Women Soldiers of the Civil War," *Prologue: Quarterly of the National Archives* (Spring 1993): 27; C. Kay Larson, "Bonny Yank and Ginny Reb," *Minerva* (Spring 1990): 33; C. Kay Larson, "Bonny Yank and Ginny Reb Revisited," *Minerva* (Summer 1992): 35.

44. Rita Mae Brown, *High Hearts* (New York: Bantam, 1986).

45. Jill Canon, *Civil War Heroines* (Santa Barbara, CA: Bellerophon, 1991).

46. Hall, *Patriots in Disguise,* 46-97.

47. C. J. Worthington, ed. *The Woman in Battle: A Narrative of the Exploits, Adventures, and Travels of Madame Loreta Janeta Velasquez* (Hartford, CT: Belknap, 1876).

48. Hall, *Patriots in Disguise,* 132.

49. Ibid., 20-26.

50. Blanton, "Women Soldiers."

51. Larson, "Bonny Yank and Ginny Reb."

52. Larson, "Bonny Yank and Ginny Reb Revisited."

53. Blanton, "Women Soldiers."

54. Bell I. Wiley, *The Life of Billy Yank* (Baton Rouge: Louisiana State University, 1978), 337.

55. Mary Elizabeth Massey, *Bonnet Brigades* (New York: Alfred A. Knopf, 1966), 84.

CHAPTER 12: AGAINST HER WILL

1. National Archives Record Group 153, Records of the Judge Advocate General's Office (Army), entry 15, Court-Martial Case File, file number MM2471, cited as RG 153, MM2471.

2. RG 153, MM2478.

3. RG 153, MM2407.

4. RG 153, MM854.

5. RG 153, MM3057.

6. RG 153, General Court-Martial Order (GCMO) #161, March 28, 1865.

7. RG 153, GCMO #160, March 28, 1865.

8. RG 153, GCMO #268, January 1865.

9. RG 153, GCMO #181, April 7, 1865.

10. RG 153, GCMO #101, March 15, 1864.

11. RG 153, GCMO #137, May 31, 1864.

12. RG 153, GCMO #119, May 26, 1864.

13. RG 153, GCMO #92, May 12, 1864.

14. RG 153, GCMO #151, May 26, 1863.

15. RG 153, GCMO #165, August 30, 1864.

16. RG 153, GCMO #263, August 30, 1864.

17. RG 153, GCMO #151, June 4, 1864.

18. RG 153, GCMO #154, June 6, 1864.

19. RG 153, GCMO #193, July 6, 1864.

20. RG 153, GCMO #167, June 16, 1864.

21. RG 153, GCMO #194, July 8, 1864.

22. RG 153, GCMO #258, August 24, 1864.

23. RG 153, GCMO #199, July 18, 1864.

24. RG 153, GCMO #84, February 15, 1865.

25. RG 153, GCMO #390, August 1, 1865.

26. RG 153, MM2468.

27. RG 153, NN751.

28. RG 153, #145, May 26, 1863.

29. Robert I. Alotta, *Civil War Justice,* (Shippensburg, PA: White Mane Press, 1989), 58.

30. I. S. Curtis, letter dated March 27, 1912, typescript in the collection of R. K. Krick.

31. Vicksburg *Herald,* August 13, 1865.

32. National Archives RG 153, entry 18, PC-29, file 31, courtesy of M. M. Musick.

33. Charles W. Turner, *Civil War Letters of Arabellas Speairs and William Beverley Pettit of Fluvanna County, Virginia* (Roanoke, VA: Roanoke Lithography, 1988), 155.

34. Reid Mitchell, *The Vacant Chair: The Northern Soldier Leaves Home* (New York: Oxford University Press, 1993), 167.

35. Louis F. Kakuske, "Pursuit Through Arkansas," *Civil War Times Illustrated* XIII (February 1975): 36–43.

36. Mitchell, *The Vacant Chair,* 170.

37. Alotta, *Civil War Justice,* 30.

38. Edward Dicey, *Six Months in the Federal States* (London & Cambridge: Macmillan, 1863), cited in Henry Steele Commager, *The Blue and the Gray* (1950; reprint, New York: Fairfax Press, 1982), 515.

CHAPTER 13: AN OFFICER AND A GENTLEMAN

1. National Archives Record Group 153, Records of Judge Advocate General's Office (Army), entry 15, Court-Martial Case Number NN109, cited as RG 153, NN109.

2. RG 153, MM3059.

3. RG 153, GCMO #426, August 16, 1865.

4. RG 153, MM2450.

5. RG 153, GCMO #187, June 24, 1863.

6. RG 153, GCMO #90, March 4, 1864.

7. RG 153, GCMO #380, November 24, 1863.

8. RG 153, GCMO #389, December 7, 1863.

9. RG 153, GCMO #249, July 30, 1863.

10. RG 153, GCMO #665, December 22, 1865.

11. RG 153, GCMO #209, July 7, 1863.

12. RG 153 (GCMO # unavailable), April 19, 1864.

13. RG 153, OO1440.

14. RG 153, MM2588.

15. RG 153, GCMO #140, April 4, 1864.

16. RG 153, MM2582.

17. RG 153, NN807.

18. RG 153, MM2448.

19. RG 153, NN111.

20. RG 153 (no order number given), 8th Army Corps, Baltimore, June 15, 1863.

21. RG 153, GCMO #279, September 2, 1864.

22. Felix Gregory de Fontaine (Personne, pseud.), *Marginalia* (Columbia, SC: Steam Power Press, 1864), 122.

23. Terry L. Jones, *Lee's Tigers* (Baton Rouge: Louisiana State University Press, 1987), 26.

24. National Archives Record Group 92, Records of the Quartermaster General, Consolidated Correspondence File 1794–1890, "Walker, Henry Harrison."

25. Noel Yancey, "The Cause of Righteousness," North Carolina *Spectator,* May 11, 1989.

26. RG 153, GCMO #561, October 6, 1865.

27. RG 153, GCMO #567, October 13, 1865.

28. RG 153, MM2434.

29. RG 45, Subject File: NJ, Jamison, Dr. T. W., box 286.

30. Carl Sandburg, *Abraham Lincoln: The War Years,* vol. 1 (New York: Harcourt, Brace & Co., 1936), 373.

31. RG 153, GCMO #330, October 8, 1863.

32. Roy P. Basler, ed., *The Collected Works of Abraham Lincoln,* vol. 6 (New Brunswick: Rutgers University Press, 1953), 539.

33. Navy Department, General Order No. 43, December 7, 1864.

34. Diary entry by Marsena Patrick, provost marshal, Army of the Potomac, Thursday, August 18, 1864.

CHAPTER 14: GENERALS NUISANCE

1. National Archives Record Group 107, Records of the Office of the Secretary of War. "Statements dated 1872 concerning Gen. H. Judson Kilpatrick's affair with a woman during the Civil War," in "Letters, telegrams, reports and other records concerning the conduct and loyalty of Army officers, War Dept. employees, and citizens during the Civil War, 1861–1872," box #2.

2. Walter Hebert, *Fighting Joe Hooker* (1944; reprint, Gaithersburg, MD: Olde Soldier Books, 1987), 1-97.

3. William A. Craigie, *A Dictionary of American English* (Chicago: University of Chicago, 1942).

4. Carl Bode, ed. *The New Mencken Letters* (New York: The Dial Press, 1977), 552.

5. Norman A. Eliason, Tarheel Talk: *A Historical Study of The English Language in North Carolina to 1860* (Chapel Hill, NC: UNC Press, 1956). Suggested by Whitmel M. Joyner.

6. Robert A. Wilson, ed. *Playboy's Dictionary of Forbidden Words* (Chicago: Playboy Press, 1972).

7. William Morris and Mary Morris, *Morris' Dictionary of Word and Phrase Origins* (New York: Harper & Row, 1971).

8. Allan Work, *Everyday Words from Names of People and Places* (New York: El Sevier, 1980).

9. Milton H. Shutes, "Fighting Joe Hooker," *California Historical Society Quarterly* 16, no. 4, (December 1937): 309.

10. Hebert, *Fighting Joe Hooker,* 169.

11. Ibid., 180.

12. Ibid., 251.

13. M. A. DeWolfe, ed. *Home Letters of General Sherman* (New York: Scribner, 1909), 250.

14. Shutes, "Fighting Joe Hooker," 315.

15. Willliam T. Sherman papers, Manuscript Division, Library of Congress, reel 8, letter dated 16 September 1864.

16. Hebert, *Fighting Joe Hooker,* 317.

17. Shutes, "Fighting Joe Hooker," 313.

18. Dumas Malone, ed. *Dictionary of American Biography,* vol. 9 (New York: Scribners, 1936), 150.

19. Ibid., 151.

20. Bruce Catton *Gettysburg: The Final Fury* (Garden City, NY: Doubleday, 1974) 41.

21. New York *Tribune,* May 21, 1899.

22. Malone, *Dictionary of American Biography,* vol. 9, 152.

23. Ibid., vol. 2, 123.

24. B. A. Botkin, ed. *A Civil War Treasure of Tales, Legend and Folklore* (New York: Random House, 1960), 178: "Beauty and the 'Beast': Butler's 'Woman Order.'"

25. Douglas S. Freeman, *Lee's Lieutenants: A Study in Command,* Arlington Edition, vol. I (New York: Scribners, 1946), 784.

26. National Archives Record Group 94 (Adjutant General's Office), Special File (PI 17, entry 286), also RG 107, TR#1, Special File #19, box #3, also Provost Marshal's File RG 109, s.v.: Annie E. Jones.

27. Unsigned note in the handwriting of Bvt. Brig. Gen. Ezra A. Carman, U.S.A., in National Archives RG 94: Records of the Adjutant General's Office, "Antietam Studies," box 2, in folder labeled "Report of Brig. Gen. John R. Jones, Cmdg. Jackson's Division, Artillery of Jackson's Division. (Noted by M. Musick), R. K. Krick cautions: "Carman was not creating a hoax here, he genuinely believed what he heard, but neither is this confirmed." *Caveat lector.*

28. Joseph G. Bilby, "An Officer and a Gentleman . . . Sort Of," *Military Images* 13, no. 4 (January 1992).

29. Robert K. Waitt, Jr. In a personal communication (1993), Waitt stated that the original of the Clara A. dairy was in the possession of Stuart O. Harrison until Harrison's death. Waitt states that he, Douglas Freeman, Earle Lutz, and Clifford Dowdey all examined the original, and that document expert Harrison Cassidy pronounced the paper, the ink, and the pen strokes typical of the 1860s. Waitt was executive secretary of the Richmond Civil War Centennial Commission. The current location of the diary is unknown. Mr. Waitt recalls that the diary was a bound notebook, about 7 by 9 inches. Some pages were loose, others were stained. Some entries were in pencil, but many were in ink.

30. Waitt, from his 1963 notes. Personal communication, 1993.

31. David Ryan, unpublished manuscript cited by Waitt. McNiven was Waitt's maternal grandfather.

CHAPTER 15: CLERICAL ERROR

1. National Archives Record Group 107, Office of the Secretary of War, Letters Received, Irregular Series, 1861–1866, T-22. Courtesy of M. Musick and M. H. Madaus.

2. Roy P. Basler, ed., *The Collected Works of Abraham Lincoln,* vol. VI (New Brunswick, NJ: Rutgers University, 1953), 226.

3. *Poughkeepsie Daily Eagle,* July 21, 1866, page 3, courtesy Dutchess County (New York) Historical Society.

4. Papers of Charles Colcock Jones, with the permission of Tulane University.

CHAPTER 16: LOVE

1. Susan Cooper, personal communication, 1991, and *San Francisco Chronicle,* February 8, 1987.

2. John D'Emilion and Estelle B. Freedman, *Intimate Matters: A History of Sexuality in America* (New York: Harper & Row, 1988), 78–80.

3. B. A. Botkin, ed., *A Civil War Treasury of Tales, Legends and Folklore* (New York: Random House, 1960), 124.

4. Rita Mae Brown, "Oh, Southern Men—Oh, Southern Women," *Civil War Times Illustrated* 26 (June 1987), 49.

5. Robert W. Waitt, Jr., "A Kinsey Report on the Civil War," address to the Kentucky Civil War Round Table, autumn 1963, copy in Kinsey Institute vertical file.

CHAPTER 17: AFTERMATH

1. Allan Gurganus, *Oldest Living Confederate Widow Tells All* (New York: Alfred A. Knopf, 1989).

2. Fyodor Dostoyevsky, *The Brothers Karamazov* (New York: Modern Library College Edition, McGraw, 1951).

3. Pension application 322554, filed in Philadelphia, January 5, 1885.

4. National Archives RG 153, General Court-Martial Order #13, August 3, 1871.

5. Chris Emmett, *Fort Union and the Winning of the Southwest* (Norman, OK: University of Oklahoma Press, 1965), 248–361.

6. Carol Leonard and Isidor Walliman, "Prostitution and Changing Morality in the Frontier Cattle Towns of Kansas," *Kansas History* 2, no. 1 (spring 1979).

7. Charles Stuart, "Women's Rights and Wrongs," New York *Citizen,* June 20, 1867.

8. *G.A.R. Souvenir Sporting Guide* (Chicago: Wentworth Publishing, 1895). Original pamphlet from the collection of Robert W. Waitt.

Bibliography

ৰ

BOOKS

Adams, George W. *Doctors in Blue*. New York: Henry Schuman, 1952.

Alotta, Robert I. *Civil War Justice*. Shippensburg, PA: White Mane Press, 1989.

Basler, Roy P., ed. *The Collected Works of Abraham Lincoln*. New Brunswick: Rutgers University Press, 1953.

Bingham, Hiram. "Missionaries versus Man-of-Warsmen." In *A Hawaiian Reader*, edited by A. Grove Day and Carl Stoven. Honolulu: Mutual Publishing, 1959.

Billings, John D. *Hardtack and Coffee*. 1888. Reprint, New York: Time-Life Books, 1988.

Blanchard, Calvin. *The Secret History of a Votary of Pleasure: His Own Confession*. New York, 1866.

Blumenthal, Walter H. *Women Camp Followers in the American Revolution*. New York: Ayer, 1974.

Bode, Carl, ed. *The New Mencken Letters*. New York: The Dial Press, 1977.

Botkin, B. A., ed. *A Civil War Treasury of Tales, Legends and Folklore*. New York: Random House, 1960.

Brown, Rita Mae. *High Hearts*. New York: Bantam, 1986.

Burt, Jesse C. *Nashville: Its Life and Times*. Nashville: Tennessee Book Co., 1959.

Butler, Benjamin F. "Beauty and the 'Beast': Butler's 'Woman Order.'" In *A Civil War Treasury of Tales, Legend and Folklore*, edited by B. A. Botkin. New York: Random House, 1960.

Canon, Jill. *Civil War Heroines*. Santa Barbara, CA: Bellerophon, 1991.

Carden, Maren Lockwood. *Oneida: Utopian Community to Modern Corporation*. Baltimore: Johns Hopkins Press, 1969.

Cohen, Morton N. *Lewis Carroll's Photographs of Nude Children*. Philadelphia: Rosenbach Foundation, 1978.

Commager, Henry Steele. *The Blue and the Gray*. 1950. Reprint, New York: Fairfax Press, 1982.

Cox, John Harrington. *Folk Songs of the South*. Hatboro, PA: Folklore Associates, 1963.

Cummings, Kate. *Kate: The Journal of a Confederate Nurse*. Edited by R. A. Harwell. Baton Rouge: Louisiana State University, 1959.

Cunningham, Horace B. *Doctors in Gray*. Baton Rouge: Louisiana State University, 1958.

Current, Richard. *The Lincoln Nobody Knows*. New York: Hill and Wang, 1958.

Darrah, William C. *Cartes de Visite*. Gettysburg, PA: Darrah Press, 1981.

Dannett, Sylvia. *A Treasury of Civil War Humor*. New York: Yoseloff, 1963.

De Fontaine, Felix Gregory [Personne, pseud.]. *Marginalia*. Columbia, SC: Steam Power Press, 1864.

Degler, Carl. "Women's Sexuality in the Nineteenth Century." In *The American Family in Social-Historical Perspective*, edited by Michael Gordon. New York: St. Martins, 1978.

D'Emilio, John and Estelle B. Freedman. *Intimate Matters: A History of Sexuality in America*. New York: Harper and Row, 1988.

De Wolfe, M. A., ed. *Home Letters of General Sherman*. New York: Charles Scribner's Sons, 1909.

Donald, David H., ed. *Gone for a Soldier: The Civil War Memoirs of Private Alfred Bellard*. Boston: Little, Brown, 1975.

———. *Lincoln's Herndon*. New York: Alfred A. Knopf, 1948.

Dowdey, Clifford. *Experiment in Rebellion*. Garden City, NY: Doubleday, 1946.

Drago, Harry. *Notorious Ladies of the Frontier*. New York: Dodd, Mead, 1969.

Eliason, Norman A. *Tarheel Talk: A Historical Study of the English Language in North Carolina to 1860*. Chapel Hill, NC: University of North Carolina Press, 1956.

Emmett, Chris. *Fort Union and the Winning of the Southwest*. Norman, OK: University of Oklahoma Press, 1965.

Folmsbee, Stanley J., Robert E. Corlew, and Enoch L. Mitchell. *History of Tennessee*. New York: Lewis Historical Publishing Co., 1960.

Fowler, F. C. *Life: How to Enjoy and How to Prolong It*. Moodus, CT, 1896.

Freeman, Douglas Southall. *Lee's Lieutenants: A Study in Command*. New York: Charles Scribner's Sons, 1946, Arlington Edition.

Glass, Paul and Singer, Louis C. *Singing Soldiers*. New York: Grossett & Dunlap, 1968.

Green, Constance McLaughlin. *Washington: Village and Capital, 1800–1878*. Princeton, NJ: Princeton University Press, 1962.

Hall, Richard. *Patriots in Disguise*. New York: Paragon House, 1993.

Hebert, Walter. *Fighting Joe Hooker*. 1944. Reprint, Gaithersburg, MD: Olde Soldier Books, 1987.

Herndon, William. *Herndon's Lincoln*. New York: Appleton, 1892.

Himes, Norman E. *A Medical History of Contraception*. Baltimore: Williams & Wilkins, 1936.

Holzer, Harold, et al. *The Lincoln Image*. New York: Charles Scribner's Sons, 1984.

Hoobler, James A. *Cities Under the Gun: Images of Occupied Nashville and Chattanooga*. Nashville: Rutledge Press, 1986.

Horn, Stanley F., ed. *Tennessee's War, 1861–1865, Described by Participants*. Nashville: Tennessee Civil War Centennial Commission, 1965.

Jones, Terry L. *Lee's Tigers*. Baton Rouge: Louisiana State University Press, 1987.

Katz, Jonathan. *Gay American History*. New York: Discus, 1976.

Kincaid, Robert L. *Joshua Fry Speed: Lincoln's Most Intimate Friend*. Harrogate, TN: Lincoln Memorial University, 1943.

Kinsey, Alfred C., et al. *Sexual Behavior in the Human Male*. Philadelphia: W. B. Saunders, 1948.

Langley, L. L., ed. *Contraception*. Stroudsburg, PA: Dowder, Hutchinson & Ross, 1948.

Leech, Margaret. *Reveille in Washington: 1860–1865*. New York: Harper, 1941.

Leyland, Winston, ed. *Gay Sunshine Interviews*, vol. I. San Francisco: Gay Sunshine Press, 1984.

The Libertine Enchantress, or the Adventures of Lucinda Hartley. New Orleans, 1863.

Logsdon, Guy. *The Whorehouse Bells Were Ringing and Other Songs Cowboys Sing*. Urbana, IL: University of Illinois, 1989.

Long, Everett B. *Civil War Day by Day*. New York: Doubleday, 1971.

McCarthy, Carlton. *Detailed Minutiae of Soldier Life*. 1882. Reprint, New York: Time-Life Books, 1982.

Massey, Mary Elizabeth. *Bonnet Brigades*. New York: Alfred A. Knopf, 1966.

Mattood, James and Kristine Wenburg, eds. *The Mosher Survey of Sexual Attitudes in 45 Victorian Women*. New York: Arno, 1980.

Michener, James A. and A. Grove Day. *Rascals in Paradise*. New York: Random House, 1957.

Middleton, Lee. *Hearts on Fire*. Coolville, OH: Alberta Taylor Civil War Books, 1993.

Mitchell, Reid. *The Vacant Chair: The Northern Soldier Leaves Home*. New York: Oxford University Press, 1993.

Mohr, James C. *Abortion in America: The Origins and Evolution of National Policy 1800–1900*. New York: Oxford University Press, 1978.

Murtagh, John M. and Sara Harris. *Cast the First Stone*. New York: McGraw-Hill, 1957.

Newhall, Beaumont. *The History of Photography.* New York: Museum of Modern Art, 1964.

Nicolay, John G. and John Hay. *Abraham Lincoln: A History.* New York: The Century Co., 1890.

Packard, Francis Randall. *A History of Medical Science in the United States.* New York: Hoeber, 1931.

Paglia, Camille. *Sexual Personae.* New York: Vintage, 1991.

Philocomus [pseud.]. *The Love Feast, or a Bride's Experience—A Poem in Six Nights.* N.p.: Associated Female Press, 1865.

Pivar, David. *Purity Crusade: Sexual Morality and Social Control.* Westport, CT: Greenwood, 1973.

Randolph, Vance. *Pissing in the Snow.* Urbana, IL: Illini Books, 1986.

———. *Roll Me in Your Arms.* Fayetteville, AR: University of Arkansas, 1992.

Robertson, James I., Jr. *Soldiers Blue and Gray.* Columbia, SC: University of South Carolina Press, 1988.

Rosen, Ruth. *The Lost Sisterhood: Prostitution in America.* Baltimore: Johns Hopkins, 1982.

Rudolph, E. L. *Confederate Broadside Verse.* New Braunfels, TX: Book Farm, 1950.

Sahli, Nancy. *Women and Sexuality in America: A Bibliography.* Boston: G. K. Hall, 1984.

Sandburg, Carl. *Abraham Lincoln.* One Volume Edition. New York: Harcourt, Brace, 1954.

Sanger, William W. *The History of Prostitution.* 1858. Reprint, New York: Eugenics Publishing, 1939; AMS Press, 1974.

Sears, Stephen W., ed. *For Country, Cause and Leader.* New York: Ticknor & Fields, 1993.

Shively, Charley. *Calamus Lovers: Walt Whitman's Working Class Camerados.* San Francisco: Gay Sunshine Press, 1987.

———. *Drum Beats: Walt Whitman's Civil War Boy Lovers.* San Francisco: Gay Sunshine Press, 1989.

Shorter, Edward. *A History of Women's Bodies.* New York: Basic Books, 1982.

Simmons, Dawn L. *A Rose for Mrs. Lincoln.* Boston: Beacon Press, 1970.

Smart, Charles, ed. *The Medical and Surgical History of the War of the Rebellion.* Washington, DC: Government Printing Office, 1888.

Smith, Daniel S. "The American Sexual Revolution—Evidence and Interpretation." In *The American Family in Social-Historical Perspective,* edited by Michael Gordon. New York: St. Martins, 1978.

Smith, Gene. *Lee and Grant: A Dual Biography.* Secaucus, NJ: Blue and Gray Press, 1988.

Sokolow, Jaime. *Eros and Modernization: Sylvester Graham, Health Reform and the Origins of Victorian Sexuality.* Rutherford, NJ: Fairleigh Dickinson University, 1983.

Sparks, David S., ed. *Inside Lincoln's Army.* New York: Yoseloff, 1964.

Speed, Joshua F. *Reminiscences of Abraham Lincoln.* Louisville, KY: Morton & Co., 1884.

Steiner, Paul E. *Disease in the Civil War.* Springfield, IL: Charles C. Thomas, 1968.

Stepp, John W. and William I. Hill, eds. *Mirror of War: The Evening Star Reports the Civil War.* Englewood Cliffs, NJ: Prentice-Hall, 1961.

Strozier, Charles B. *Lincoln's Quest for Union.* New York: Basic Books, 1982.

Sullivan, Constance. *Nude Photographs: 1850–1980.* New York: Harper & Row, 1980.

Turner, Charles W., ed. *Civil War Letters of Arabella Speairs and William Beverley Pettit of Fluvanna County, Virginia.* Roanoke, VA: Roanoke Lithography, 1988.

Twain, Mark and Charles Dudley Warner. *The Gilded Age.* 1873. Reprint, New York: MacMillan, 1972.

United States War Department. *War of the Rebellion: Official Records of the Union and Confederate Armies.* 128 vols. Washington, DC: 1880-1901.

Van Swieten, B. *The Diseases Incident to Armies with the Method of Cure,* translated from German. Philadelphia: R. Bell. Printers, 1776.

Way, Frederick. *Way's Packet Directory 1843–1983.* Athens, OH: Ohio University, 1984.

Wiley, Bell I. *Embattled Confederates.* New York: Harper & Row, 1964.

———. *The Life of Billy Yank.* New York: Bobbs-Merrill, 1951.

———. *The Life of Johnny Reb.* Baton Rouge: Louisiana State University Press, 1971.

Wilkie, Franc B. *Pen and Powder.* Boston: Tichnor & Co., 1888.

Williams, Frederick D., ed. *The Wild Life of the Army.* East Lansing: Michigan State University, 1964.

Wilson, Ephraim A. *Memoirs of the War.* Cleveland: Bayne Publishing, 1893.

Zall, P. M. *Abe Lincoln Laughing.* Berkeley: University of California, 1982.

Zissner, Hans. *Rats, Lice, and History.* Boston: Printed for the *Atlantic Monthly* by Little, Brown, 1935.

ARTICLES AND EXCERPTS

Bilby, Joseph G. "An Officer and a Gentleman . . . Sort Of." *Military Images* 13, no. 4 (January 1992).

Blanton, DeAnne. "Women Soldiers of the Civil War." *PROLOGUE: Quarterly of the National Archives* (Spring 1993).

Brandt, Allan M. "AIDS in Historical Perspective." *American Journal of Public Health* 78 (April 1988).

Brieger, Gert H. "Health and Disease on the Western Frontier." *Western Journal of Medicine* 125 (July 1976).

Brown, Rita Mae. "Oh, Southern Men; Oh, Southern Women!" *Civil War Times Illustrated* 26 (June 1987).

Bullough, Vern and Martha Voght. "Women, Menstruation and Nineteenth Century Medicine." *Bulletin of the History of Medicine* 47 (1973): 66.

"Captain Newcomb and the Frail Sisterhood," *American Heritage* 33, no. 4, (June–July 1982).

Cooper, Susan. "Love Letters of the Past." San Francisco *Chronicle* (February 8, 1987).

Gilbert, Arthur N. "Doctor, Patient and Onanist Diseases in the Nineteenth Century." *Journal of the History of Medicine* 30 (1975): 217.

Jones, James Boyd. "A Tale of Two Cities: The Hidden Battle Against Venereal Disease in Civil War Nashville and Memphis." *Civil War History* 31, no. 3, (1985).

Kampmeier, Rudolph. "Venereal Disease in the United States Army: 1715–1900." *Sexually Transmitted Diseases* 9 (April 1982): 100.

Kaser, David. "Nashville's Women of Pleasure in 1860." *Tennessee Historical Quarterly* 23 (December 1964): 4.

Kakuske, Louis F. "Pursuit Through Arkansas." *Civil War Times Illustrated* XIII (February 1975): 36–43.

LaPointe, Patricia M. "The Disrupted Years: Memphis City Hospitals 1860–1867." *West Tennessee Historical Society Papers* (1984).

Larson, C. Kay. "Bonny Yank and Ginny Reb." *Minerva* (Spring 1990).

———. "Bonny Yank and Ginny Reb Revisited." *Minerva* (Summer 1992).

Legman, G. "'Unprintable' Folklore." *The Journal of American Folklore* 103 (July–September 1990).

Leonard, Carol and Isidor Walliman. "Prostitution and Changing Morality in the Frontier Cattle Towns of Kansas." *Kansas History* 2, no. 1 (Spring 1979).

Murphy, Lawrence R. "The Enemy Among Us: Venereal Disease among Union Soldiers in the Far West, 1861–1865." *Civil War History* 31, no. 3 (1985).

Musick, Michael. "Spirited and Spicy Scenes." *Civil War Times Illustrated* 12 (January 1973).

Park, Edward. "Could Canada Have Been Our Fourteenth Colony?" *Smithsonian* (December 1987).

Press, Donald. "South of the Avenue: From Murder Bay to Federal Triangle."

Records of the Columbia Historical Society of Washington, D.C. 51 (1984).

Seifert, Donna J. "Within Sight of the White House." *Historical Archaeology* 25, no. 4 (1991).

————. "Mrs. Starr's Profession." Paper presented at the 1992 Society for Historical Archaeology Conference, Kingston, Jamaica. January 8–12, 1992.

Shutes, Milton H. "Fighting Joe Hooker." *California Historical Society Quarterly* 16, no. 4 (December 1937).

Stearns, Carol Z. "Victorian Sexuality: Can Historians Do It Better?" *Journal of Social History* 18 (1985).

Stuart, Charles. "Women's Rights and Wrongs." New York *Citizen* (June 20, 1867).

Twain, Mark. "Some Thoughts on the Science of Onanism." Privately printed pamphlet, cited by Jacob Blanck, *Bibliography of American Literature* II, item 3580, 1957.

Wallace, R. "United States Hospitals at Nashville." *The Cincinnati Lancet and Observer*, n.s., vol. 7 (1864).

Weiner, Hollace. "The 'Outing' of Historical Leaders." San Francisco *Sunday Chronicle—Sunday Punch* (August 15, 1993).

Yancey, Noel. "The Cause of Righteousness." North Carolina *Spectator* (May 11, 1989).

MANUSCRIPT COLLECTIONS

Public Library of Cincinnati, Cincinnati, Ohio
    Bert Fenn Papers
Duke University, Durham, North Carolina
    John McClean Harrington Papers
James Frasca, Croton, Illinois
    Personal Collection
Michael Hammerson, Highgate, London, United Kingdom
    Personal Collection
Gary Hendershot, Little Rock, Arkansas
    Personal Collection
Kinsey Institute, Bloomington, Indiana
    Waitt Papers
Roger Long, Port Clinton, Ohio
    Personal Collection
Ohio Historical Society, Columbus, Ohio
    Patrick Keran Papers

Tennessee State Library and Archives, Nashville, Tennessee
        Civil War Collection, Federal Papers
Tulane University, New Orleans, Louisiana
        Charles Colcock Jones Papers
Western Reserve Historical Society, Cleveland, Ohio
        William M. Chambers Papers

NEWSPAPERS

Fredericksburg *Christian Banner.*
New York *Citizen.*
Poughkeepsie *Daily Eagle.*
Richmond *Daily Dispatch.*
Richmond *Daily Whig.*
San Francisco *Chronicle.*
Vicksburg *Herald.*

Index

🖋